The Existential Jesus

The Existential Jesus

John Carroll

COUNTERPOINT

BERKELEY

This edition published by arrangement with Scribe Publications, Australia.

Library of Congress Cataloging-in-Publication Data

Carroll, John, 1944–
 The existential Jesus / John Carroll.
 p. cm.
 Includes bibliographical references (p.   ) and index.
 ISBN 978-1-58243-465-0
 1. Bible. N.T. Mark—Criticism, interpretation, etc. 2. Jesus Christ—Biblical teaching.
 I. Title.
 BS2585.52.C37 2009
 226.3'06—dc22

                        2008034659

Cover design by Sandy Cull
Interior design by Scribe
Printed in the United States of America

COUNTERPOINT
2117 Fourth Street
Suite D
Berkeley, CA 94710

www.counterpointpress.com

Distributed by Publishers Group West

10 9 8 7 6 5 4 3 2 1

Contents

THE ENIGMA OF BEING

The enigma of *being* confronts all humans. It does so whenever another walks in the door. We take in a presence: the person opposite is more than his or her attributes. Stripping away the colour of the hair, the age of the face, and whatever we know about the life story, there remains this ethereal concentration of being. In the place of empty space, a charged field of some kind of force manifests itself. It is a field with its own phantasmal shape. It lives more as a distillation or essence than as a character or personality. Behind each of these existential forms lies the big presence in the culture of the West—that of Jesus.

Jesus is the archetypal stranger. He appears from nowhere, shrouded in mystery, but soon is gone. While others see him charged with brilliant and terrifying charisma, he himself struggles along his life-path. He is the existential hero—solitary, uprooted from family and home, restless, always on the move and, until the mid-point in his mission, blind to where he is going. He has no occupation, nor worldly power. He chooses followers, tries to teach them, but they remain foolishly obtuse. Everything he attempts founders. Increasingly feared and misunderstood by those closest to him, increasingly hated by the authorities, he withdraws into troubled introspection. The people rise in outrage against him.

This is the Jesus portrayed in the earliest recording of his life, the first Gospel, that of Mark. By the end of the story, he has lost confidence in any God up above. He himself is all there is — he alone. The climax to his life is six hours of torture nailed to a cross. It ends in a colossal scream, as he breathes his last. There is no resurrection from the dead. The story closes inside an empty tomb, with three women fleeing, out of their minds with fear.

Mark's story is an 'enigma'. This English word was taken over directly from the Greek — *ainigma*. Aeschylus used it in the most profound of all classical Greek tragedies, *Agamemnon*, to mean 'dark saying', or 'grimly prophetic riddle'.[1] Mark's story is one long and complete *dark saying*.

Why is he the 'existential' Jesus? Because the normal identifying markers of the self have been stripped away from him — family, friends, a past, an occupation, and even an anticipated life-path. In effect, all he can proclaim about himself is: 'I exist.' His story then becomes a quest for the *I* that exists. What is the nature of his being? What powers may he draw upon? How should he live in relation to the one thing that he has been given: his own existence?

'What is truth?' Pilate will ask Jesus. That is indeed the question. Of course, there are material facts. And there are moral truths. But these are the lower and middle orders. The question is about higher order, or 'capital T' truth. If Truth exists, what is its substance? Which is its domain? Or is it an illusion?

We are haunted by the Truth that we suspect lies behind things. On the surface, events and their emotional currents fill the mind. These are the things that happen between birth and death — people encountered, children raised, jobs performed, homes built, schedules and pastimes, achievements and failures, loves and griefs. A myriad of such threads weave the cloth of an individual life.

Yet somehow the subterranean truth is everything. It is like a mysterious stranger encountered on an afternoon walk, an intrusive and unwelcome companion who is fleetingly there, then gone. Only afterwards, in reflection, one comes to fear that this was the vital encounter, and it may have been missed.

Emmaus

The imagination is full with its promise—that it might tap into the source of vital energy, injecting the zest and dynamism that is lacking; that it might bring illumination to a life, and provide the key to what it is all about, bestowing meaning. Conversely, without such a truth, or truths, life sinks into routine—lacklustre in mood, absurd in content, ultimately futile. Without these truths, we might be on the wrong train, at the wrong time, going in the wrong direction. So we fear, but are not sure. The 'truths' are our signposts.

So we explore ancient sites seeking some timeless authority—a blurred inscription in stone, a sculpted face, a special place with sacred presence. So we plunge into romance, dreaming that the other might be the one. So we form families in the hope of redemptive cosiness, and steadfast belonging, or a new generation that will rise higher. So we search for a central life-activity—a 'vocation'—for work that is more than a profane job. So we build nations, cities, and institutions, imagining that if we get the form right, then what we have made will be more than bricks and mortar; a sort of perfection that will endure. In a modest way we have similar dreams about a memo; an essay; a well-decorated, clean, or orderly room; and, especially, a performance at sport.

When reality strikes back, as it inevitably does, much of this turns out to have been an illusion. It's an illusion that at best redeemed life for a while, before popping like a soap bubble. However, if *redemptive illusion* is all there is, the truth about human life, the whole truth—if we are honest—is that it swings between the absurd and the horrible.[2] There is nothing more. Here is the starting point for the Jesus Story.

The modern West's most influential literary work, *Hamlet*, orbits around the question, 'To be or not to be?' Truth, it implies, is to do with the nature of 'being'. And many today do seek a richer conception of the self — the site where it is imagined that important truth dwells. Hence the wide appeal of Eastern philosophy, with its greater emphasis on inner consciousness. Hence the prevalence of theories and therapies that promise the self more understanding of its own nature.

European philosophy itself, in the twentieth century, swung back to focus on *being*.[3] This was a return to the beginning. At the historical start of Western culture, in classical Greece, the inscription carved in stone over the entrance to the sacred oracle, in Delphi, commanded: *Know thyself!* The essence of each individual living human — the *I* — holds the secret. What each person really wants to know dwells here: 'Who am I?'

The West has one supreme teacher on being. Only one has fathomed its depths. Through the grand course of Western culture, from Homer to us, most is to be learnt about the *I* from Jesus. His own way of putting it was, '*I am*'. This teaching is not abstract like philosophy. The philosopher, at most, supplies a body of dictums that may be pondered sagely in the mind, but fail to engage viscerally with the fundament of the self.

The Jesus teaching comes in the form of a story. As such it is down-to-earth, and graspable. It speaks through the narrative account of the life of one man — and his own wrestling with his mission. It compels us to engage with his experience and what he learns — to walk in his shoes.

It is within the mystery of the narrative that Truth resides. Such has been the experience of a university reading group I have convened for a decade. We meet for an hour a week during semester to discuss, one chapter at a time, books from the New Testament and the Hebrew Bible—itself otherwise known, in the Christian tradition, as the Old Testament. Our group of seven is diverse, not particularly reverent, and interested mainly in the text in itself—what it has to say, and how it says it. I have convened the group out of an interest in the foundational religious texts of our culture; also, as someone with a deep intuition of a sacred order governing the human condition; and as someone for whom Jesus is a central but obscure presence. I have never been a practising Christian.

Twice the reading group has read Mark—although with a largely different membership. Both times the experience has been astonishing—quite unlike that of group-reading any other books of the Bible. After Mark, everything else would disappoint.

From early on, a sense grew of us entering a tightly closed and shadowy place in which the atmosphere pulsed with a strange charge. In spite of the confines, it was like the tang of mountain air. Once in, there was no way out. If only one could follow the threads, decoding them as one advanced, one might enter some illuminated chamber. And there were many glimpsed illuminations. Everyone instinctively knew that, for all the other members, themes reverberated through the intervening days, waiting to be taken up at the next meeting. Sessions regularly ended in perplexed euphoria. By the close, the group had gelled into a kind of informal sect, without doctrine, simply bound by a sense of shared awe. A journey undertaken together had, in some elusive manner, changed lives.

Jesus, as he is commonly identified and understood, is a creation of Christianity, the religion founded in his name. This is Christ the Saviour, mediated through his churches.

Western civilisation and its culture are deeply and pervasively Christian. There is the architectural authority of the grand medieval cathedrals, from Amiens and Bourges to Cologne, Milan, and Westminster Abbey. There is St Peter's in Rome, with Michelangelo's dome, Bernini's interior, and his piazza in front, the whole a projection in space and volume of the phenomenal and seemingly timeless influence of the Vatican. Then, like satellites, there are the hundreds of thousands of imposing stone churches in villages and towns throughout the Western world. There is the art, from stained-glass windows and medieval icons to the consummation of Western painting and sculpture — the Renaissance virtuosity of a Donatello, a Raphael, a Poussin, their work centring on Christian images and Christian stories. High poetry, just in English — from Milton, Donne, and Herbert to Hopkins and Eliot — is explicitly Christian. The novel, the story, and film all draw extensively on Christian archetypes. Then there is the music, from Gregorian chants to hymns, carols, requiem masses; the Western tradition reaches its pinnacle in the cantatas and Passions of Bach — devoutly Christian music.

Yet much of this seems like a past that has been lost. The social influence of the Christian churches has been in relentless decline for two centuries. Its influence over family life and morals, the cogency of public pronouncements by bishops, the reputation of priests, even the ceremonial control of births, marriages, and funerals — all have dissipated. The modern West is overwhelmingly secular and humanist in its habits, tastes, and beliefs.

The United States is sometimes cited as the exception to the secularisation of the West. Religious strains continue to reverberate in American culture. In politics, the stock rhetoric of 'God bless America' sometimes cloaks a kind of Old Testament belief in the 'chosen people' carrying out God's mission in the world. Many hundreds of Christian radio and television stations network the country. Christian books regularly chart amongst the nation's best-sellers. A third of Americans, according to opinion polls, hold to a fundamentalist belief in the literal truth of the Bible. A majority in 2002 said they believed that the apocalyptic predictions in the Book of Revelation will come true.

Yet the counter-case is just as plausible. Whilst 85 per cent of the American population is nominally Christian, only 20 per cent regularly attend church, and the figure is falling—a smallish but significant minority.[4] This compares with a minuscule 5 per cent of the population in other Western countries.[5] Moreover, examining what Americans spend their time doing, and with what degree of passionate engagement, gives one of the most telling readings of the culture. Work, sport, family, and leisure prevail. All of them are thoroughly permeated by the consumer way of life. One of the best indicators today of popular taste is the content of the most-watched television shows: the list is pervasively secular, dominated by sport, soap opera, police and medical dramas, comedy, sitcom, and 'reality' and chat shows.

The waning of Christianity as practised in the West is easy to explain. The Christian churches have comprehensively failed in their one central task—to retell their foundation story in a way that might speak to the times. They have failed at what the ancient Jews called *midrash*—the art of reworking stories so as to bring them up to date. The church Jesus is a wooden residue of tired doctrine about a benevolent and omnipotent Lord God up above, the Trinity, the forgiveness of sins, Holy Communion, resurrection from the dead, and so forth—little of which has cogent mainstream resonance today.

This is not just a recent problem. From the outset, the churches have practised a systematic negation of the Jesus of the first Gospel. And Mark provides the definitive telling of the story that governs the three that follow—Matthew, Luke, and John. Harold Bloom puts it that Mark invented Jesus.[6] The churches have not wanted anything to do with Jesus the teacher of the deep truths about human identity. They have made him superficial and boring, a background prop for their own creeds, rituals, and power. This history of denial and falsification has finally caught up with the clerical elites and their priesthoods.

It is a mark of the cultural and psychological maturity of the modern West that individuals have come to make their own judgments about what they find plausible in answer to the three big questions of meaning: *Where do I come from?*, *What should I do with my life?*, and *What happens to me when I die?* In the end, the highest authority has become the individual's own conscience. The vast majority have turned their backs on the churches, and have come to roll their eyes dismissively at Christian doctrine. Mark's existential Jesus would approve.

It is not, moreover, that the churches may claim some other source of authority on the life and teaching of Jesus. The four stories are all we have. There are a few other fragmentary accounts and collections of sayings found later, notably two 'gospels' attributed to Thomas and Peter; but these texts add very little, as do the Letters of Paul. There is no independent evidence about the historical figure of Jesus. The only two non-Christian testimonies to mention him—one, Jewish, from around 90AD, and one, Roman, from two decades later—record little more than that a Jesus Christ lived, and that he was crucified.

Churches have a necessary logic they must obey if they are to survive. They are communities of individuals. To bind those individuals together into a cohesive whole, and make them dependent, they must build a body of moral laws—'Thou shalt nots'—then proclaim and sanction them, punishing those who break them. Churches are ethical institutions. To gain legitimacy here, they are in need of a charismatic foundation figure who was a moral teacher.

Also, they usually call for a Jesus who is benevolent and forgiving, one who comforts those who suffer. Hence he has been projected as the Good Shepherd—Jesus the meek and mild, a gentle figure of sweetness and light. From such a characterisation derives the children's 'little Lord Jesus' who 'lays down his sweet head'.

Mark's Jesus is not remotely like any of this—and he is not interested in ethical teaching. Worse, he identifies all churches with the withered and stonyhearted. He exposes their nature as innately driven to suppress Truth. Truth is their lethal enemy.

This conflict comes to a head over the word 'sin'. As if to confirm hostilities, church Christianity has distorted Mark's text—through skewing the translation of his words in a direction to suit itself. It has falsely projected the image of a moralistic Jesus preoccupied with *sin*. The Greek word translated as 'sin' used by Mark—*hamartia*—means 'missing the mark', as in a badly aimed spear-throw. It can also mean 'character flaw'. Mark's Jesus is concerned with the righting of being, or the restoring of a character that is out of balance. This is an issue of *being*, not of *morals*.

Churches are not the only groups that Mark targets. A church is one example of human community. It is not inherently different from others—whether family, club, society, school, company, suburb, or town. It is merely representative.

Mark's Jesus teaches that the person is the locus of Truth. His perspective is individual-centred and anti-tribal. Whatever the virtues of a community for human well-being —most commonly in the form of family—that is not where a person will find who he or she is, or what is meant to be. Indeed, group traits and attachments have to be stripped away. Matthew will coin the image of the 'whited sepulchre, beautiful on the outside, but inside full of dead men's bones'. In effect, Mark portrays all churches as whited sepulchres.

Whether a role of any significant depth remains for 'church'—both in itself and as a paradigm of community—will be taken up later in this book. A church strives, at best, to become a *sacred community*, bound by some enthusiasm that inspires its members with more than just the practical or functional business of the group.

The sociological signs are that the modern West has entered a post-church era. The West seeks its answers to the big questions outside the stone walls, and especially in everyday life in the secular world. Its new altars are modest and obscure—at home, at work, in sport, and in nature.[7] However, without the security of community or institution—to provide boundaries and direction—it is all the more in need of a Teacher. So it is time to return to the beginning, before the churches were built, when there was Jesus alone, and his story. Who was this man who shaped the Western world?

There are four distinct characters projected in the different versions of the story—Mark's Jesus, Matthew's Jesus, Luke's Jesus, and John's Jesus.

What do we know with some confidence about the four Lives of Jesus, or Gospels? We know, firstly, that they were all written in Greek; not in the Aramaic that Jesus himself almost certainly spoke; and not in the Hebrew that was the main written literary language of the Jewish culture from which he came. They are not translations from earlier Aramaic or Hebrew texts. They are, literally, Greek stories. This is surprising and significant.

No manuscripts have survived from the first century. The oldest discovered fragments of the stories date from the early second century, a hundred years after the death of Jesus. The first complete manuscript dates from around 350AD. None of this is surprising, given an age in which manuscripts had to be copied by hand. For comparison, the oldest complete surviving manuscript of Plato's writings is from a thousand years after his death.

The most authoritative version of the Lives today, The Greek New Testament, has been produced by the collaboration of biblical scholars, working eclectically with the manuscripts and fragments, trying to find the most plausible and consistent variants. Around 3000 of these manuscripts exist, copied between the second and seventeenth centuries.[8] Wholly authentic or autograph Gospels, in the sense of exactly what the author wrote, or dictated, do not exist—only approximations of them. Nevertheless, little controversy remains over the content of the four texts.[9]

We do not know the identities of any of the storytellers for certain, or indeed whether one person wrote each Life. Many scholars assume that the original texts received heavy editing at the hands of others, which helps to explain contradictions between the stories, and discontinuities within the narratives. According to this view, it is the heavily edited versions that became accepted as the canon in the second century, when collections of Christian writings were being brought together to form what would become the New Testament. Indeed, there are troublesome sections in all four Lives that the reader is tempted to explain away as evidence of bad editing, faulty copying, or the author having a bad day.

The consensus today is that Mark wrote first, around 70AD.[10] Then came Matthew, who worked from Mark—copying out something like 80 per cent of his text virtually word for word, with minor amendments. He also added significantly—his text is more than 50 per cent longer than Mark's. For example, the story of the birth of Jesus and the Sermon on the Mount first appear in Matthew. Matthew, in complete contrast with Mark, presents a handbook for building churches. Matthew's is the most Jewish Jesus, his role spelt out as a continuation and fulfilment of themes from the Hebrew Bible.

Chronologically, Luke comes third, also working off Mark's text, repeating much of it whilst reorienting Jesus towards the Good Shepherd figure taken up later by the churches. Luke adds important stories—Mary Magdalene at the house of Simon the Pharisee, the Supper at Emmaus—and he alone recounts the parables of the Good Samaritan and the Prodigal Son. Matthew's and Luke's are the Gospels that have been favoured by most churches. Indeed, the early church showed little interest in Mark's Gospel, which fell into disuse.[11]

In comparison with Mark, Matthew lacks pungency, terseness, and subtlety; the narrative is clumsy and dramatically incoherent. Luke has moments of literary flair, and adds key episodes and parables, but lacks the dramatic lucidity and intensity of Mark. Neither Matthew nor Luke exhibits any of the depth and challenge of the first Gospel.

Most biblical commentators have taken John to be different in style and intent from the first three Lives, which are referred to collectively as the *Synoptic* Gospels—meaning, they view Jesus from the same perspective or point of view. Scholars assume that John wrote a couple of decades later than Mark, although there is no hard evidence supporting this. The argument put in this book will be that John, like Matthew and Luke, writes with Mark's Gospel in front of him; but he was the one, the only one, who understood the profundity of the very difficult text he was reworking. He develops those parts of the first Gospel that he finds important but embryonic or sketchy in the original, and he provides short narratives to flesh out some of Mark's most cryptic teachings. His Jesus is different—magisterial, detached from his own trials, in control of his destiny, knowing exactly what he does. John's Jesus complements Mark's.

This book is in two parts. Part One retells Mark's story of Jesus. In it, I provide a translation into English from Mark's 'common' Greek, as it is called—which means a relatively simple form of the language, in spite of the complexity of its subtext. The translation is accompanied by my interpretation and is indented to distinguish it. I have based it in the main on the King James Authorised English Bible. To produce it, I have relied on my knowledge of classical Greek, supported by reference to extensive scholarly commentary, and more recent translations (notably, the New Revised Standard Version). Occasionally, I have used the William Tyndale translation from 1526 that provided the core for the King James edition and, later, many of the poetic phrases and lines that have so influenced modern English.

I have, at times, translated more literally from the Greek than standard versions do—especially where Mark's directness or pungency has been compromised. As one example, Mark writes 'they feared the great fear', which has usually been lamely rendered as 'they feared exceedingly'. Also, I have rendered crucial terms such as 'sin', 'Holy Spirit', 'forgiveness', and 'faith' differently than many readers will be used to, and I have provided explanations for doing so in each case.

Everyone who becomes absorbed in the story is going to try to make their own sense of it—that is how this extraordinary work functions. This means wrestling with the words in the text and their range of possible meanings. Questions of language and interpretation become central, and are often difficult to resolve.

The whole exercise requires its own constant exchange, backwards and forwards, between the interpreter's own blurred sense of self and life-path, and the story's coding of parallel human lives. And new meanings, ones that strike a vital contemporary chord, are encrypted here.

My experience has been that immersion in the story, struggling with it, forced me into the position, again and again, of asking *Who am I?* in the narrative. Different answers appear. It is as if this story's method is to possess the reader through its characters, in order to provide a range of mirrors back on the viewing *I*.

In effect, this is a story with six characters. There is Jesus, and there are five distinct modes of response to his teaching and his presence. Part Two of this book ('They Who Follow') looks at the five characters who represent the different reactions to Jesus. Part Two draws heavily on John's Life of Jesus.

Truth is mythos. This is the axiom that underpins this book and its method. *Mythos* was the classical Greek understanding of culture: a body of timeless, archetypal stories from a long time ago. This is myth in the sense of a charged narrative about larger-than-life — even semi-divine — figures whose lives set the pattern for the way things human have been ever since, and always shall be. Homer's *Iliad* showed the way.[12] *Mythos* is not 'myth' in the sense of the merely fictitious — tales that project events that did not really take place.

Mythos, however, is not concerned with the historical Jesus — what this man actually did and said in Palestine around the year 30AD. It happens, of course, that we know virtually nothing about him. The only point worth making here is a negative one: if it could be categorically proved that Jesus never lived, there would be a problem for the story. The same is true for the Trojan War and the credibility of *The Iliad*. There is this odd ambiguity about *mythos* in the Western tradition. Its two pivotal stories are not based on historical evidence, yet both depend on some belief that their characters lived and that the events happened.

Much biblical scholarship since the mid-nineteenth century has been in search of the historical Jesus, and in particular what Jesus actually said. It scrutinises the Gospels for the 'authentic' Jesus, deciphered from the hybrid one that it presupposes was fabricated by the four storytellers and the other editors writing decades after the crucifixion. In part, the aim is to bring legitimacy to Christian doctrine, aspiring to base it on what the real Jesus taught. This tendency turned into a caricature of itself in 1985, with the foundation of 'The Jesus Seminar' — a group of fifty-or-so scholars who meet regularly to vote on what Jesus actually said and did. They have produced their own colour-coded Gospels: red text for what they believe Jesus definitely said; pink for what he probably said; grey for his ideas but not his words; and black for words that they hold to be altogether false.

The academic quest for the historical Jesus is paralleled by tourists or pilgrims visiting the city of Jerusalem today. Their expectation of finding the sites where the key events happened is satisfied by ruins, churches, gardens, streets, and tombs that mark the spot. All are fanciful. Many, like the Church of the Holy Sepulchre, are ludicrously fake.

The example of the Via Dolorosa, marked out by the Crusaders, is typical of this exercise in historical futility. There is a negligible chance that this street, supposedly marking the path Jesus trod while carrying his cross from the place of his trial to his execution, is genuine. The trial probably took place at Herod's Palace, on the opposite, west side of the city to where the Via

Dolorosa starts. And the crucifixion might have taken place almost anywhere in the densely built rabbit-warren of alleys that comprises the northern part of the Old City today—or even beyond it.

The one plausible parallel is that Jesus himself found Jerusalem a cold, hostile, unholy city, occupied by zealous, moralistic clerics, squabbling religious sects, money-grubbing merchants, and dense, swarming crowds. Modern Jerusalem is not so different.

One commentator has condemned the very quest for the historical Jesus as idolatrous.[13] And, indeed, such a quest is not only largely futile, but it searches for Truth where it does not dwell, in the sort of material evidence that is studied in a science laboratory. We shall see how Mark mocks those who seek truth in the surface facts. We only know Jesus through his story—as *mythos*. Oscar Wilde, in *De Profundis*, referred to the 'four prose-poems about Christ'.[14]

Anyone who writes about Jesus today is reliant on a mountain of Christian theology, textual scholarship, and biblical commentary. Furthermore, theologians have made their own diffuse contribution to Western culture, well beyond the bounds of their field. Many of the modern disciplines in the humanities derive wholly or in part from medieval theology—philosophy, literary criticism, iconography, philology—just as works of literature, art, and music have been informed by biblical interpretation.

However, biblical scholars have shown a striking incapacity to step outside their disciplines to understand the way that narrative works. This is a notably acute handicap in relation to Mark, given his tactical use of enigma, and the interweaving throughout of themes which typically surface with no more than a hint or an obscure conundrum. He repeatedly uses his subtext to tangle the threads of surface meaning. Part of Mark's working method is dramatic paradox. Mark is a virtuoso storyteller who cannot be understood from outside the logic of his own art.

Also, most biblical commentators are practising Christians, and their work periodically suffers from the wearing of doctrinal blinkers. Even the doyen of modern scholars, Raymond E. Brown, whose work has been invaluable to the background research for this book, has times when the fact that he was a Roman Catholic blights his interpretation. At one point, he even makes it explicit that because later Christian theology won't allow a particular reading of Mark's text, he cannot accept it as valid.[15] The Protestant theologian Rudolf Bultmann concludes that Jesus' main message was an extension of the Old Testament. It was intended to focus on the end of the world and the Kingdom of God.[16] This is a bewilderingly implausible reading of Mark, as the work to follow should demonstrate.

Two of the West's most eminent literary critics, both secular men, have acknowledged the superiority of Mark's Gospel as a work of literature. Harold Bloom writes, 'A substantial number of Americans who believe they worship God actually worship three major literary characters: the Yahweh of the J writer, the Jesus of the Gospel of Mark, and Allah of the Koran.'[17] Bloom added later that 'whoever composed Mark is a genius still too original for us to absorb'.[18]

The British critic Frank Kermode devoted a whole book to Mark, *The Genesis of Secrecy*, that I found more useful than all the biblical scholarship I have read. Kermode explores how story works, through a textual analysis of what is arguably the most cryptic major narrative in Western culture: Mark's Life of Jesus.

The major aid in reading Mark's text has been John's own Life of Jesus, and vice versa. It is extraordinary that one story should attract two storytellers of peerless rank. We cannot imagine a second Homer, nor a second Shakespeare.

Also, three of the masters of Western art have provided ways into the *mythos* that Mark and John created. Donatello, Raphael, and Poussin rethink the Jesus story, and translate it into visual imagery. After John, they are the ones who have seen what Mark saw.

Why, it might be asked, would anyone write yet another book on Jesus? For two millennia this story has been told and retold, interpreted and reinterpreted, many thousands of times—in writing, painting, sculpture, drama, and music. The Bible—that is, its Jesus sections—is by a vast margin the most published and written-about work in the West.[19]

The justification for this book is simple. We cannot live without *mythos*, without answers to the three big questions that life poses. As the Australian Aborigines put it in relation to their own quite different *mythos*—which they called the Dreaming—if you lose contact with the founding, archetypal stories, you wither away and die. It is only the conjoining of an individual's own story with the Dreaming parallel that inspires life, transforming it out of profane ordinary time and its banal routines.

Jesus is the core of the Western Dreaming. His presence is vital to our civilisation and its individuals. He is known by his story. Mark composed the first and most potent version. It is time to retell the first Gospel, and reflect upon it in the context of today. My principal aim is to restore the story, a bit like a conservator working on an Old Master, the painting grimy with stained varnish and the encrustations of time. My hope is to introduce new viewers, in a new time, to the splendour of the work; to suggest to those already familiar with it to take another look; and to read it in a fresh way, drawing new meanings out of it.

What emerges is a mysteriously enigmatic, existential Jesus whose story has not been retold elsewhere, and whose teachings have not been spelt out as they are here.

This Jesus learns through his own bitter experience to reject temples and churches. What he finds himself left with is nothing, apart from his own story. So he invites those who have ears to hear to join him, to stand in his shoes, and to learn from his tragic journey. By the end, the total accumulation of what he has done and what he has said is stripped back to one single teaching: all you need is his story. You don't even need him, only what his story teaches — a *dark saying* about *being*. Mind, he himself is that mysterious stranger intruding on the afternoon walk, fleetingly there and then gone, his own presence everything.

The story is a self-contained numinous object. It is like a precious stone with complex internal faceting, flickering planes of light, within which shadows — strangely difficult to glimpse — flit and shimmer. Here dwells the radiance.

PART ONE

The Story

CHAPTER ONE

THE SOWER

When he appeared, as Mark tells it, he came out of nowhere, with no past — except for a single reference to Nazareth in Galilee, his hometown. There is no birth narrative. There is no Virgin Mary, mangers, shepherds by night, or three wise men from the east. In this, the first story written about his life, he has no childhood. The only mention of kin is an early, dismissive refusal by him to see any of them — 'Who is my mother or my brothers?' No trade is noted, or education. Other sources will suggest he was in his early or middle thirties. He is what will become, in the culture of the West, the mysterious stranger. The implication is that his earlier life, about which we are told nothing, was inconsequential. Whether it was ordinary, wayward, or wasted, it did not contribute to who he is. His presence will be known, for as long as he remains, through his mission, which starts now.

Yet Mark's opening words are about birth or, rather, genesis: *In the beginning was the Story.*

These first words of Mark read tersely in the original Greek: *Archē tou euaggeliou.*[1] John, whom I am taking to be the great interpreter of Mark, provides his midrash: *En archē ēn ho logos* — 'In the beginning was the word.' Mark's third word, *euaggelion*, translates as good message or good tidings, travelling into Old English as godspel or gospel. Hence the attributed title,

The Gospel of Mark. John adapts *euaggelion* into *logos*, which is usually translated as 'word', but which might equally be rendered 'story'. As we shall see, John means both. By the end of Mark's narrative it will be apparent that the good message is the story itself, as told here.

The Story is what was, in the beginning. It is the source of all things that are. *Creation* is being recast — in contrast and in opposition to *Genesis* in the Old Testament, which has God in the beginning creating all things. This is a tactical opening — to supersede the Hebrew Bible. The implication is clear: that Bible got it wrong. Forget the past! Scrap the holy texts! This Story is a new start. It abolishes the old.

God is replaced by the man whose Story is about to be told. Mark opens by setting up the answer to the first of the big questions, 'Where do I come from?' John, in his opening chapter, will likewise make it clear that Jesus replaces God.

It was around the year 30, in a remote province of the Roman Empire during the reign of Tiberius. Suddenly he was there, by the river Jordan:

> And he was baptised in the river, by the preacher from the deserts, John, who came clothed in camel's hair bound with a leather belt, eating locusts and wild honey. John, given to the preacher-way of lecturing, 'Sinners repent, or be damned!' now said, 'One is coming after me, greater than I, whose sandal strap I am not worthy to bend down and untie. I baptise with water, but he will baptise with sacred *pneuma*.'
>
> As he came up out of the water, he saw the heavens split open and pneuma descended upon him, like a dove. A voice came from above, 'You are my beloved son in whom I delight.'

> Immediately, the pneuma drives him into the
> wilderness—for forty days. There among the wild beasts
> he was tempted by Satan, and the angels served him.

From the outset, he is on his own. The solitariness is stark. Many are around, but he alone sees the heavens part. He alone senses the pneuma descending over him—it, rather than the water, is the medium of his baptism. He is bathed in pneuma—his first companion. He alone hears the voice.

'Sacred pneuma' is traditionally translated from the Greek—*pneuma hagion*—as 'Holy Spirit' or 'Holy Ghost'. In the original Greek it is not capitalised.[2] The church tendency to conceptualise it as an entity loses the pneuma associations with wind, breath, and spirit—its range of Greek meanings. I shall leave 'pneuma' untranslated throughout.

Pneuma is 'the wind that bloweth where it wills, and thou hearest its sound, but canst not tell whence it cometh, and whither it goeth'. This is how John, taking Mark's cue, will timelessly project it. It is the charged wind, the cosmic breath, the driving spectral force. It is also the directing power that drives the stranger into the wilderness. And it manifests itself in unsound forms within deranged individuals.[3] John will refer to 'pneuma the god'.[4]

Propelled by his ethereal companion, he strays through the desert, where nothing grows. It is the territory of John the Baptist, the wild man who watered his head, outside the bounds of human law and community. Is he lost? Is he resisting the call to become whoever he is, to do whatever is demanded on the path he does not yet foresee? Maybe, like any man, he fears the enormity of what is to follow, that even he might not be up to it. He may be wishing for an ordinary life; or at least some power, given his special being, over worldly affairs.

He is tempted, but we are not told by what—apart from Satan. He enters into some state of darkness—perhaps mania or madness. Is he tempted by power or desire, the realm of sin and damnation that the wild man preaches against? If so, is he tempted to counter his own human instincts by becoming the preacher, and speaking from out of the source of his own weakness? Then, at least, he would know where he was going. Meanwhile, benevolent higher powers—angels—look after him.

Forty is the number of punishment. Forty days he foundered in the void.

Then he regained his balance. To summarise Mark, he returned to Galilee to begin—John the Baptist had just been imprisoned. At first he preached, like the preacher, as if feeling his way, not quite knowing how or where. He also went to the temple where he taught, for he discovered he was a teacher. In fact, *teacher* will quickly become his major role.[5] Drawing many to him, he spoke with an inner presence, not like the others repeating doctrine out of books.

In these early days he discovered he had special powers. When he chose, he could miraculously heal the sick. For a brief interlude he did so—first a man convulsed with unsound pneuma, then a leper, a quadriplegic, and a man with a withered hand. His reputation spread. Masses flocked to him, in spite of the fact that he had taken to the road. They flocked from Galilee; from Judea; from the coastal towns; from beyond the Jordan; and even from Jerusalem, a hundred and fifty kilometres away. He had begun a ceaseless journeying—at the pressured, impatient pace that would mark his short time.

Still unsure himself about how to proceed, unclear about his mission and who he is, he goes up the mountain. When he comes down, he tries out a new tactic—to teach through parables:

He began to teach again, by the sea. Because of the size of the crowd he got into a boat, to sit in the sea, with the crowd nearby on the land. He taught them many things in parables.

'Listen,' he said to them, 'See! The sower went out to sow. Some seed fell by the road and birds ate it. Some fell on stony ground, and immediately it sprang up, for there was no depth of earth, but the rising sun scorched it, and because it had no root it withered. Some fell among thorns where it was choked. But other seed fell on good earth and it thrived. He who has ears to hear, let him hear!'

When he was alone later, those around him, including the twelve, asked him about the parable. He said, 'To you, it has been given to know the mystery of the divine kingdom. But to those outside all things are created in parables, so that

[and he continued by quoting Isaiah]

'Seeing they may see and not perceive; and hearing they may hear and not understand; lest they turn and their sins be forgiven them.'

Then he questioned them, 'Do you not know this parable? If not, how will you know all parables?'

The only part of this episode that is not puzzling is the parable itself — of the sower. The parable is clearly elaborated while everything that surrounds it is cryptically condensed. He has engineered an extravagantly vivid physical setting. He sits by himself, on a boat, separated by water from the crowd pressed together along the shore. Behind them is the mountain. Behind him is the open Sea of Galilee. This sea is more like a lake, which still today has a timeless, otherworldly enchantment to it. He has chosen a place of rare beauty and serenity as the site for his teaching. In this particular scene, he has sat himself in a boat as Lord of the Lake.

The size of the crowd is stressed. Slightly later in the story, Mark will be specific: five thousand follow him to a remote, inhospitable spot behind the Sea of Galilee, not far from where the current crowd has gathered. Five thousand was a huge assembly for the time. Its like would only have been seen with armies massing for battle. Further, the crowd would have been drawn mainly from a sparsely populated region of rural villages and fishing hamlets — where travel was by foot. A modern scholar has estimated the population of Nazareth, one of the few 'towns', at around two hundred people.[6] Capernaum, at the north end of the Sea of Galilee, chosen by the teacher for his base, could not have been much larger. The enormity of the crowd crammed by the water signals the potency of his charisma, and reputation, from early on in his mission.

He starts with a beguiling invocation, like a shaman storyteller, in the form of a double imperative: 'Listen!' and 'See!' Seeing and hearing are later picked up in his riddle to the twelve, as he twists the words of Isaiah, ripping them out of context, into a paradox.

But this parable seems straightforward — unparadoxical. Does surface clarity hide a deeper mystery? He seems to say that he will use the parable as a teaching device, so that those who see will not gain insight; so that those who hear will not understand.[7] If this is the case, why does he bother? Teaching would seem to be pointless.

He enacts a division of people into types. Within the crowd there are twelve special followers whom he has chosen, most of them simple fishermen from around the Sea of Galilee. They constitute some sort of elite. Within them he has selected a favourite three, nicknaming them. Simon he renamed Peter or, in Greek, *Petros* — which means 'rock' or 'stone'. James and John, the sons of Zebedee, he called, enigmatically, 'sons of thunder'. Thus there was a new identity, as if reborn, and the warmth of personal names. It seems he hoped for trust and intimacy with his chosen twelve, an inner circle that he could train to act on his behalf, forging a sacred bond that would steel their resolve. And also, perhaps, he hoped that this community around him might ease his solitariness.

'Listen!' and 'See!' introduces a dualism. There are those who understand the *mystery*, and this group is initially identified as the twelve and a few others. They are the insiders. Insiders already know. Then there are the outsiders. It is necessary to speak to them in parables, which he proceeds to do. But, don't imagine, he warns obscurely, that this is so they might gain some understanding. On the contrary!

When the twelve question him afterwards about the parable he realises that they have not understood it. It appears he had been deluded in his attempts to collect followers and form a band. The twelve are not insiders. To separate them from the crowd was premature. They do not know the mystery. Worse, they do not even comprehend a simple parable — one that true insiders would see in a blink. So what are they capable of understanding? His separation from the land, the water calm beneath him, gestures to a sense of the precariousness of the footing of others, led by the twelve, all of whom he has left on firm land. Mark describes him as sitting 'in the sea' — he is alone. His enthusiasm about his chosen followers deflates, and he has hardly started.

Another seed is being sown: the seed of his own doubt, as indicated by his abrupt shift in perception of his chosen followers.

Does he himself know the nature of the *mystery*? Does he know how it might be revealed? The only knowledge which counts is that which comes from inside. But what might this mean? The parable is all about seeds. Maybe the encrypted story will reveal the mystery, in spite of what he says about parables. All we can do, at this point, is wait and see. And to follow his double command: listen.

What also does it mean to say that outsiders are born from parables, their seed? Does he refer to encrypted stories? Is it the function of deep stories not to be understood, but just to lodge somehow in the deep substratum of being, and infiltrate the housing psyche? Is he developing a theory of knowledge and interpretation? Is this a first sign about how his own story will work?

After questioning the twelve about what they know, he — the teacher — provides his interpretation of the parable:

> The sower sows the word [*logos*]. Those beside the road are ones who have the word taken away by Satan the instant it is sown in their hearts. Those on stony ground hear the word with joy, but they have no root in themselves, so their era [*kairos*] is brief. The moment they are put under stress or persecuted, because of the word, they stumble. Those amongst thorns hear the logos, but they are preoccupied by the cares and pleasures of the world, so they choke. The word sown on good ground bears fruit prodigiously.

This interpretation hardly adds anything, seeming almost intentionally dry and lacklustre.[8] It strengthens the sense that this particular parable is easy to understand. Calling the seed the *word* does no more than beg the question of what it is. Perhaps he is merely underlining his point about parables being inherently paradoxical, and that teaching is the bringing of a fundamental story into focus, then blurring it, lest the listeners gain the impression they understand something.

The interpretation does provide a fragmentary clue to one element of the parable — that concerning stony ground. His sudden uneasiness about the twelve brings to mind his renaming of Simon, which seems to have been rash. The Greek word in this sower parable for stony ground is *petrōdes* — metaphorically, the home of *Petros*. Simon belongs on stony — or rocky — ground, the matter out of which he is formed.[9]

When Simon the fisherman was called to follow, he heard the word with joy. But the forewarning is that he has no roots, so the moment there is stress, or fear of persecution, he will wither. Outsiders, blind by definition to the mystery, deaf to the word, will stumble. On rocky ground, men stumble. They return to the horizontal, as they were in the beginning. He had hoped that the first among the twelve would be a rock, firmly placed, a sure support for himself and for others; but he is, in reality, stony ground. The Greek verb for stumble, *skandalizō*, contains the further thrust of 'offend', 'outrage', and 'scandalise'. The heat of the sun is an offence to those with frail roots.[10]

The quick-flourishing seed on stony ground shrivels up the moment the sun comes out. It cannot take heat. Mark had earlier recounted that at Simon's house the teacher had once taken the mother-in-law by the hand — for she was fevered — lifted her up, and restored her.[11] This was no act of mercy or confirmation of family ties, but a sign of Simon Peter's future. Fever is fire in the wrong place. It is a cue that his family has a diseased relationship to fire, or heat. *Fire* will grow in metaphorical significance as this story unfolds, becoming *light*.

To make further progress in understanding the parable, we need to pause and return to the teacher's two principal acts of healing, carried out earlier. The quadriplegic who walks, and the man with the once-withered hand, both contribute to the fabric of the sower story:

> He returned to Capernaum. After a few days news got around he was in a certain house, where many gathered, so there was no room, not even at the door. Four came carrying a paralysed man. When they could not get near because of the crowd they climbed on the roof. They broke through and lowered the bed on which the man lay. When he saw their trust he addressed the paralysed man, 'Child, your sins have been forgiven you.'

The scene is high drama. With hordes of the *dis-eased* jammed into the room, pressing upon him, he had been interrupted by the ceiling above his head being broken open. A contraption then lurches down on ropes towards him, four faces staring down framing the open sky. Struck by this ludicrous interruption from above, a parody of the sacred pneuma that had descended on him, and moved by their trust,[12] he spoke directly to the flat-out, helpless man.

Feeling his way, he chose his words with care. 'Your sins have been forgiven.' These words inflamed the intellectuals,[13] crammed in among the crowd, looking on. He sets the first stake in the ground of his new metaphysical territory. The intellectuals hear the words through the ears of their religion, understanding him to be talking about transgression, immoral acts, and forgiveness. According to their Jewish beliefs, only God has the power to forgive sins, so this miracle worker was blaspheming, his words outrageously impious.

Hamartia, the Greek word for 'sin' used by Mark, may alternatively be translated as 'flaw'. Aristotle, over three centuries earlier, had used the same word to mean 'character flaw' in his theory of tragedy—and Greek culture, with its philosophy, was well known in the time and place in which this story is set. The origins of hamartia carry the sense of 'missing the mark', as in a faulty spear throw.[14] Likewise, *aphiēmi,* the word for 'forgive', might be understood differently as 'send away', 'dispatch', or 'set free'.

Here, the teacher continues the transition out of the medium of water. At his first appearance, river baptism was superseded by immersion in pneuma. Water evokes the ethical domain. It purifies and cleanses. It washes away sin. It is the medium of the preacher, and of Jewish religion. His focus is not on virtue and justice, not on good and evil—in either the character of individuals, or their acts. Mark makes this explicit with repeated use of the word 'pneuma'.

So, while the intellectuals hear him say to the prostrate man, 'Your sins have been forgiven you', there is a quite different, pneuma version of the same words. Mark's Greek is like a trick image here: viewed one way, it looks like a vase; viewed another, like two faces in profile. The pneuma perspective reads something like, 'Your disturbed nature is righted.' Or, 'Let the flaws be gone.' Or even, 'You are freed from paralysed being.'

> He knew in his pneuma how they thought, so he turned on them abruptly, 'Why do you question these things in your hearts? Which is easier to say to this paralysed man, 'Your sins are forgiven.' Or, 'Arise, Take up your bed and walk!' The son of man has the authority to right those who are unhinged.'

Here, he fuels the boiling confusion of the intellectuals by switching from moral forgiveness—which they understand, and which they forbid him to enact—to pneuma. Their Jewish religion requires them to obey the moral law, and the rituals and practices of their church that follow on from it. They would rather coldly follow the letter of that law than inspire fallen being.

Significantly, he himself appears unsure and in transition, from the old view which held that the good or godly life is good people living virtuously and justly. He is in transition to a new, pneuma perspective, which is to do with *being*, and its balance.

> He turned to the bed-ridden man, 'I say to you, Stand up, take your bed and go home!' Immediately, the man rose, picked up his bed, and strode off.

The quadriplegic is not told to sin no more. He is told to stand up. The teacher has made his own fateful decision. Purification by water has given way to inspiration by pneuma.

The paralysed man is the human condition. His normal state is prostrate. In the horizontal, the plane of the corpse, he is unable to move until the transforming pneuma settles on him. This happens through the medium of the teacher with 'authority'—*exousia*, literally meaning 'out of being', or 'from out of the essence'. It is direct contact with essential being that frees the spirit to stand up, and achieve the vertical. Right being departs, holding its bed like a triumphal lance, or an anticipatory cross. It is only in the vertical, like a tree, that a person may both sink roots into the earth, and rise up to meet the wind that bloweth.[15] The Story has planted its opening metaphor.

And pneuma rules:

> Surely, I say to you that all sins will be forgiven the sons
> of men, and whatever sacrilege they speak, but he who
> profanes sacred pneuma will never be forgiven, but judged
> into eternity.[16]

Without the sacred breath there is nothing—dispirited life is
death. Pneuma is the higher power that animates, uplifting and
inspiring. Not to breathe is to choke, to become choked up. The
teacher proclaims that there is one act for which there is no
redress, no way back, no redemption. He has arrived at his sole
and unique command, superseding the entire moral law. Thou
shalt not profane pneuma—pneuma the god. Nothing else
matters.[17]

He implies that to fail in relation to pneuma leaves an unholy
wound. The wound festers and turns to rancour—the
compulsion to defame pneuma and those who carry it.
Pneumaphobia is born. This is fear of pneuma, a fear with
malicious intent.[18] Pneumaphobia is the lowest condition into
which humans can sink, turning into the source of evil. His new
medium is starting to breathe through his teaching presence,
sowing its own categories.

He had wandered into synagogues at this time, and taught.
That his authority was over pneuma, rather than worldly affairs,
made them a logical choice. But temples, indeed churches in
general, were trouble. He saw the corruptions of the Jewish
church, and he challenged its ways with predictable contempt:

> He entered the synagogue again where there was a man
> with a withered hand. The Pharisees watched him closely
> to see whether he would heal him on the holy day of the
> week, the Sabbath, so they might accuse him. He addressed
> the man with a withered hand, 'Step forward!' He

questioned the Jews who were scrutinising his every move, 'Is it lawful on the Sabbath to do good or to do ill, to save life or to kill?' They were silent.

He was fuming, his anger rising at what he saw as their stonyheartedness. So he commanded the man, 'Stretch forth your hand!' The forward-thrust hand was restored.

For the first time during his mission, he loses his temper. This is a man with supernatural powers, and immense reserves of assurance and self-control. Moreover, he has just switched his own focus to righting being. Now hamartia strikes him, throwing him off-balance. What has rattled his composure?

On the surface, this episode is a calculated confrontation with the synagogue, the entire Jewish religious elite, and its law-centred culture. More, that law was given by the hand of God, on the mountain, to Moses, their great leader, and from it derive all the rituals and customs of the 'chosen people'. As a starting point, he is rejecting rule by law — in this sense, perhaps in any sense — in favour of individual judgment, guided by compassion. If a man needs healing, and you have the power, then you do it, irrespective of whether it is Saturday or Sunday when it is forbidden to work, inside the holy sanctum of a church, or out in the market-place. Anybody with feeling and sense knows this.

He has no reason to lose his temper over such a paltry matter. He is hardly so naive about human motivation and the innate coerciveness of any social group — their stonyheartedness. The anger must be triggered by deeper cares. Perhaps it is at what their suspicion and hostility indicates. The church — and this probably means any church — will turn into his deadly enemy. All human institutions, even at their most necessary and best, are bound to resist him — given that he has just renounced the role of the moral teacher.

The fuming with anger signals inner discontent. He has probably assumed that he will build a church, gathering followers as John the Baptist did. That would be the obvious and easy way. Indeed, chosen followers accompany him into the synagogue as the doubts mount. Standing before him are Pharisees guarding their temple, seething with hatred. Behind him are chosen followers who may prove no different from the Pharisees.

His first move in this episode is from outside the temple to inside it. It is the Sabbath. His first command is 'Step forward!' The implication is that the deformed man is part of a crowd inside the church, and is asked to separate himself from it, like a soldier commanded to step forward from the ranks on parade.

Further, the stepping forward is in counterpoint to the opening movement, the teacher's entry into the synagogue. Motion in; motion out. Step forth out of the church, for metamorphosis is not possible within its walls. The second command, 'Stretch forth your hand!' continues the momentum, from inside back out, as if he is calling those he calls to leave the church, to free themselves from the yoke of human collectivity. It helps explain why he has singled out this particular affliction. His anger is at the logic of churches, and it feeds his instant recoil. Symbolically, the temple is the domain of the withered, which must be drawn outside — hand beckoning hand — to be made whole.

Let us return to the teaching parable. To date, the Story has provided two pathology metaphors — paralysis in the plane of a corpse, and the deformed hand.[19] The sower parable contrasts four different places where seed falls, but its main interest is in stony ground. The teacher spends most time in his interpretation with those who have initial enthusiasm, but no root in themselves. They wither once the sun gets too hot.

Also, men stumble on stony ground. Their centre of gravity

is awry. Lacking balance, they topple. We know their essential character — for it has already been sketched. They are the paralysed man. In them, the standing up is reversed. He strode off brandishing his bed like a triumphal lance; they fall down.

Stumbling is paralleled by withering. Those who are born with no root in themselves will shrivel in strong light — the blueprint is Peter. Again, the teacher has prepared the metaphor. We already know the *withered*. The movement of the rootless is in the opposite direction to that of the man with the deformed hand. He comes out; they go in. There are withered hands that are restored; there are embryonic beings that wither. The implication is that Peter belongs inside the church.

The theme of 'time' is also introduced in the sower parable — and in relation to those on stony ground. The theme invokes two Greek words with contrasting meanings. There is *chronos*, as in chronological time, measured by clock and calendar. There is alternatively *kairos*, with the more mysterious sense of epic time, the measure by which the grand and significant events in a life are sequenced. A kairos instant may be forever, the moment in which a person is torn out of the oblivion of everyday being and finds the truth that transforms the life — lighting it, or darkening it, eternally.

On stony ground, it is irrelevant whether a human plant is short-lived or long-lived in terms of hours, days, and years. As the teacher says in his interpretation, the deeper sense is that there is little kairos. Letter-of-the-law communities and their occupants live in chronos time. Monday, Tuesday, Wednesday ...; Friday, Sabbath Saturday, Holy Sunday ... As his journey draws inexorably towards its climax, much will hinge on 'the hour', a kairos conception. Kairos is powered by pneuma.

The sower parable is the first 'impression point' in the Story.[20] All stories—whether spoken, written, painted, composed, or filmed—are governed by focal images, dramatic climaxes, and lines of force. A few highly charged events or sequences through the story act as anchors of meaning. It is these intensity nodes and vectors that *impress*—pressing on the reader's attention. They pressure the lead motifs.

Impression points lodge in the subconscious of understanding, needling the psychic nerve. They draw the lines of the rest of the text to them—as subordinate. Their own tendrils of significance feed through the work as a whole, structuring it, articulating beyond their surface role. They orchestrate its drama—its pace, its moods, and its climaxes—as a means of making its themes resonate. Deep engagement with the story is dependent on them.

I shall retell Mark through the pressure nodes in his narrative. They will be dwelt on at length (as with the Sower) while intermediary detail is left out. The power of the sower parable is illustrated by the way it subordinates the pair of healings—of the quadriplegic and the withered hand—to its own logic. It turns their role in the narrative into that of 'teaching stories', rather than the 'miracle stories' that they first seem.

To make the role of the first impression point—the Sower—clearer in this chapter, I have done some minor reordering of Mark's sequences. I shall not take this liberty with the text again. I have taken it here because Mark's narrative momentum does not get going until the Sower appears in his fourth chapter. Thereafter the momentum hardly falters.

Impression points are the seeds that, taken collectively, provide entry into the subtext in which the *mystery* lies buried.

Following the sower episode by the Sea of Galilee, the teacher continues his instruction to the twelve. As they become increasingly bewildered, intimidated by his obscure talk about insiders and the mystery, the parables become shorter and more difficult:

'For him that has, it shall be given; and for he who has not, what he has will be taken away.'

'The divine order is as if a man should scatter seed on the ground, and sleep by night and rise by day, and the seed should sprout and grow, he himself not knowing how.'

'To what shall we liken this order, with what parable shall we signal it? It is like a mustard seed which, when sown on the earth, is smaller than all other seeds; but when sown it grows larger than all cultivated herbs, and shoots out great branches so that the birds of the heavens may nest in its shade.'

This sequence marks the end of his attempt to teach by using parables. The parting image is of the word needing the right soil in which to grow, in the night and unattended. Equally, it must be the right seed, and here as everywhere things are not as they seem, the smallest becoming the greatest. Insiders are made from what is within. They have the one thing that matters, yet more shall be given them. Outsiders lack, but even the little that they have shall be taken away. This seems unfair, unjust, and at odds with any normal human conception of a moral order. This teacher is decidedly not a Good Shepherd.

The first phase of his mission ends with an allusion to the genesis of insiders, and to the mystery—but no sign yet as to its form. Warnings have suddenly sprouted around him. Beware of knowing. His knowing is 'in pneuma'. He disparages 'knowing in your heart', never mind 'letter of the law' obedience to handed-down custom and belief.

His brief phase of teaching through parables has left the uneasy impression that the vital riddle, that of the sower, may be little more than a judgment on the twelve he has chosen. As a consequence, the mini-parable about seed sown in the night is a caution to himself. He should give up trying to cultivate followers. They are the herbs overshadowed by the vast mustard tree. Insiders will appear when they appear. He should give up sowing seeds.

His teaching is in the process of turning into a monologue—for there are no insiders to understand the mystery, and his parables are impenetrably opaque to others. As if mumbling aloud to himself, his short parables reflect on his opening experiment in folly.[21] If it is futile to cultivate insiders, perhaps the most he can do is try to grow like the mustard seed. Then, whichever birds wish to do so may nest in his shade.[22]

He has flung himself into his mission, travelling as if hounded by the shortness of the time left. Constant movement has marked his healing and teaching, from place to place, at a furious pace. Likewise, events force him to question himself and what he is doing. They force a pressured sequence of revaluations. He is not a moral preacher, like the wild man from the desert, or like those who inhabit churches. He has miraculous healing powers, but they mean little to him. Nor is it his way to gather a band of followers, and train them. If he is a teacher—and about this, too, he has become unsure—he teaches by parable, not doctrine.

Unwittingly, the true subject of his teaching has become himself. And, so far, he himself is his only student.

The effect is immediate. He changes direction in his journey, away from teaching, and into doing. He needs to grow himself into a commanding tree.

CHAPTER TWO

FEARING THE GREAT FEAR

In the evening of the same day he said to the few around him, 'Let us cross over to the other side.' They took him with them in a boat, other small boats following. And a great wind stormed in, and waves dashed into the boat so that it was foundering. He was asleep on a pillow in the stern, so they woke him, 'Teacher, you don't care that we perish?' Once aroused, he reproached the wind and said to the sea, 'Quiet, be silenced!' The wind abated and there came a great calm. He turned to them, 'Why are you so afraid? How is it you have no trust?' And they feared the great fear, saying to one another, 'Who is this that the wind and the sea hearken to him?'

On the other side of the Sea of Galilee, in the region of the Gadarenes, the moment he left the boat a man met him, one with unsound pneuma, who dwelt among the graves. Even with chains nobody could bind him, for he had often torn shackles to bits, pulled chains apart. Untameable, through all the night and all the day, in the mountains and amongst the tombs, he would scream out and hack himself with stones.

From afar, seeing the boat arrive, he ran down and prostrated himself, crying out with a great voice, 'What are you to me, son of the highest god, I implore you not to torment me.' He was responding on the instant to the command that met him, 'Come out, you unsound pneuma, from this man!' To the following question, 'What is your name?' the man replied, 'My name is Legion, for we are many.'

Legion pleaded with him relentlessly not to send his *daimones*—the spirits that possessed him—out of the region. The *daimones* themselves implored him to send them into a herd of pigs that was feeding near the mountain. He immediately gave them permission, so the unsound pneumata came out, and entered the pigs, and the entire herd of around two thousand hurtled down the steep hill into the sea and drowned. The swineherds fled, and reported these things in the town and in the country. The people then, flocking to witness what had happened, saw Legion sitting, clothed and of sound mind. Afraid, they began to urge the teacher to leave their borders.

As he got back into the boat, Legion pleaded to be with him. But he forbade it, saying, 'Go to your home and report to those who are yours what the Master[1] has done, and the empathy[2] he has shown you.' So he left, proclaiming what had happened, and all were in wonder.

Once the teacher had recrossed the sea a vast crowd met him, including Jairus, one of the elders of the synagogue. He went up and fell at his feet, begging, 'My little daughter is close to death, please come with the power of your touch, so she may live.'

So he went. Now a certain woman had been haemorrhaging for twelve years and spent all her money on doctors who had merely made her worse—under whose influence she had suffered much. When she heard about him she came up behind in the dense crowd and touched his garment. Immediately the flow of blood stopped and she knew she was cured of her curse. He felt power had drained out of him, so he turned around, asking, 'Who touched my clothes?'[3]

The twelve were incredulous: 'You see the crowd jostling you and you ask, "Who touched me?"' He was looking around to see who had done this. The woman, although lost in the crowd, was in fear and trembling, knowing what had become her. She prostrated herself before him and told all the truth. He said, 'Daughter, your trust has saved you. Go in peace, and be free from your scourge.'

While he was still speaking some came from Jairus' house, announcing, 'Your daughter has died. Why trouble the teacher any more?' The teacher immediately reassured the head of the synagogue, 'Fear not; only trust.'

Allowing no one to follow him apart from Peter, James and John, he went to Jairus' house. Observing an uproar of weeping and wailing, he entered, charging, 'Why such commotion and distress? The child is not dead, but sleeps.' They ridiculed him. Accompanied by the father and mother, and the three, he went in to where the child was lying and took her by the hand, saying, 'Dear little girl, to you I say Rise.'

Immediately the girl, who was twelve, stood up and walked around. And they all wondered with ecstatic wonder. He strictly ordered that no one should know, and that she should be fed.

He begins this new stage in his journey by crossing the sea. The mythic resonance of crossing over the great water is one of transformation, from one state to another. Whether it presages a change of consciousness, or of psychic bearings, or of life path, ultimately it signifies the conversion from life into some meta-life form. It is accompanied by a great storm — nature in upheaval — so that the flimsy boat carrying its anxious human band is threatened with catastrophe. That same water is about to be populated by two thousand demons. A storm is needed to clear the air.

Panic ensues. The twelve do not know the *mystery*; so, once the great wind strikes, they lose their bearings. There can be no trust without affinity with the mystery. Just as Peter has the wrong relationship to fire, so here they are all out of tune with wind, a pneuma mode. And they are at sea on water, which is odd given that they are fishermen, and should be at home in a boat, on the sea in which they used to cast their nets. He has obliterated early lives, so even regular founts of security no longer help. The scene mocks those who have normal human training and experience of storms at sea.

The upshot is increasing bewilderment among the twelve about who he is and what he is up to. In one single day, they undergo their own, life-determining metamorphosis. Men who have given up everything, to follow the man who, they hope, will lead them to the mystery, find themselves blinded by chronic insecurity. The new mood rises that will govern their remaining time in his company — fear. Mark puts it that they now 'fear the great fear'. Theirs is thus a sort of anti-initiation — uprooted from the old order, they fail to sink new roots. It is set as an anticipatory contrast to what happens to the three strangers who now cross his path.

Nature's fury had given way, under his command, to the great calm. But not only Nature was in tumult. On the other side, he is immediately confronted by human fury, and at its most extreme. Legion is untameable barbaric violence. His raging is mainly directed against himself as he tears at his own flesh, purging his inferno through incessant screaming. He is out of his mind, like a mad animal—a rabid dog or a wounded bull. More specifically, he is inwardly tormented by unsound pneuma. The deranged pneumata are referred to by the word *daimones*—in Greek mythology, lower spirits or half-gods. Alternatively, a person's *daimōn* may be a positive force that acts as a guide or protector in life—Socrates claimed his *daimōn* would intervene, guardian-angel like, whenever he was about to do something foolish. In Legion's case the implication is not only that there are multitudes of them, but that they are unsettled, or in the wrong place—a hamartia problem.

Legion feels at home only among the tombs. He belongs among the dead. Other humans are desperate to chain and shackle him. Their response to rampaging pneuma is to tie it down, lock it up. Better no spirit than the jungle—untamed pneuma leads directly to the graveyard. Human order depends on straitjacketing pneuma.

Legion, who is many, is the first to meet the Master in his new role, and after storm over water. He is the one who sees him coming. Also, his mode of encounter is to cry out with a loud voice. A great voice or, in Greek, *mega phōnē*, will signal key moments later in the story.

Legion is, in part, the Master's other self, not so different in essence—we recall his own rage in the temple. And to gain a broader sense of his waywardness, we only need to dwell on the extravagant image of him sleeping on a pillow at the stern of a boat that is foundering, in the midst of a howling storm, his twelve shaking him awake in whimpering panic. Both beings are governed by pneuma, and so belong together. Both are dynamos of mighty passion—roaming among the tombs, withdrawing up the mountain, crossing the *daimōn*-infested waters.

Mark began with the beginning, when there was the Story, the beginning which is now. It is Legion who is instructed to go and tell the story. Legion is the first. We know by now that the chosen twelve will not be asked: they are told to keep secret the healing of the girl. Their new condition — of great fear, of permanent inner storm — is set in contrast with Legion sitting quietly and in sound mind, a human incarnation of calm. Also he is clothed, in a sign of his new state of civility.

Legion had been a deranged animal roaming the mountains. The story closes with two thousand mad pigs hurtling down the mountain to their death. The sea is now possessed by *daimones*, making it even more threatening for those who may need to cross over it. The *daimones* leave the impression that it is their natural home, where they belong. The people, hearing of the swine, and seeing Legion sitting in all his superb calm, become like the twelve — afraid. It is the union of the two who have the power of pneuma that sparks off the great fear — like a howling gale over water buffeting the flimsy boat of normal human gathering. They all now want the Master out of their region. His presence is too unsettling. Human community can no longer house him.

An exile by his own destiny, by his own chosen path, he crosses back over the sea and finds himself engaged with two women who are critically sick and in need of their own crossing over. These are rite-of-passage stories, from one life-stage to another, at either end of maturity — at least on the surface. We may assume the older woman who is haemorrhaging is stuck in menopause. Unable to transform into elder being, she is bleeding to death, her vitality and all her resources draining away. Doctors of the body merely aggravate her suffering. In touch with the right power, or force, she is renewed. Many touch his robe, but only she is receptive to its potency; the obtuse twelve see only the profane, exterior facts. That she may now tremble in fear before the teacher is itself a sign of right order—she is free to live. It is 'truth' she now speaks, and all of it.

Jairus, too, is an elder, with the sense to approach the man who may save his daughter. Aged twelve, she is on the threshold of puberty—another blood metaphor. Biologically, she is about to become a woman. Metaphysically, the change into adulthood requires the death of the child-self, followed by rebirth. Her standing up is a sign that the blood, or life-force, has started to flow—a seed may germinate. This requires his presence, his touch, and his word.

Jairus receives the definitive double-command: 'Fear not; only trust.' As a true elder, he has found the proper relationship to the one who has given up on cultivating insiders who cannot trust him, and who are, therefore, in his presence, reduced to fear. The older woman has intuitive trust, so she touches his robe. The fear that follows is *right fear*—fear of the one with the power. Right fear is the holy emotion, expressed by the bowed head, the eyes lowered—she prostrates herself. It is the sacred shame that every human feels in the vicinity of higher authority, and in the vicinity of a violation of higher order.[4] This is what he means by there being no way back from profaning pneuma. Pneumaphobia is not to be forgiven—it is not to be redeemed.

The menopausal woman, like the dear little girl, has been in the condition of the living dead for twelve years: one, in a state of pre-human childhood; the other, post-human purgatory. Legion has gone from being a wild animal to a calm storyteller. In all three, delinquent forces have been tamed.

From teaching by parables he has moved into living as a parable. And the birds—three of them—flock to nest in his tree. The motif is initiation, the metamorphosis universal to human societies. All cultures require their members to be subjected to an ordeal through which the old self — usually it is the child self, but not necessarily so — is systematically annihilated, until the person is reduced to nobody, a non-being. Then, through some form of introduction into the deep mysteries and truths, the initiate is brought back to life with a new persona, forged in the crucible of ordeal by fire. The new persona is geared to maintaining the sacred meaning.[5]

The daughter was thought to have died, before rebirth into her adult self. The woman's ordeal lasted for twelve years of acute, life-draining *pathos* — suffering. Legion, only at home among the dead, was himself a cauldron of teeming spirits hotly driving him around the mountains, his volcanic might tearing shackles apart. In all three cases of initiation, as he enacts it, the great fear is overcome. Trust rules. Legion is the exemplar, sitting calmly, his own presence now an intimidation of the unsettled, they who have not; and a centre of gravity for the poised, they who have.

The sequence of metamorphoses has left him with three would-be insiders. He then reverts to one last attempt to make something of the twelve:

> He travels with them back to his own country, only to be met by incredulity among the people. They are scandalised that one of their own has gained such powers and wisdom — this carpenter, son of Mary, brother of James, Joses, Judas, and Simon, his sisters also known locally. He said to the twelve, 'A prophet is not without honour, except in his own country, among his kin, and in his own house.' Here he finds that his teaching and healing are ineffectual, and is astounded at the lack of trust.

He seems shaken by what he is learning—'astounded'. His hoped-for new family—the twelve—is disintegrating. He seeks out his childhood place of belonging. Under duress, humans go back home. But the return home proves naive on his part. His own people do not want to know him—as he has become. They only want him as he was, outwardly normal like themselves—with a trade, a mother, and brothers and sisters. This was the younger person whom Mark did not bother to portray. Although they do recognise his powers and wisdom, this only serves to make them more hostile.

His failed homecoming confirms his growing suspicions about himself. The way to *know thyself* so far is a journey of negations—crossing off what he is not, stripping away old or imaginary selves. He is not a man with his father's trade, not from Nazareth, and not one of the people of Galilee. He has no mother, no brothers, and no sisters. At this point, he is best known by what he is not.

> He gives the twelve instructions. They are to proceed in pairs, taking nothing for the road, apart from a staff—not food, money, or spare clothing. He provides them with the power over unsound pneumata, and they go forth healing the sick, and preaching repentance.

Finally they have a role. But it is not his role. That they have taken to the road lecturing against immorality brings to mind the preacher John the Baptist:

> King Herod heard, for the teacher's name had become well known. He concluded that John had risen from the dead. Herod had arrested John and imprisoned him, because of his wife Herodias—she had previously been

his brother Philip's wife. John had told Herod it was unlawful for him to marry his brother's wife. Herodias held this against the Baptist. But she had failed in her ambition to have him killed, because Herod feared John as a just and holy man, and protected him—listening to him, and accounts of what he did with pleasure.

Herod's birthday offered her an opportunity. During a banquet for the eminent and powerful in Galilee, the daughter of Herodias danced for Herod and his guests. They were enchanted, so the infatuated king promised the girl, 'Ask whatever you wish and I shall give it to you, up to half my kingdom.' She consulted her mother who told her to demand the head of John the Baptist.

She returned in haste to the king and said, 'I want you to give me, without delay, the head of John the Baptist on a serving dish.' The king was acutely grieved, but because of his oath, taken in front of his guests, he could not refuse. He dispatched an executioner. John was beheaded in prison and his head carried into the birthday banquet on a plate and given to the young woman, who then presented it to her mother.

Meanwhile, the twelve had returned, reporting to him all they had done and taught. He wanted to withdraw to the wilderness. But news spread through the towns of his movements, and crowds flocked to the place where he went. Almost sick with pity, he then spent the day with them, teaching. Towards evening the twelve urged him to send the masses away, as the place was remote and there were no supplies. He told them to give the multitude food. They protested that they had only five loaves of bread and two fish. Commanding them to seat the people in groups, he took the loaves, broke them and divided the fish.

Everybody there was fed—five thousand men. Twelve baskets full of leftovers were then collected.

He has become profoundly ill at ease. In his first days, when doubts hounded him, he withdrew to the wilderness. This time, his agitation is compounded by the crowds that cling to him. The people's lack of direction, their helplessness, gets to him. Against his inclination, he spends a day teaching. His inner circle is proving stonily unresponsive. They return from their trial on the road, in pairs, healing and preaching, reporting on their success. They immediately regress in his presence to a state of not trusting. They prove incapable of feeding the people. His response is to seek solitude:

> So, after the feeding he made the twelve take a boat and precede him to the other side of the Sea of Galilee, to Bethsaida. He sent the crowd away. When they had all gone, he left the wilderness and went up the mountain.
>
> It was evening and he was alone. From on high he saw the boat in the middle of the sea with the twelve struggling to row into a rising head wind. At about the fourth watch of the night he approached, walking on the water. He wanted to pass them by, but seeing him and taking him for a phantasm they all screamed out in terror. He spoke to them, 'Courage! **I am.** Don't fear.'
>
> He approached and got into the boat. The wind abated. They were astonished beyond measure. Because they were stonyhearted, they had not understood the loaves.

The first phase of his mission, as Mark tells it, reaches its climax here, with him alone at night on the mountain, suddenly distracted by the sight of the twelve struggling to make headway across the sea. They are not even in danger, these Galilee fishermen — unlike the previous time crossing over, when a heavy sea was about to swamp their boat.

Questions pose themselves. What impels him down to the water, in the dark, and out across it, approaching the boat yet only intending to pass by? What impels him to fatefully urge them to have courage, knowing the instruction to be futile, and then to follow it with, 'Don't fear!', given that this will have the opposite effect — inducing fathomless terror? Above all, what impels him in the middle of the wind-chopped sea, in the depth of the night, to insert the two words that will become his pivotal message, introducing it here: '*I am*'? It is placed, as if in parenthesis, between the words 'courage' and 'fear'.

One clue is provided in the adjacent story of Herod, Herodias, and the beheading of John the Baptist. King Herod Antipas, ruler of Galilee by Roman authority, misreads the new teacher. He takes him to be another preacher who has come to root out moral corruption — John returned from the dead. The king's confusion brings the conflict between the ethical order and pneuma to a head.

Herod has a troubled conscience about the execution of John. His own moral balance had been overthrown by his wife. Knowing his weakness, she has used her beautiful daughter (Salomé, as named in other sources) to seduce him. Salomé is ravishing, dancing wantonly before him.[6] Drunk with inflamed spirits — wine and fantasy — a corrupted pneuma presence, he loses control. There are further undercurrents in the story. Either Herodias is jealous at her husband lusting after her daughter, or she is so contemptuous of him that she doesn't care. In either case, her resentment is spiked, manifesting itself as a need to humiliate him — which she does.[7]

Herod's control is in the ethical domain: he admires the

moralist preacher, whom he used to listen to with pleasure. This moral control loses out to the enraged scheming of a woman whom he fails to shackle, whose haemorrhaging force has not been cured. Herodias and Salomé pair with the menopausal woman and Jairus' daughter. Mark refers to the unnamed Salomé as *korasion*, the same word the teacher had used to address the twelve-year-old. *Korasion* ranges in possible meanings from an affectionate term for a girl, to damsel, maiden, and young wife.

This mother-daughter coupling represents failed initiation, the riot in their blood raging against feeble male attempts to stop it. Once the dancing tease gains power, the hysteria of hate works its fill. Without death in order to be reborn, there is toxic rancour. It manifests itself in one of the most hideous images in Western culture: the severed head of the preacher carried aloft on a plate by this triumphant young woman into a banquet of drunken men, and then presented to her drooling mother. Seductive sensuality turns into vicious blood-lust. The corrupted female erotic finds its consummation in orgiastic sadism.[8]

Herod's case is illustrated in the sower parable—when the word is choked by worldly pleasures, cares, and insecurities. He represents all men who have the wrong authority. He is taunted by his own beheaded morality, exhibited before him on a serving dish. Beheading, as numerous Renaissance paintings of this scene later make clear, is displaced castration—symbolic of powerlessness.[9]

Herod is linked with John the Baptist, his story that of the emasculation of the ethical. He suffers symbolic castration at the hands of his own hamartia, or imbalance. Salomé scorns her impotent stepfather, and Herodias humiliates her weak husband-king.

John the Baptist died by the sword he lived by. That his mission was on the ethical plane, directing sinners to repent, meant his death would take the form of a great evil—a violation of the ethical order.[10] His seat of understanding is the head, from where he speaks; it becomes the site of his death. But the Master's new teaching locates knowing in sacred pneuma. The ethical has no power in itself, and withers without pneuma. Only pneuma, mediated through the Master, may still the vortex of blood. The ethical does not have power over either blood or spirit forces. It lacks *passion*.[11]

The cultural transformation that occurs when the power of pneuma displaces the ethical is highlighted by the fact that the teacher does not begin his mission until John the Baptist is imprisoned. The old order has given way to the new. King Herod is the neutered foil to the new Master—the one with power.

The dancing Salomé at night in the palace before the feasting men, out of their normal minds with drink, serves to cue the reader's imagination for walking on water. The walking also occurs at night, before the twelve, who in turn are out of their minds—with fear. In both cases, the watchers are overwhelmed by impassioned fantasy: eros in the palace, and dread on the sea. The scene-setting associations suggest that the Master executes his own exotic dance over the water, before the twelve whom he has called to follow him.

The twelve have good cause to be at their wits' end. He is himself in a wild, charged state of being, gliding across the choppy sea in the dark, coming close, then put off by their chill panic. Is it his own anger driving his change of mind in mid-step, or the first stab of the inner torment unto death he will suffer? In response to their screams, he changes direction a second time; but before approaching the boat, and still at some distance, he voices his taunting command. He knows it will only sink them further into terror.

In fact, he *is* a sort of phantasm. With the unnerving wind creating a mind-storm, they might well see him as a frenzied dervish whirling towards them, or a spectre hovering with shadowy intent. What powers he may now draw upon—the two thousand *daimones* who know him intimately under the surface, at his command while at home beneath his feet, the rising wind whipping across the darkened sea. In another parallel with Salomé at Herod's banquet, he is, in his own kind of way, naked before his followers.[12]

How dreadful it would have been, as Kierkegaard concluded, to be one of the twelve.[13] They have willingly uprooted themselves. They were simple folk—fishermen and others. But even the most astute of worldly men or women could not have done better in their circumstances. Anybody in their shoes would have been thrilled by the charisma, which must have been electric. The huge gathering of five thousand in a remote, inhospitable spot gives us some indication of his phenomenal reputation. The twelve have been specially chosen by this messiah celebrity with supernatural powers. Their own people want to see him, to hear him, to witness his miracles—to flock as near to him as they can. The crowds come from all points of the compass, some trekking from two hundred kilometres away, even from Jerusalem. These twelve, his chosen confidantes, must have been dumbstruck with awe.

Under his tuition, they might gain their own magical powers, their own purpose and vocation, perhaps even knowledge. They imagined they had found the way, and that this way would be easy—the path to a promised land, as members of a cosy, select band bound by camaraderie. Something along these lines would have been their misty dream-image of the future. But, from very early on, the dream began to dissolve. The sower set the test. The shift to parable bewildered them, as did his talk about insiders and outsiders and, above all, his reference to the mystery. Then the uneasiness began to rise, the lack of surety, the fear. Fear makes foolish, more foolish than their normal selves had ever been. They became scared of him, unnerved by his presence.

The concluding judgment of the twelve is that they are stonyhearted. According to their ancestral Jewish culture, this condemnation is severe. 'Callous of heart' is a description of the spiritually dead. So the twelve are now subject to a third role-casting—these fishermen whom he called with hope and enthusiasm so little time ago, whom he reinvented as ethical preachers going out in pairs with minor healing powers. They are identified with those who oppose him, the pneumaphobic. They are no better than Pharisee intellectuals.[14]

'Because they were stonyhearted, they had not understood the loaves.' Mark himself appends this judgment, after the Master has got into the boat and the wind has abated. The twelve have not understood the loaves. Mark here diverts the narrative, throwing in a reference which sounds like it is meant to help with interpreting the story. But it leads the reader in the opposite direction, creating obscurity.

He sent the twelve out on the road in pairs, without food or money. The implication is that if the mission is right—if it is true vocation—the necessities will be provided. The followers will not have to worry about such profane matters as daily bread. Hence, their anxiety about feeding the five thousand indicates that they lack trust. Likewise, on the sea, they are terrified by something out of the ordinary, these fishermen subjected to a mere breath of headwind. Worse, their endemic fearfulness, induced by their bewilderment about who he is, makes them so jumpy that they take him to be a ghost. They no longer recognise their Master. The better they know him, the more alien he becomes—like some huge and dark supernatural presence rising over them.

Mark seems to deliberately pitch his text so as to disorient and unsettle us. The reader is forced into multiple interpretative strategies. But, at best, they seem to work in part, chasing elusive threads of meaning. Beneath the surface, things are a bit like the two thousand *daimones* — and why were there so many of them?

How, for instance, are we to read the twelve baskets of scraps? Is it a reference to the twelve, or to the twelve years of bleeding? Then the five loaves, the two fishes, the five thousand men — is this some numerological puzzle? Or, perhaps more likely, has Mark thrown in a false lead? That the followers are now condemned for not comprehending the loaves reminds us of parables that are introduced so as not to be understood.[15]

Whilst the Master has clear and profound reasons to be fed up with these twelve seeds sown on stony ground, their shoots withering before his eyes, Mark supplies an oblique one. We, the readers, are left in fear that we, too, do not understand the loaves. Or that, if they are included as a decoy, we do not understand what matters.

By now, his opening foray is over. He was initiated in his beginning by the heavens opening and by pneuma descending on him from above. He was driven into the wilderness for his first forty days of doubt. Then he returned to choose followers, whom he would embrace and make his own, teaching them by his own doings, training them to take over when he would depart. He also tested the way of the preacher. He worked miracles, only to find they drew crowds to him as if he were a cheap vaudeville magician. He sought to address multitudes of five thousand, with the result that he himself became drained and rattled, needing solitude on the mountain. And those multitudes, he supposed, remained unchanged, returning home with little more than confused reports about a remarkable experience.

At the outset, he had charged into action; but the 'Follow me!' to his hoped-for insiders rang hollowly in his own ears from the moment he started to teach. From there, his mission narrowed into claustrophobic introspection — his bitter mood characterised by the harsh treatment of the twelve during their two boat crossings. He has found himself incapable of initiating anything. At the most, three anonymous people happen across his path.

During his dark dance over water, before reluctantly approaching the screaming twelve, he asserts: 'Courage!' It sounds more like an imperative addressed to himself. He is the one under duress. His imagined vocation with his chosen companions is sinking around him, plunging like one of Legion's *daimones* beneath the waters. He has to find a power he may draw upon. He does so in his authority over himself, his centre of gravity in what he terms '*I am*'. Within primal being, he proclaims, as if to buoy himself up, there is no fear.

He has gained more clarity about his way. Its end is *I am*, dependent on the elusive pneuma, in the hope of learning the mystery, which exists in kairos time. It is a solitary mission, focussed on himself and what he learns. But these are mere abstractions, a neat theorem that is little better than doctrine. The mask gives no sense of what lives behind it. To see what lies behind the mask we need, according to Mark's opening cue, to know the full story.

Finding himself diverted for the second time on water, he is forced into a desperate teaching strategy — to instruct by fear. Friendliness hasn't worked. He will try to make the twelve more receptive by deliberately and systematically heightening their anxiety. As he turns on them, it is unclear to what degree his wild performance is guided by cold-blooded deliberation and detachment. He seizes the psychic jugular, pitching them into nightmare. He himself — their hero, guide, deliverer — reappears before them as a monstrous phantasm. The joy of being with him in the early days — the adoring crowds, the healing of the paralysed man, the withered hand in the temple — all too soon have given way to bewilderment over the meaning of the parable, and loss of the mystery. And now a horror climax is reached in these boat crossings. His last chance with them is that fearing the great fear may obliterate the original, ordinary human self — as had the near-death sickness of the twelve-year-old girl.

He can hope, if they do not respond to the initiation ordeal by his hand, that someone else might. The dear little girl may find the path, or perhaps the woman bleeding her life away, or deranged Legion — anyone, someone, apart from himself. Even about himself, we are led to suspect, from Mark's gist, he cannot be sure.

He is close to fearing the great fear himself. The first time on water he had slept peacefully through a storm. Immediately after, there were three encounters; each one, like the bleeding woman's touch, drew power from him. Going home to Nazareth, he finds he is not wanted. He does not belong. He withdraws to the wilderness; but the five thousand follow, and he struggles through a day of teaching. The day ends with him discovering that the twelve, in spite of their experience on the road healing and preaching, have no trust. So he withdraws, going up the mountain by himself.

Seeking solitude, he chooses the mountain. The Greek gods lounged high up and apart on Mount Olympus, looking down on tiny mortals far below as they pursued their petty dreams and performed their silly antics.[16] He is not much like that. Rather, there is the precedent of Legion, storming around the mountains, screaming out and hacking at himself with stones. What we do know is that he is up there most of the night. Although deeply distressed, he keeps an eye on the Sea of Galilee.

The wind rises. John, in retelling this episode, will call it an *anemos megalos pneontos* — 'a great blowing wind' or 'a great breathing wind'. There is a suggestion of howling pneuma low over the sea, the head-wind supernaturally charged. The Master notices that far out on the water his chosen twelve, rowing their small boat, are panicky. So he descends — or, is it more like the mad pigs, with him hurtling down to the water? He is demonic with sacred force, his *being* so plentiful and sound that, from the shore, he charges out across the waves. His dancing self, enfleshed in his pneuma element, phantasmal, godlike, executes its debut step. And proclaims its truth.

Up on the mountain of old, the God of Moses named himself — *I am that I am*. Up on the mountain of the new time, alone, it is not his God whom he meets. It is himself. Coming down, in the depth of the night, he is changed. Others believe him to be out of his mind, or a spectre — not surprisingly, for now the sacred rage is within.[17] Dancing across the water, he announces: '*I am.*'

CHAPTER THREE

FIRE ON THE MOUNTAIN

He travelled to the region of Tyre and Sidon. Wanting no one to know, he entered a house, but could not escape. A Greek woman whose young daughter suffered from unsound pneuma found him, came to him and fell at his feet. She implored him repeatedly to cure the girl, but he denied her, 'Let the children first be fed, for it is not good for the bread of children to be thrown to dogs.'

She responded, 'Master, even the little dogs under the table eat the children's crumbs.' He replied, 'For this word go; the *daimōn* has left your daughter.' Once home, she found the girl in bed, cured.

The Greek woman rebukes him for his prejudice. He refuses her repeated plea to save her daughter on the grounds that she is not a Jew. Greeks, as Gentiles, were scorned like dogs because of their ritual impurity. He has angrily slandered the woman as sub-human. However, she is not fearful in the face of humiliating dismissal, calmly taking him on. She makes him aware of what he is doing, and he corrects himself.

The episode is straightforward. In the aftermath of his confrontation with the twelve on water at night, he finds himself without a mission, with no alternative but to keep travelling, restless and distracted. The sacred rage has faded. When he arrives in a new region, he wants only to hide. Bad-tempered in response to the Greek woman's intrusion on his solitude, he is ungracious, even crudely abusive. He is so run down that he regresses into the role of a moralistic, letter-of-the-law Jewish teacher. In fact, he has become his own example of they who lack trust and balance. We can hear him, as Mark puts it, groaning deeply in his pneuma.

Then he crosses the sea, for a third time with his followers:

> On the other, eastern side, at Bethsaida, a blind man was brought. He took him by the hand and led him out of the town. He spat into his eyes, laid his hands on him, and asked whether he saw anything. Looking up, the blind man said, 'I see men that like trees I see walking.'
>
> He then put his hands on the man's eyes and made him look up. He was restored, once again seeing everyone clearly. He sent him home, instructing, 'Do not enter the town.'

His first move is to take the blind man out of the town. This time there is no resistance to healing — and no sighing to the heavens, as in other recent miracles. He knows the significance of the encounter. The man with the withered hand had been ordered out of the temple. The town is the place of human community. What is about to occur does not belong within settled human habitation. Insiders live outside.

He leads the man by the hand — the two of them alone, such is Mark's inference. Once outside the town, he spits into his eyes and touches them. He has to ask whether the man now sees anything. He has lost much of the flair and confidence of his earlier healings, when he knew precisely the effect of his moves.

His powers are waning.

The man looks up. As usual with Mark, the story is cryptically condensed. The head may have drooped in melancholy, at his endemic blindness; or it may have been lowered in submission, perhaps in hopeful reverence. Looking down may be a way of evading the ordinary and everyday, in order to concentrate on the extraordinary. Then again, looking down is the essential human condition, seeing nothing—as in oblivion, or permanent forgetfulness. Blindness is a metaphor for this normal state.

The man looks up. What he sees are men like trees walking. Mark's Greek employs the verb 'to see' twice in the shortish sentence. As if vision shimmers before his half-open eyes, he sees then does not see; he half-sees, twice sees. Is it a hallucination, a vision in the double sense? Or is it a slowly clarifying inner vision? If the two are outside the town by themselves, what are other men doing there? Perhaps they are trees, like dead men walking.

The potency of this one line will generate recurrences through Western literature, not the least in a Shakespeare midrash in *Macbeth*, where the principal character's end is signalled by him seeing a wood of trees on the move. From this moment, Macbeth is a dead man.[1] Macbeth had, early on, made the enigmatically Mark-like metaphysical observation, 'Nothing is but what is not.'

It takes a second intervention to fully heal the man's blindness. That he then sees all men clearly brings with it a suggestion of perception into deeper truth. This is what the twelve do not have. In part, another initiation story has been included, a rebirth to true seeing—perhaps initiation stories are the only ones that matter. Life is either anxiety about bread and counting baskets of scraps, or it is looking up and seeing the blur of trees moving like men.

Is it the other way—men on the move, somehow looking

like trees? As Legion had entered the narrative as another self, so does this blind man. He serves as a device, a medium for the Master who, standing in his shoes, the two of them alone outside the town, is starting to see his own future. It is he who is the dead man walking. The tree will reappear as the cross. This is the moment — we are in kairos time — of his first true seeing. Until now he had been proceeding blindly and making mistakes — just like any normal man.

He begins to know more than what he is not — more than the nothing, which is but what is not.[2]

In the background here, as a situating point of reference, there may be the Greek understanding that *oblivion* is the normal human state. This understanding was at the core of classical culture, for the Greek word for truth — *alētheia* — means literally 'without lethe'. Lethe was the place of oblivion, or forgetfulness; later, the river running to the underworld. To drink its waters was to sink into a state of forgetfulness. Death was eternal oblivion. Truth is the rare condition of seeing through the mists of oblivion — a condition of clarity or illumination.

Yet, clear seeing may be no more than a beckoning ideal for humans. In real life, the best may be the middle stage, of blurred vision. Even it seems rare — coming that close to the mystery of the enigma.

The brief, extraordinary saga at Bethsaida ends with the seeing man being ordered to stay out of the town. Truth means exile. The sociographic lines are firming.

Next, he journeyed north from Bethsaida, through the towns of Caesarea Philippi. On the road he asked the twelve, 'Who do people say that I am?' They answered, 'Some John the Baptist, others Elias, and others one of the prophets.'

He asked them, 'But you, who do you say that I am?' Peter answered, 'You are the Christ.' He warned them to tell no one about him, then began to instruct them that it was necessary for the son of man to suffer much. He spoke candidly that he would be rejected by elders, chief priests and intellectuals, and be killed, but rise after three days. Peter took him aside and began to reproach him.

Turning around and seeing his followers, he denounced Peter, 'Get behind me, Satan, for you are not mindful of the things of God, but the things of men.'

Having summoned the crowd together, with the twelve, he spoke:

'Whoever is willing to follow me, let him deny himself and take up his cross. For whoever wishes to save his soul will lose it, but whoever loses his own soul on account of me and my Story will save it. What will it profit a man if he gains the whole world but loses his soul? Or, what will a man give in exchange for his soul? For whoever is ashamed of me and my words in this lost generation, him the son of man will be ashamed of hereafter.'

This is a call. In Mark's narrative it is unique for the Master to teach like this — directly and in formulae, not in parables, and not speaking in the mode of an inward meditation. The declamation is made to an anonymous crowd that includes the twelve. The teacher had just revealed the manner of his death. And here are the first of two references he will ever make to the *cross*. The cross is sown like a seed in the text, but we are given no sign as to what it might grow into. It is the sequel to the *mystery*.

The episode pivots on his outrage at Peter, who has pulled him aside for an intimate exchange — as he had, just before, pulled the blind man aside, out of the town. But instead of a climax in prophetic revelation, he turns on his leading follower and levels the astonishing accusation that he is under the sway of satanic impulses.

The encounter with the blind man had the deeper significance of marking his own awakening. It took two stages; the first, a blurred, dream-like insight into the future. As if it were 'through a glass darkly', to draw on Paul's words,[3] he sees men like trees walking. Only thereafter may he see clearly. He has witnessed his own destiny, face to face. From the beginning he had miraculous healing powers and phenomenal charisma; shortly into his mission, he could charge down the mountain and out across the water. But he was not clairvoyant: he did not have prophetic insight into his own future. With the blind man, this changes.

He is now free to pass on what will happen to him — the decisive events. It is the first time he foretells his end. The effect on others is one of negation, as had been the case when they were on water, with his words, 'Courage! *I am*. Don't fear.'

At this moment of climactic gravity, Peter is without empathy. His mind is full of 'the things of men'. His rebuke is out of fear for himself — fear that he will be left without a Master, left to his own meagre resources. A follower is lost without a leader. Here, fear makes selfish.

Peter's higher fear is of the Master's teaching, which is being reoriented, at this juncture in the story, to centre on pathos. *Pathos* is the Greek word that, in its double meaning of 'experience' and 'suffering', equates human vitality with tragedy. A life without experience is nothing; but experience is, of its nature, fused with suffering.

There is the oblivion of the loaves, or there is life. Life is fed by the suffering unto death. In the particular story about to unfold, the people with political and religious authority will turn on him, and so will the custodians of culture, the intellectuals. To follow this man risks death. Peter's great fear is taking shape. The charge, 'Whoever is ashamed of me', is loaded against him.

The trigger for the Master's fury in this scene is the response to the central *being* question, 'You, who do you say I am?' Peter's answer draws on stock Jewish theology, which at the time was anticipating a *messiah* (the Hebrew word that translates into Greek as *christos*). The 'Christ' was literally an anointed one who, it was hoped, would come to free the people from oppression—from Roman rule. The thrust of Mark's narrative is that the title *Christ* is wrong. He is teacher and Master, but he never claims to be the messiah. Indeed, his rage against Peter implicitly rejects the Jewish vocation of messiah; in effect, he is asserting that, 'I am not Christ.'[4] 'If you think I am', he implies, 'it is the devil who drives your thoughts.' More generally he is saying, 'I am not who you think I am.'

In identifying him with the messiah, Peter is in effect asserting, 'You are a Master, charismatic, with *daimonic* powers, a man who amazes and frightens me, so you must be the saviour prophet anticipated in Jewish writings.' Peter has little capacity for a new understanding, so he resorts to the categories of the church in which he was brought up. He has not moved beyond the obsolete temple. It is where they who stumble and wither belong.

The 'soul' (*psuchē*) has also been introduced as a category. Peter has exchanged his soul for a defensive and mindless parroting of doctrine. He represents the typical human response to acute, disorienting anxiety—here, a sickness of soul not body. To give its cause a name, however hollow or arbitrary, is to control it, and thereby anaesthetise its pain. 'You are the Christ.' The greater the anxiety, the more dogmatic will become defence of this doctrine as absolute truth.

Peter represents churchgoer, therapy patient, and indeed almost everybody, all those who take pride in their opinions and associations — all who in effect assert, 'I am x' or 'You are y'. Much that is human 'gains the world'. Indeed, the Master will soon shame a rich man who seeks to follow him — his failing is not that he is rich, but that he is attached to the world of his many possessions, as necessary to his sense of himself.

Peter is treated harshly. The Master called him, named him, taught him, and did what he did in front of him. Surely, it is *his* failure of judgment. Yet we have before us, already, the contrasting example of the berserk one — Legion. Once calmed, Legion is sent out into the world to tell the Story; whilst Peter, when under self-induced pressure and questioned, stutters out false platitudes about saviours. What Legion achieves is true recognition. The Master's anger at Peter is over the follower's total failure to recognise who he is.

Peter has a natural affinity with messiah, or saviour, thinking. He represents a common orientation. The messiah is in polar opposition to pathos — suffering. The Master's teaching here is not new, for central to classical Greek culture was the tragic vision that it is only after the annihilation of the I, a release from the bonds of the normal human self, and its everyday desires and insecurities, that it is possible to join the primal wholeness of being.

'Saviour thinking' carries with it the optimist illusion that I can change, and my world can change — I can be saved from who I am, and transported out of the damaged society of my birth into a land of milk and honey. In effect, thus speaks Peter. Such a view is also incompatible with kairos, which determines the hour in which what matters will be — including a different logic of metamorphosis. Legion is exemplar. Peter rebuked the teacher precisely over his kairos talk about the end.

What is new in this story is the *cross*: it has neither Greek nor Jewish precedent. We see it, at this stage in the story, only in the blurred form of men like trees walking. And pneuma is new, which breathes in the beyond of being. And the Master himself is *sui generis*: no figure remotely like him comes before, or after, in the culture of the West.

There is one category that the Master chooses for himself, and only one: 'son of man'. He uses it in part to negate 'messiah' and 'son of God' — there is no mention in the story so far of a heavenly father above. It is the *son of man* who will suffer unto death. But what does he mean by this term, which has bewildered interpreters ever since?[5] He is a human being, no more than any other; just a man. He had earlier referred to others as 'sons of men' — by inference, simply meaning 'human' or 'mortal'.[6]

There are deeper resonances. He is the quintessence of humanity, in its Platonic form or ideal. Those who kill him will kill the essence of *being*, the descendent of all that has come before, in its purest distillation. Then there is another son of man: he who was born to serve. And, finally, we should — as always with Mark, when in doubt — assume a twist, a riddle. Perhaps the Master is providing another sign of who he is not. He is not a son; he has no father. His parentage is generalised. He is essential humanity. He is *I am* with no name.

Six days after announcing the cross he went up on a high mountain. As if to provide his own reply to his central probe, 'You, who do you say that I am?' he took Peter, James, and John with him. The four were alone:

> On the mountain, he was metamorphosed before them.[7]
> Shining were his clothes, white like snow, such as no

earthly bleaching could achieve. And Elias and Moses appeared to them, talking with him.

Answering, Peter says, 'Master, it is good for us to be here; let us put up three tents, one for you, one for Moses, and one for Elias.' Peter did not know what he should say, for the three were terrified.

A cloud appeared, overshadowing them, and a voice came out of the cloud, 'This is my beloved son. Listen to him!' Then, suddenly looking around, they saw they were alone with him.

On the descent, he ordered them to tell no one what they had seen. At the bottom, they found the others arguing with the intellectuals surrounded by a large crowd. Immediately the people saw him, all were astounded, and came running in welcome.

Let us interrupt the story here, for this short episode is compressed. Stalled in his mission, short-tempered, low in spirits, his powers enfeebled, travelling at a furious pace through all the regions around the Sea of Galilee, and as far as Tyre and Sidon on the Mediterranean, backwards, forwards, crossing and recrossing the sea, weighed down by his first sighting of the ghastly future he is about to meet, he receives a second baptism. At the start, in the first instance, on the threshold of his mission, he had stood in the river, and the pneuma descended, bathing him. This time, his baptism comes as fire on the mountain.

He bursts free from the sludge of his way, down below, on the plane of everyday humans. The king of the Greek gods, Zeus, had announced himself in shafts of lightning spearing through the night sky; for mortals, just to look on him directly was to be incinerated. The God of Moses also appeared in the form of fire, in the burning bush. Now it is he who manifests

Shining, like a god, his robe a brilliant white.

A cloud appears overhead, overshadowing them, which we may interpret as black and threatening. Although no question has been put, Peter in 'answering' blurts out, in terror at what he sees, that it is fortunate they are there so they can erect tents. The Greek word for tent, *skēnē*, also translates as 'tabernacle' or 'temple'.

This episode is 'over-determined', to use Freud's term: there are several motifs conflated into one, all happening concurrently. Divinity is in the cloud, but Peter misreads it profanely as looming rain, and wants to provide shelter from the storm for the three holy men. Peter's second misreading is to equate the three men. Continuing his messiah interpretation, he thinks his Master belongs among the Hebrew leaders and prophets.

Third, and without knowing what he is doing, Peter is anticipating his own future—building churches. His irrepressible 'answering', when out of his mind with fear, is to construct a temple. The darker side of this reflex recalls shallow roots and the withered hand. He will retreat inside the church. Not up to the mystery, he regresses to the protection of the worldly community—then, now, and to come. Churches, one and all, are the same. The subtext is that the three tents—or churches—are for Peter, James, and John.

Peter is terrified by the Shining. Huddled inside his temple-tent, he will not have to look on it. The climax to his warped kinship with fire has arrived. His mother-in-law had fever; seed shooting on stony ground withers when the sun rises; and now his Master is bathed in fire. Peter switches to his native medium, water. He is a man of water. Water puts out fire. The natural state for water is in the horizontal; fire rises in the vertical.

Here is Peter's answer to the question that has not been put. A riddle is implicit in the text, and it parallels the riddle that

Oedipus solved to free ancient Greek Thebes from the curse of the Sphinx. Oedipus was questioned as to what it was that moved on four legs in the morning, two at noon, and three in the afternoon. The answer was man, which meant himself — his story hinged on the fact that he did not know himself. Peter's riddle, too, is about the question of his being, of who he is.

James and John also fail the *know thyself* test. Their nickname — sons of thunder — turns out to have been satirical. They might be linked with the Greek divinity (Zeus was known by thunder as well as lightning), but they also misread the cloud as a rainstorm. When granted access to sacred Shining, they remain bogged in the profane. In contrast with the voice out of the cloud naming its beloved son, they are the offspring of bad weather.

The theory about churches and their role is extended in this episode. Churches are ethical institutions, their main function being to protect against moral wrong — symbolised by the black cloud of dirty, drenching water from above. Churches, by their nature, are hostile to fire. They need to extinguish it. The foundational Christian church, in Rome, has made baptism by water, administered to the human infant, its prerequisite entrance-ritual. By contrast, pneuma prefers heat, and its correlate, light.[8]

Elias and Moses are ancestors. Heroic or big-man ancestors are meant to bestow authority and legitimacy. In this case, they were the two great Jewish religious leaders. He is observed talking with them. Moses on Mount Sinai during his earthly mission had conversed with his god. On the high mountain of the new time, they pass on their baton. He takes over their role.

The voice from the cloud also has precedents from the Hebrew Bible. Moses had seen his god in the form of a dark cloud during the crossing of the Red Sea, as he led his people out of Egyptian captivity.[9] The divine intervention here seems to be directed at the favoured three. They are instructed to listen to their Master. The story has already made it plain, however, that such a command is wasted — unless a miraculous transformation takes place. It is the Master who is undergoing metamorphosis, not the three.

The voice from the cloud seems superfluous. Maybe the significance of the intervention is rather in the recognition, 'This is my beloved son.' Of the three Greek words for love, here it is *agapē* — not *eros* (sexual love) or *philia* (friendship). Agapē is selfless love, perhaps with the inflection that its source is divine: sacred love. He is the offspring of sacred love. Primal *being* is born of higher love.

The divinity in the black cloud is a dying god. This is the second and last time he intercedes in the Story. It will turn out to have been his farewell, in the form of an exit blessing. The great Jewish founding fathers and spiritual leaders have been superseded, and so has their God.[10] He, too, is passing the baton.

Hence, the Shining. From the darkly blurred vision down below of men like trees walking, he has journeyed up, high on the high mountain, where lightning ignites him. The Shining is too brilliant for ordinary men to look upon, so they go into hiding. On high, he completes his two-stage initiation — by pneuma, and then by fire. Having shed the skin of the initial phase of his mission, he is ready for the end. *I am* has undergone metamorphosis — he is not who he was. Charged with the strength and nerve to face what he sees, and a *being* fitted to the hour, he may now advance along his way.

On his return to the plane of common existence, people see him as radiant, and run to him in welcome:[11]

> He asked the intellectuals what they argued over. Another
> in the crowd spoke up, 'Teacher, I brought my son to you

because he has a mute pneuma. Wherever it seizes him it throws him down, and he foams at the mouth, grinds his teeth, and goes rigid. I asked your followers to free him but they were incapable.'

He responded, 'O generation without trust, how long shall I be with you? How long must I put up with you? Bring him to me.'

They brought the boy, and the pneuma, on seeing him, threw convulsions, and the boy collapsed, rolling about foaming at the mouth. He asked, 'For how long has this happened to him?'

The father replied, 'Since childhood. Often it threw him into fire, and into water, to destroy him. If there is anything you can do, help us, have sympathy.' In turn, he was answered, 'If you have the power, all things are possible for one who trusts.' At which the father cried out, 'I trust, Master, help my distrust.'

Seeing a crowd running towards them, the teacher rebuked the unsound pneuma, 'You, dumb and deaf pneuma, come out of him, and forever leave him alone.' It cried out, threw the boy into violent spasms, then left. The boy was like a corpse; many said that he had died. The teacher grasped him by the hand, raised him, and he stood up.

After entering a house, the twelve asked privately, 'Why were we unable to dispel it?' He replied, 'Nothing is powerful enough to free this kind, but prayer.' Immediately they all departed together and passed through Galilee, for he did not want anyone to know.

Raphael would take Mark's cue and link the healing of the mad boy to the metamorphosis on the high mountain. In his huge painting of *The Transfiguration* (c.1518–20), the boy looks up and sees the Shining, which no one else can look upon. The boy is instantly cured.

Here, as in the case of Legion, it is a *daimōn* trapped inside the person that throws him into furied thrashings around with foul emanations from the mouth—in one case frothing, in the other incessant screaming. While untamed, it threatens to destroy the character that houses it. It brings volcanic vitality.

The demon-possessed are better off than the pneumaphobic twelve, or the once-favoured three who were present at the Shining. Legion and the mad boy both know their Master—Legion has roamed amongst the mountains as well as the tombs, anticipating the site of the Shining. The boy is the one, the only one, who obeys the voice commanding them on the mountain to 'Listen to him.' Harold Bloom, in his reflections on Mark's text, puts it that only the demonic in us sees the Master.[12]

This is another episode that centres on initiation. The disturbed pneuma wants to pitch the boy into the two media for baptism—water and fire. Is it to kill him outright? Or must he die in order that he may rise anew? The frothing at the mouth and the violent convulsions suggest death spasms, confirmed by the body going rigid. The crowd thinks him dead. The demented boy reads water accurately in its recent cloud manifestation. He reads it as the divinity, and listens. He sees fire in the form of the Shining. He sees it clearly, and is himself metamorphosed. He is the one with the right relationship to water and fire—elements that are trying to kill him. Each lethal element in the story is non-lethal—a potential medium for *truth*. At each marker, the boy's move is right; that of Peter, wrong.[13]

The father plays a role, too. He trusts enough to bring his son along, and is desperate enough to try anything. The Jewish doctors, using their science, have proved useless. So have the twelve, even with their special powers. The father, like the blind man who ushered in the journey up the high mountain, needs a two-stage transformation. He admits to being halfway: 'I trust, Master, help my distrust.' He represents most humans at their best, and receives favour.

This man's confession is set in the context of the Shining. The teacher has just descended to the plane of everyday humanity, only to be met by disputing crowds and bewildered followers. Groaning at a generation without trust, he is irritated that he must immediately return to battle with contrary pneumata. Nevertheless, the father's main role is to prepare the way for the person whose story counts—his son.

Pneuma cannot be released from its demonic state by knowledge. The teacher tells the twelve, and in private—as if disclosing one of the mysteries—that it may only be freed by prayer. Which leads to the question of what is prayer, and whose prayer? The story provides the answers.

Raphael, in his *Transfiguration*, captures the essentials of the story. He bypasses the surface detail of the narrative—above all, the direct command to the *daimōn* to come out—and attributes the cure to the mad boy looking up and seeing the Shining. The Renaissance artist is taking liberties with the story in his midrash, yet Mark invites this condensation by conjoining the two episodes, and providing a series of oblique cues as to the nature of prayer.

It is the prayer of the boy, who is also a beloved son, which saves him. The prayer is not in the form of a meditation or voiced mantra, kneeling with head bowed and eyes closed. Prayer is looking up and seeing the light. The blind man looked up to see men like trees walking, then he saw clearly. Raphael also depicts the plane of everyday human life as down in the dark, a swirling upheaval of confusion and fear, a boy writhing in his loving father's arms.

Prayer is not a technique that can be learnt. It is not a form of worship to be enacted ritually, or at will. It is outside the control of the individual. It is pneuma-like, and pneuma-dependent. It is not given to us to know whence it cometh, or whither it goeth.

The Master's role in 'prayer' is simply to be who he now is. We are back to the mustard tree. Any words to the deranged boy are secondary.

Along the way, in this middle phase of his mission, he has two important conversations or, rather, encounters. They are not with big-man ancestors. The subjects are a blind man and a mad boy. In both cases, it is primarily the teacher who has his eyes opened. He is starting to make out the answer to the question, 'You, who do you say that I am?' The answer involves the power of his Shining.

His groan on returning to the crowds down below is not just at the twelve, and the demands of his way. Prayer, and its nature, is at the core of the twin episodes of metamorphosis on the high mountain and the mad boy. He foresees the prayer to come, when it is he who will be reattempting the incandescence, alone in the Garden in the depths of the night—his last night—his followers all fleeing, ashamed of him, a time when there will be no light. 'How long shall I be with you?' has a double edge.

CHAPTER FOUR

THE BLACK STUMP

S oon after the Shining, he departed Galilee — leaving behind forever the serenity of its lake and green hills, the rural fishing and farming location he had chosen for his mission. He turned south, heading for his final destination. On the way, he again warned the twelve what would happen.

They drew near Jerusalem. At Bethphage and Bethany, near the Mount of Olives, opposite the Temple mount, he sent two of the twelve ahead with instructions to enter the village nearby, where they would find a young donkey tethered, one on which no man had sat. They should untie it. If anyone questioned, 'Why are you doing this?' they were to reply, 'The Master has need of it.'

They went and found a young donkey in the street tethered to the outside of a door. While they were untying it some bystanders challenged them. They replied as commanded and were given permission.

They brought the donkey to him, placed their cloaks on its back and he mounted. Many carpeted the road ahead with their cloaks, while others spread foliage that they had cut from the trees. Ones going before him, and ones following were crying out, 'Hosanna! Blessed is he who comes. Blessed is the coming kingdom of our father David. Hosanna in the highest!'

So he entered Jerusalem, and into the Temple. Having looked around at all things, he then left and went back down to Bethany with the twelve. The hour was already late.

Once on the road next morning, he was hungry. Spotting a verdant fig tree from afar he went to see if he might find something on it. He found nothing but leaves, for it was not the kairos time for figs. Reacting, he said to it, 'May no one eat fruit from you ever again, into eternity.' The twelve heard.

They came up to Jerusalem. Entering the Temple he began to throw out those buying and trading, and he overturned the tables of the moneychangers, and the chairs of those selling doves. He would not allow anyone to bring a vessel through the Temple. He taught, 'Is it not written that my house shall be called a house of prayer for all nations? You have made it a den of outlaws.'

The intellectuals and chief priests heard him and plotted how to kill him. They feared him, for all the people were marvelling at his teaching.

When it was late he left the city, returning again down to Bethany. Next morning, as they were passing by, they saw the fig tree dried from its roots up. Remembering, Peter said to him, 'Teacher, look! The fig tree you cursed has withered.'

The triumphal entry into Jerusalem, as it came to be known, ends with the cursing of an innocent tree — its crime being that it doesn't fruit out of season. The entry itself is celebrated like a victory parade by his followers. But they are identifying him with the Jewish messiah, come to restore David's kingdom once founded on Mount Zion in Jerusalem.[1] He is given the attributes of the saintly king — riding on a donkey unpolluted by other humans, metaphorically virginal, even its feet protected from having to tread on dirt. Freshly cut greenery is symbolic of fertility. The enthusiasm of the followers, hymning and dancing ahead, chanting and skipping behind, contrasts with the indifference of the Jerusalem inhabitants — no one meets him, no one greets him.

His own focus during this first entry into Jerusalem is solely on the Temple. The Second Temple, built fifty years before by Herod the Great, dominated the city — as the Muslim Dome of the Rock, on the same site, does today. It was one of the splendours of the Roman world, its built-up precinct huge, occupying a 500 metre-by-300 metre rectangle, around half of all the space contained within the city walls. The building itself was grand — 40 metres long, 10 metres wide, and 20 metres high, the height of a dozen men. And it was the key institution, both religious and civic, in Judea. The treasury of the nation was housed there. The physical magnificence of the Temple reflected its supreme place at the heart of the culture of the Jews.

The implication is that he enters the Temple by himself, makes a clinically thorough inspection, then leaves. What the twelve observe is hardly: 'Hosanna!' — a joyful welcome of the messiah into the holy city. He is more the stranger, the hostile intruder into a hill fortress.

He has himself provided the messiah cue, by fulfilling an Old Testament prophecy:

Rejoice greatly, O daughter of Zion; shout, O daughter of Jerusalem: behold, thy King cometh unto thee: he is just, and having salvation; lowly, and riding upon an ass, and upon a colt the foal of an ass.[2]

He stamps his authority on the scene from the start with his foretelling of the fetching of the donkey. Is he taunting his followers with their messiah confusion? Is he setting them up, and Mark's bewildered readers with them, with the sort of born-again joy and illumination that will characterise so many who will later join the churches founded in his name? Is it the naivety of his followers that is mocked in the choice of a virginal animal? Is he, so to speak, riding *them* up the mount, and into the empty city, and from there straight into the Temple?

Given the darkly portentous perspective that Mark has built up for us by this point in his story, the 'triumphal' entry has a ludicrous aspect — both comic and pagan.[3] It is as if the Master has formed his own procession, mimicking a Dionysian festival. In Greek mythology, the god Dionysus — alternatively known as Bacchus — leads in revelry his band of satyrs and other debauchees, including the drunken, fat old lecher, Silenus, riding on an ass.[4] This association is not fanciful in the overall context of the wildness of Mark's portrait of the teacher who dances across a stormy sea in the middle of the night.

The entry into Jerusalem seems like some tragic-comic pantomime. We have cause to suspect he is playing with his audience.

What is serious is his shutting down the business of the Temple and its cultic practices — banning vessels needed for religious ceremony. Once inside Jerusalem, his mood is grim and angry. Mark's description of his first sortie, when he inspects the Temple, is clinically terse, implying a mood of severe, detached coldness. On his second sortie, he empties the Temple with a raging ferocity. He disqualifies it, leaving it void.[5] This is no restoration. Indeed, he has taken up residence at the Mount of Olives, situated, as Mark stresses, across from the Temple Mount, a kilometre away. He journeys backward and forward — his place opposite and opposing, as in a battle encampment, with the village of Bethany the seat of his power.[6]

This is cultural war. It is very strange that he meets no direct resistance. He is one man, on his own, pitted against an entire culture, mounting his violent attack in the midst of crowds of the enemy, gathered in their central meeting-place. They fear him. His authority must be darkly intimidating, inducing momentary paralysis.

The purging of the Temple is framed by the cursing of the fig tree. What sort of man is this, with such anger in him, anger that is seemingly arbitrary in its target? The tree is verdantly alive, in full leaf — spring growth — but it is not the season for figs. The twist seems to be kairos: in ordinary chronos time the tree is normal and healthy, but it is not ready now that the hour has arrived. Death is its order of being.

The metaphor is once again over-determined, with a number of charged inflections. The corrupted Temple is being cursed — it will never fruit again. The man with the withered hand had to be drawn outside the Temple to be cured; the fig now has its sap dried up, from roots to branch tops, in one day. *Withered* is the constitutive state of churches.

Furthermore, on the next morning, as they are passing by on the way back up to Jerusalem, it is Peter who observes, 'Teacher, look! The fig tree you cursed has withered.' By this stage in the story, what has been revealed to Peter is ominously clear — he is the fig tree. His exclamation is poignant in its terrible naivety. Peter still understands nothing — and now we have entered kairos time.

Mark provides a hint, nevertheless, that Peter might be starting to awaken. He describes Peter as 'remembering'. The surface reading is that he merely recalls the day before when the Master cursed the tree. But, perhaps, there is the first flickering here of connecting threads—withered hands in Temples, stony ground (roots are again mentioned), stumbling, the transformation on the mountain and the dark cloud, and even his own repeated misunderstandings.

Mark invites the reader to stand in Peter's shoes. What must it have been like on that spring morning, with the town of Jerusalem looming above them, for the twelve to stop in front of the stark, blackened tree, dead from the roots up, its leaves withered, the solitary tree that only the day before had been full of abundant life? Their Master has, just the day before, raged through the Temple, evicting its occupants—cursing the inner sanctum of the holy city of the Jews, insulting their religious leaders, provoking a climate of explosive hatred and violence. The twelve are now on their way back on the road up into a city where, they must know, the authorities are plotting to destroy them. It must have looked like he was wilfully bringing upon himself the dark fate about which he has already warned them. And, on top of all that, they are constantly out of their own minds with fear of him.

So they find themselves, on that spring morning, before the dead tree, bewildered and afraid. He says nothing. They must suspect that this is another of his parables, this time enacted before their eyes—a living parable. Are they in the vicinity of the *mystery*? Peter and the others can only stand by astonished, agog with foreboding.

It is his story. Merely one day after the triumphal entry riding on the donkey, travelling up the same road between Bethany and Jerusalem, he sets the tone for what is to come. Just as a rampaging barbarian army lays waste to all in its path, so he leaves a desolation of smouldering ruins and corpses. He scorches nature—exemplified by the healthy fruit tree. He destroys human habitation—typified by the central communal building, the Temple, and with it the culture of the Jews. All that remains standing is a dead tree. In his raging tantrum he has enacted the wasteland, and at the sacred centre of what will become the culture of the West. In a few days' time, which is kairos now, he will be nailed to that tree.

The damning of the fig is the signal that kairos is upon them. It is a shock image; a shock tactic. As a mirror inversion of the high awe of the Shining, its function is to throw all who cross his path out of the cosy routines of chronos. The fig refuses, so it dies.

His loss of composure is not surprising. The fated way he now sees ahead is inhumanly difficult to tread. So he turns on followers who have proved stonyhearted — petrified. He is the fuming firestorm, creating before their eyes a portrait from hell of what they are. Possibly, too, his anger is at his own inability to make the fig fruit — just as he has failed to make the twelve learn.

The twelve are wrong, however, to interpret the tree exclusively as themselves. It is, above all, his own fate that he conjures up in the form of the withered fig, continuing the tragic Jerusalem pantomime. This time, the phantasm dancing across the sea chanting 'I am!' has been metamorphosed into the frozen form of the anti-Shining — a charcoal vertical stump in the midst of a human wilderness of what is not.

We are in the time of his anger; it will give way to despair. He knows his hour is not quite yet. There is time to pass, and composure to regain:

> He breaks the silence before the fig tree, answering Peter, 'Have sacred trust. For I say to you that whoever commands this mountain, "Be taken up and thrown into the sea" and does not doubt in his heart but trusts what he speaks, whatever he says shall come to be.'

Continuing on to Jerusalem, he was walking around in the Temple when the chief priests, the intellectuals, and the elders came up to him, questioning, 'By what authority do you act? Who gave you this authority?' He sidesteps by saying he will only answer if they answer his question, which is whether John's baptism was from heaven or from men. They refuse to answer, afraid either way of the people, who revered John as a prophet.

He evades the vital *by what authority* question. The preceding assertion that true knowing can move mountains is addressed to the twelve, but surely it is not. It rather reads as an internal monologue, a hymn to himself as he struggles, on the threshold of the kairos end, to maintain his spirits. Its charge is rhetorical. Once he had such powers to move mountains; now they are reduced to exterminating a harmless tree. Maybe it was his discontent, his wayward mood, that cursed the fig tree—not his authority. And maybe it was his anger that purged the Temple—not his authority. His alternative strategy is to tell a parable:

A man planted a vineyard then left it in the care of farmers. At harvest kairos he sent a servant to collect his share of the fruit, but the farmers beat him up and sent him away. The man sent another servant, whom they stoned, wounded in the head, and shamefully despatched. He sent another, who was killed, then many others, who were all beaten or killed. Finally he sent his beloved son, reasoning that he would be respected. But the farmers calculated if they killed the heir then the inheritance would be theirs. They killed the son and threw his body out of the vineyard. So what does the owner do? He comes and obliterates the farmers and gives the vineyard to others.

The parable is obvious. The Jewish elite recognise that it targets them; so they hesitate to act against him, fearing the crowd. They try to trick him into denigrating Roman rule, risking a charge of treason:

> They have Pharisees and Herodians question, 'Teacher, we know that you are of the truth, and you only teach the truth of the divine way, without fear or favour to any man. Is it lawful to pay taxes to Caesar, or not?'
>
> Knowing their hypocrisy, he said, 'Why do you test me? Bring me a coin so that I may look at it.' They brought one, and he questioned, 'Whose image is this, and whose inscription?' They answered, 'Caesar's.' So he replied, 'Render to Caesar the things that are Caesar's, and to God the things that are God's.'

Time passes in the Temple, as he roams around, in the waiting room of his hour.

> Next it is the turn of some Sadducees, whose Jewish sect does not believe in resurrection after death. They pose a riddle about a woman who has had seven husbands. When she dies and rises from the dead whose wife shall she be? The teacher replies that the God of Moses is not the God of the dead, but the God of the living.
>
> One of the intellectuals who had overheard the debate then asks which is the first commandment. He replied, 'First of all commandments is: "Hear Israel, the Lord God, our Lord, is one. And you shall love the Lord your God with all your heart, with all your soul, with all your mind, and with all your strength." And the second, like it, is: "You shall love your neighbour as yourself." No other

commandment is greater than these.'[7]

The intellectual understood. He was the last who dared question the teacher. A large crowd in the Temple was listening enthusiastically. He warned them of the intellectuals, the ones who desire to parade around in long robes; love to be greeted respectfully in the marketplaces; seek the best seats in the synagogues and the places of honour at dinners; they who devour widows' houses and, for show, deliver long prayers. They will receive more severe judgment.

Now he sat opposite the treasury, passing more time, and observed many who were rich donating generously. Then a poor widow came and threw in two small copper coins. He called the twelve to him, 'This poor widow has put in most of all. For the rich gave out of their abundance, whereas she has given out of her poverty, and all she had, her whole life.'

Then he left the Temple. A follower addressed him, 'Teacher, Look. What stones and what buildings!' He responded, 'Do you not see these great buildings? Not one stone will be left upon another; not one will not be thrown down.'

He departed from Jerusalem and proceeded over to the Mount of Olives, where he sat opposite the Temple. Asked for a sign, he began his warnings, 'Watch! Many will come in my name saying "I am." Many will be deceived. There will be wars and rumours of wars. Nation will rise against nation. There will be earthquakes and famines. These are the beginnings of the birth pains.'

'Watch! They will hand you over to governments, and you will be flogged in synagogues. You will be brought before rulers because of me, as witness. But first the Story must be told to all nations. When you are arrested do not worry what to say, for the sacred pneuma will speak through you. Now brother will betray brother, to death; and father, his child; and children will rise up against parents, killing them. Because of my name all will hate you. But he who endures to the end will be delivered.'

'When you see the abomination of desolation standing where it should not—you who understand—those in Judea should flee to the mountains. He on the housetop should not return to the house; nor he in the field go back for his clothes. Woe to women who are pregnant, or who nurse infants. If anyone comes in those times claiming to be the messiah, do not believe him.'

'Watch! I have told you all these things in advance. After the desolation the sun will go dark, the moon will give no light, the stars will fall, and the higher powers will be shaken.'

[He continued by quoting one of Daniel's visions]

'Then the son of man will be seen coming in the clouds with great power and glory.'[8]

'Watch! Learn this parable from the fig tree. When its branch becomes tender and it puts forth leaves, you know summer is near. Of the day, and of the hour, no one knows, not even the son.'

'Watch! Be alert! Watch! For you do not know the kairos. It is like a man away on a journey, leaving authority to his servants, each to his own work, and the doorman he commanded to watch. Be on the lookout, therefore, for you don't know when the master of the house is coming—in the evening, at midnight, at cockcrow, or

early in the morning; lest, coming suddenly, he finds you
sleeping. What I say to you, I say to all, "Watch!"'

After this monologue on the Mount of Olives, the teacher
will next appear in Bethany. He has spent something like two
days talking in the Temple. If the triumphal entry into Jerusalem
was on the Sunday — what came to be known as Palm
Sunday — then Monday was the cleansing of the Temple. The
pause before the dead fig occurred on Tuesday morning, followed
by Temple teaching, and then again on the Wednesday, when he
also goes across to the Mount of Olives. From there, Mark takes
up the narrative with him at dinner in Bethany — possibly on the
Wednesday evening. On Thursday he will prepare for the Last
Supper, which occurs that same night. So runs the rough
chronology of his final week.

The post-fig interval of teaching is pitched in Jewish terms,
and conducted inside the Jewish Temple. Perhaps it is so he will
be understood. Even the two commandments are quotations
from the Hebrew Bible, commandments selected by him from
among many others. What status do they assume? They are of
lesser significance than his own singular law, given early in his
mission, that the one unforgivable state is pneumaphobia. 'Love
God' and 'Love thy neighbour' are important, but not ultimate.
They will not move mountains. When he cautions Peter to 'Have
sacred trust', he gestures not backwards to the old Jewish order,
but forwards, to the *mystery* contained within the black stump.

The interlude inside the Temple is cast in a different language
to his earlier teaching. It bears an altogether different logic to the
rest of his story. Perhaps the initial questioning of his authority
snaps him out of his angry and dispirited mood. He charges into
the aggressive parable of the stolen vineyard. By the next episode,
of Caesar's taxes, he is back in command, his authority on display,

and he toys with the Jewish leaders. The exchange with the Sadducees about marriage after death is like some tiresome intellectual game. Then he offers the crowd a stock caricature of hypocritical religious practice—notably out of character for Mark in its crudity. His final act in the Temple is to meditate on the poor widow, and what it means to give out of nothing, to give a whole life. In other words, a sequence that opens with the issue of authority moves into the closer focus of contrasting higher authority with the face of Roman rule, then ends with the most insignificant of copper coins.

The prelude to his prowling around in the Temple like a restless, moody lion is the withering of the fig. When he finally leaves, his attention turns back to destruction, which he now develops into apocalyptic imagery. A familiar idiom, that of kairos, returns. He orchestrates the entire following sequence, on the Mount of Olives, within a musical frame—a slowly accelerating chant, the tempo of mounting gravity, his own insistent chorus hammering 'Watch! Watch! Watch!' The incantation reaches its own climax in servants left in charge of the house, each instructed to apply himself to his own work, but not to sleep lest the Master return. Work at what you do, head down, but always be alert, for I shall return! Bide your time in your daily work; but watch, always watch!

In the midst of this sequence, like a deadly poisonous snake sleeping in the grass, is the 'abomination of desolation'. What might this perplexing expression mean? It evokes shades of some monstrous evil, a deluge of black fire scorching the earth. His coming has awakened the malevolent force—more lethal than pneuma-crazed pigs. It is the antithesis of him, yet he himself has equivalent powers, if with different intent, for he is the obliterating firestorm that withers the fig tree and lays waste to the Temple. The subtext of his 'whoever commands this mountain, "Be taken up and thrown into the sea"' is that he refers to the mountain rising straight ahead of them, the one they approach — Temple Mount. He is in the process of throwing the culture of the Jews into the sea.

But the immediate abomination to which he refers is closer at hand. After the desolation, he foretells that the sun will go dark. That, in fact, is only a couple of days away.

When the narrative recommences he is in Bethany, at the house of Simon the Leper, reclining for a meal:

> A woman came with an alabaster flask of very expensive perfume — pure spikenard. She broke the flask and began pouring it over his head. Some there were indignant at the waste of precious perfume, which might have been sold for more than three hundred denarii, and the proceeds given to the poor. They castigated her.
>
> But the Master intervened, 'Let her be. Why bother her? She has done a beautiful thing for me. You always have the poor, and can help them whenever you wish. Me, you do not have always. She has done everything. She has anointed my body for burial before the time. I say to you that wherever my story is told in the world, what this woman did will also be known, in memory of her.'
>
> Then Judas Iscariot, one of the twelve, went to the chief priests to betray him. They were delighted, promising him money. So Judas plotted the time to hand him over.

What the woman in Bethany does is *Watch*. At the opening of the triumphal entry-scene into Jerusalem he paused at 'Bethphage and Bethany near the Mount of Olives'. 'Bethphage' means 'house of unripe figs'—in other words, Bethany's other self awaits the kairos. Mark has set up the final week with a signal that it will be in Bethany that the fig will fruit.

We are back with the mustard tree and insiders. This woman has appeared from nowhere. She does not even have a name. Yet she sees the mystery. She was not present at his *watch* incantation—again, so much for teaching. In a house in Bethany, where he is simply reclining for dinner, it is she who finds him. Entering, she takes over, breaking the alabaster, filling the room with fragrance. Nor was she there when he danced across the water urging courage, proclaiming that all you need to know is '*I am!*' This is precisely what she does know. The 'beautiful thing' is her recognition, and the anointing of his head—the seat of the living *I am*. She has no fear.[9]

Luke will rework this episode from Mark and place it earlier in his story. The unnamed woman becomes a prostitute, and Simon the Leper becomes Simon a wealthy Pharisee in the Galilee town of Magdala. John reworks it again, replacing it at the same point in the narrative as Mark, but naming the woman Mary of Bethany, sister of Martha and Lazarus, and extending her story—as the one who watches, becoming the first insider taught by him. John also blurs her identity into that of the prostitute Mary Magdalene.

Here is midrash at its finest; and it helps with interpreting Mark, who is at his most cryptic in this episode. Mark's detailing is minimal. He tells us that the perfume is extravagantly expensive—three hundred silver denarii was as much as a workman earned in a year.[10] One of the very few ways for a single woman to obtain such a sum of money would have been through working as a high-class prostitute. The touching of his head, his hair, the crack of alabaster, the pouring of the precious oily liquid, the fragrance in the room, are rich with cumulative sensuality. Hers is an earthy yet selfless love. That the host, Simon, is a leper adds to the insinuation of contagious impurity, and heightens the charge of the Master's celebration of this woman: 'She has done everything. She will be remembered, with me.'

John will make explicit what is also in Mark, that it is Judas who protests about the waste of money. Mark works elusively, by suggestion and inference, in this instance going directly from the anointing in Bethany to Judas' plans for betrayal. That the chief priests offer to pay the traitor picks up the earlier money reference, identifying Judas with silver. It also signals his hypocrisy. He has no interest in the poor.[11]

In the surface text, Mark leaves those who resent the woman nameless—like her. He may be clarifying essences. Names and personalities are irrelevant to what makes an insider, and what makes a rancorous outsider. Ultimately, the Master himself is *I am* with no name.

Judas realises that this woman is alert to the kairos. She has understood 'Watch!' He attacks her out of competitive envy. Judas is the archetypal *I am not*. To be confronted with the primal *I am* was hardly bearable. Now there is a second one. Recognition of her sends him into a paroxysm of destructive rancour. She shows him up, above all to himself. He is void of the one thing that counts. This scene, as conjured by Mark, precipitates Judas into raging evil. That there is an insider, and that it is not him, arouses his last passion—to destroy the Master. The *abomination of desolation* awakens in him. The abomination of desolation is pneumaphobia, the one unredeemable condition. It is now that the early teaching about the mystery begins to work its fill.

I shall return in Part Two to the stories of both Judas and the composite figure—Mary of Bethany / Mary Magdalene. They deserve consideration in their own right.

'She has done everything,' is how the Master identified her. She has realised her mistake in setting aside precious oil for his death. She was keeping it to anoint the corpse, thus obeying the religious ritual of her time. This unnamed woman must have been a follower at a distance, hitherto unmentioned, stigmatised by her work; or a friend; or both. The metamorphosis he teaches is not the overcoming of death through resurrection—symbolised by the anointing of the dead body. *I am* shines in life, here and now. So she goes up to him, the living man, and bathes his hair in luxuriant perfume. In the charged, aromatic air, pneuma breathes.

The potency of her act is displayed in the reaction of outsiders. By now, two quite different types have been delineated—Peter and Judas. Peter is the naive one, uncomprehendingly bewildered, with no sense of *Watch*. His attention was caught by the withered fig, yet he fails to distinguish its polar and redemptive opposite—her anointing of the reclining Master's head. Only able to see himself and his own future, he is blind to she who does not stumble. You cannot see what you are not.

Judas, by contrast, is shrewdly intelligent and perceptive. He understands exactly what is happening in the Bethany room at the house of Simon the Leper. He watches. Lacking the vital essence of *being*, he cannot love. The fragrance that fills the room is poison to him. He is wrenched tight, choked with black bile—so he rages against the waste of money. Unnerved by the truth, the truth about himself, this abomination of desolation is precipitated into action. It is pneumaphobia that drives him.

CHAPTER FIVE

AND IT WAS NIGHT[1]

It is Thursday, twenty-four hours to the crucifixion:

Being the day for killing the Passover lamb, the twelve asked him, 'Where do you want us to go and prepare, so you may celebrate the Passover feast?'

He sent two saying, 'Go into the city where you will meet a man carrying a jar of water. Follow him. Wherever he enters, say to the master of the house, "The teacher asks where the lodging is in which he may eat the Passover with his followers?" He will show you to a large upper room which is ready. Prepare for us there.'

They left and went into the city, finding it just as he had said, so they prepared the Passover. When it was evening he arrived with the twelve.

As they reclined and ate he told them, 'Surely, I say to you that one who eats with me will betray me.'

They became troubled and questioned him, one after the other, 'Not I?' He replied, 'One of the twelve, the one dipping in the bowl with me. The son of man is indeed going away, just as it is written, and woe to he who betrays him. It would have been better for that man never to have been born.'

As they were eating, he took bread, blessed and broke

it, and gave it to them, saying, 'This is my body.' Then he took the cup and, offering thanks, he gave it to them and they drank from it. He said, 'This is my blood, the testament shed for many. Indeed, I will no longer drink of the fruit of the vine until the day I drink it new in the kingdom.'

After they had sung a hymn they left, heading towards the Mount of Olives. He said, 'All of you will stumble, for it is written, "I will strike the shepherd and the sheep will be scattered."[2] But after I am raised I shall go ahead of you into Galilee.'

Peter responded, 'Even if all stumble, not I.' The Master replied, 'Surely, I say to you that on this very night before the cock crows twice you will disown[3] me three times.' Peter protested effusively, 'Even if I have to die with you, I will not disown you.' The others said likewise.

They arrived at a place named Gethsemane. He said to the twelve, 'Sit here while I pray.' Taking Peter, James and John along with him, he became alarmed, filled with anguish. He told them, 'My soul is exceedingly sorrowful unto death. Stay here and watch.'

Going a little farther, he fell on the ground, and prayed that if it were possible the hour might pass from him. He said, 'Abba, father, everything is possible for you. Take this cup away from me. Nevertheless, not my will, but yours.'

Returning to find the three asleep, he addressed Peter, 'Simon, Are you sleeping? Were you not strong enough to watch one hour? Watch and pray, lest you be tested. For indeed, the pneuma is willing, but the flesh is weak.'

Once more going away, he prayed, speaking the same word. When he returned, he found them asleep again, for their eyes were weighed down. They did not know how to answer him.

Then once again he returned to them, the third time, directing, 'Sleep on, forever! Enough,[4] the hour has come. Behold, the son of man is being betrayed into the hands of the lost. Get up, let us be going. See, my betrayer approaches.'

While he was still speaking, Judas drew near, leading a large mob with swords and clubs sent by the chief priests, the intellectuals, and the elders. The betrayer had given a signal that whomever he kissed they should seize and lead away safely.

Judas went directly up to him. 'Teacher! Teacher!' he kissed him tenderly. So they grabbed him. One of the followers standing by drew his sword and struck the servant of the high priest, cutting off his ear.

The Master challenged, 'Have you come out, as against a robber, with swords and clubs to arrest me? I was with you every day teaching in the Temple, but you did not seize me. However, the script must be fulfilled.'

At this, those with him abandoned him and fled.

Now a certain young man had followed him. The young men seized him but, having only a linen cloth thrown around his body, he left it behind, fleeing naked from them.

Then the teacher was led away to the high priest, with whom were assembled all the chief priests, the elders, and the intellectuals. Peter followed at a distance, right into the courtyard of the high priest. There he sat with the servants and warmed himself at the fire.

The chief priests and council sought witnesses so they could condemn him to death, but found none. Many lied about him; however, their testimonies did not agree. Some then falsely claimed to have heard him say that he would destroy this Temple built with hands, and within three days he would build another without hands.

The high priest stood up to question him directly, 'Do you answer nothing? What about these men's testimony against you?' But he remained silent. So the high priest asked him again, 'You are the Christ, son of the blessed?'

He answered, '**I am**. And you will see the son of man sitting on the right hand of the power, and coming with the clouds of heaven.'

Then the high priest, tearing his clothes, proclaimed, 'What further need of witnesses do we have? You have heard the blasphemy! What do you think?'

They all condemned him as deserving death. Then some began to spit on him, cover his face, and beat him. They urged him to 'Prophesy!' The attendants struck him.

Meanwhile, below in the courtyard, one of the high priest's servant girls saw Peter warming himself, and charged, 'You were also with him.' But he denied it, 'I do not know, nor understand what you are saying.' He went outside into the forecourt.

The servant girl spotted him there and began to say to the bystanders, 'This is one of them.' He denied it again. A little later those around charged Peter, 'Truly you are of them, for you are a Galilean.' He began to curse, and to swear that 'I do not know that man, of whom you speak.'

On the instant, the cock crowed. Peter remembered what the Master had said, and he broke down and wept.

They come in quick succession, the evening quintet—Last Supper, Gethsemane, betrayal, Jewish trial, and denial. The prayer in the garden is not the Shining, but collapsing to the ground asking for the hour to pass. He wants to renounce even the kairos, in the dark, as events rush dizzyingly past, drawing him along.

He can still ask the three to watch. But they are so blinded—their eyes 'weighed down'—that, even at this moment of climactic portent, the dark furies of the kairos wheeling around so that one can almost hear the menacing screams, insensitive to his sorrow unto death, deaf to *Watch!* (and it is a bitter irony that *they* should start chopping other men's ears off), they fall asleep, and three times. Hence his final charge to them, 'Sleep on, forever! Enough.' He has had enough, enough of his hour, enough of they who stumble, perhaps even enough of himself. 'Endless sleep!' is what he condemns them to, and it is harsh. If they are dead to this moment of all moments, they may as well remain among the dead, forever. These are his final words ever spoken to them, and they are a dismissal: *sleep the big sleep.*[5] 'Endless sleep!'

It is horrible. Pressing on this last time of sheer and hopeless despair at his chosen twelve, the betrayer approaches him, addressing the man who has changed his life, 'Teacher! Teacher!' The surface is warm and intimate; the fact, a sniggering dynamo of hate. How can poison give birth to what follows—a tender kiss? This is not just a smiling villain, but a gently embracing human monster. And Judas is his creation.

The entire episode was prefigured in the Last Supper. A sense of fatedness broods over the day, from the first scene where he dispatches two followers to find the upper room that is prepared for what is to be. There will be a man carrying a jar of water; there will be a lodging house; there will be a master of that house. So runs the script, which he already knows.

Just as he knows that one of the twelve will betray him. That it is the one who dips in the bowl with him indicates a special bond. The bowl is a variant on the cup, the cup of destiny. It contains the wine, his blood, and the betrayer dips his hand into the blood. There is intimacy between Judas and him, the shared destiny sprouting from the fact that Judas is the only one of the twelve who understands him. Hence the kiss. The woman in Bethany had kissed him; it is she who provokes the other, Judas kiss — its negation.[6]

Destiny and its cup return with his final words during the arrest, 'The script must be fulfilled.' 'Script' is *graphai*, the Greek word traditionally translated as 'scriptures'. *Graphai* means 'writings', or 'lines', as in those drawn or etched. The lines of fate are drawn; the script must be fulfilled. He underlines the predestination of Judas and his role.

The Supper opens with his first decree that one of them will betray him. It closes with his second, and final decree that all who have assembled together that evening will stumble. They have just sung a hymn together, after his blessing the bread and offering the wine — suggestive of communal flare and conviviality. This is a rare moment of cosy brotherhood. Dramatically, the sequence echoes the triumphal entry into Jerusalem, the dancing and singing as a prelude to the striking dead of the fig tree. The musical rise and fall is repeated, as are the warnings to *Watch!*

For him, the Supper has been a ritual, one in which he presents himself for sacrifice, offering his body and his blood to the future. He makes it clear that those who are about to sacrifice him are the very twelve reclining and eating around this table — from the betrayer who dips with him, to the rest who will all stumble.

Under prosecution at the Jewish trial, he remains almost entirely silent. What is there to say? The council calls on many to testify against him, including the charge that he said he would destroy the Temple, and would within three days rebuild it without the use of hands. The council takes the testimonies to be lies — which is odd, given that he has, in fact, emptied the Temple, and is in the process of enacting its total destruction. That a true accusation is taken to be false may indicate that the Jewish elite are so bewildered by him that they bungle the prosecution. They have reason to condemn him to death, out of self-preservation, yet end up judging him on bad grounds.

The high priest becomes so agitated that he gets to his feet in the midst of the noisy throng to question him directly. He is troubled that the teacher remains silent, for this suggests that he has an inner authority, and that the council does not intimidate him. He seems to have no fear of them. But the high priest's real anxiety is expressed in his final question, 'You are the Christ, son of the blessed?' He suspects that the Messiah predicted in Jewish scripture, sent to save the chosen people, might be here — and that they are about to put him to death. Which means that he knows the truth of the charge that the chief priests are hypocrites who have turned the Temple into a den of outlaws, profaning their office. From his own Jewish perspective, the high priest may be about to condemn his people's saviour to death. Little wonder he is on edge.

The final question from the custodian of the Temple does provoke an answer, but for a quite different reason. It is the same *Who am I?* question the teacher himself put in the murky time when he slowly awakened to his own mission, just preceding the mountain Shining — the question Peter wrongly answered in the same terms now used by the high priest. That was when men looked like trees walking. Now he provides the decisive answer himself, and not one that proclaims he is Christ the messiah, son of the blessed. He uses the cue, breaks his silence, and reminds all those present, including himself, who and what he is—'I am! (*egō eimi!*)'

His *watch* hymn had prepared this ground, with him warning, 'Many will come in my name saying "I am".' Here is the answer to the *by what authority* challenge.

Peter's final act in the story is to curse his teacher, the man who has made everything possible, who has opened the door through which the rock has found itself unable to pass. Peter's excessive protestation, 'Even if I have to die with you, I will not deny you', already contains the seed of its own evil. He protests too much. The next moment, when asked to watch for an hour, merely an hour, he falls asleep—not just once, but three times. After the second awakening he shows some embarrassment ('they did not know how to answer him'), but promptly falls asleep again. The third time he is told not to bother waking up. So Peter *has* died with him, but not in the sense he anticipated a little earlier.

Peter's boast has been like the performance of the cock that will sound his end—a puffed-up parody of courage. Three sleeps prepare the way for three denials. The content is telling. After the arrest, Peter follows at a distance. He enters the courtyard of the high priest. At this stage, he shows more courage than the others, fearing but not fleeing. He moves guiltily, hovering in the vicinity of his own humiliation. He sits, like an unwelcome stranger, with the servants, and warms himself at a fire in the courtyard beneath the council assembly proceeding above.

The Greek word used by Mark for 'fire' is *phōs*, as in phosphorescent, literally 'light'. The cycle of Peter's skewed relationship to fire—from his mother-in-law's fever, to the sun that withers seed on stony ground, to the metamorphosis on the high mountain—reaches its climax in his attempt to warm himself on the threshold of the denial. In fire he seeks the light, the Shining that he failed to see, the 'Pray!' that he failed to heed.

His is a story of gruelling, remorseless, tragic failure. The simple fisherman has tried his hardest. He was drawn to the light; he has followed and obeyed. At times he even thinks he knows, and boasts about his fidelity. It is all too human — he would like the boast to be true, to be him, Simon the trusty rock, and here his better self speaks, only to be harshly countermanded.

Peter's first denial takes the specific form, 'I do not know.' By his third denial, the tempo has heightened, with him swearing, 'I do not know that man.' And he curses. It may be that, at this very moment in the assembly hall above, his Master is pronouncing for the last time the logos — 'I am!' Like two voices singing a duet on different sides of the stage, 'I am' is accompanied by 'I do not know'. 'I do not know I am; I know I am not.'

During the Last Supper, each of the twelve had chanted, one after another, 'Not I?' *Not I* is a contraction of *I am not*. In denial, Peter is no more than their representative, to be identified forever by *I do not know* and *I am not*. Here is the bitter aftertaste of that supper, its ultimate meaning. Peter's curse is that 'I am not', and he curses the man who has confronted him with his own rootlessness. When the light goes out in the courtyard it will be endless sleep.

Earlier this very evening in Gethsemane, that not-known and cursed man had already, when he woke Peter up, reverted to addressing him by his original name. 'Simon, are you sleeping?' he had asked him. 'Were you not strong enough to watch one hour?' The rebuke is tender; but, for Simon who became Peter, the initiation has been annulled. The message is: return to who you were before you met me — return to oblivion. So the ultimate curse on Judas applies equally to Peter: 'It would have been better for that man never to have been born.' In Peter's case it is spoken with warmth, sadly.

In the garden, Peter is dead tired. He falls asleep out of spiritual exhaustion. He is already — in his being and soul — in denial. His repeated falling asleep indicates that he does not want to be re-awoken. Endless sleep is his own choice. He has had enough. He has had too much. So his final act after the untimely awakening is to utter curses. He hates his Master, the Master who should have known better than to call him. The curse of Simon Peter becomes the climax of his denial, and his curse is on himself and his life. The denial, at its kernel, is the denial that *I am*.

James and John also fall asleep. They had once asked the Master, after the metamorphosis on the high mountain, that they might sit next to him in his splendour. The arrogant and foolish sons of thunder received the pained reply, '*You don't know what you ask. Are you able to drink the cup I drink, and be baptised with the baptism I am baptised with?*'

Everything that is not becomes shut up in itself. Peter is trapped in his own inability to know, and is left to curse; Judas, knowing, is consumed by his own void, hating what he knows. The one person with poise is the woman in Bethany. Not preoccupied by self, not fearful of whom she might be, she is free to *watch*, and to recognise him. She is the only one alert to the exceeding sorrow unto death. She is the only one free to love. She does a beautiful thing. And, because of her, he is not alone.

There is another woman. She is also nameless. The servant girl, too, does only one thing — she speaks the truth. She confronts Peter, only to be told a lie — that he does not know what she is saying. She then follows him out into the forecourt and accuses him again. She is outraged at his lie. She will not be fobbed off. He will not escape her.

She has no status, no power, and no name. She is a woman; she is a servant; and she is young. She is in breach of the social conventions of her time in challenging a man, and one perhaps old enough to be her father.[7] Her only authority is that she speaks the truth, and it is so potent that she nails Peter. He cannot squirm free. She is the cock crowing, awakening him to what he has done, to what he is. That she has no worldly authority, nor personal attributes, makes her voice one of pure, unselfconscious innocence — outraged that a man can lie about something as important as his relationship with the man who called him.

This woman represents all humans at their best: nameless servants of truth, defending its order. Her power is such that she knocks the wind (pneuma) out of Peter, whose flesh is willing — that is, bragging about how he will die with his Master. She crushes him with shame, so completely that he may never recover. This is the power of truth. She is the anonymous voice of *endless sleep*.

The story that Mark tells is radical here, as ever. In scrapping the normal attributes of the self — in this episode, worldly rankings and statuses — it makes all humans equal. It is democratic two millennia before its time.[8] *I am* is not clothed in customary finery.

The servant girl echoes the woman in Bethany in her capacity for seeing, and then in acting on what she sees. They are both watchers. Perhaps she is outraged more at the truth, rather than the lie, in Peter's 'I do not know' denial. Unconsciously, instinctively, she knows the Truth. She is appalled that this man Peter who, as she charges, was one of his followers, and therefore spent time in his company — that he, with all this advantage — should not *know*. Peter is a disgrace. Just as her other self, the woman who anoints, is counterpoised to Judas, the servant girl is counterpoised to Peter. She feels violated in her deepest being by human blindness, as personified in him. Her eyes are not weighed down.

The cock was predicted to crow twice, but Mark's narration has it only sounding once, on the third denial. The servant girl accuses Peter twice, the subtext being that there are two different charges: one of lying denial, one of not knowing. She is the rooster, sounding Peter's death. But there is one further and deeper reading: the cock, like a number of Mark's metaphors, is richly over-determined. Peter has been called twice. The first time, the teacher by the Sea of Galilee called the fisherman to follow, nicknaming him the rock. Now, the second time, there is the call of the cock at dawn on crucifixion Friday. It cancels the first. Peter curses the Master; the cock crows; Peter reverts to Simon; then, endless sleep.[9]

There is another youth. A young man is suddenly there, in the Gethsemane garden, clad only in a linen cloth. He has appeared from nowhere. All we are told is that he has followed the teacher. Who is he and where has he come from? Mark inserts him as a further enigma at this critical juncture late in the text. A new presence, he arrives hard on the heels of the twelve abandoning the Master and fleeing. The implication is that the young man is more courageous, of a higher rank than the twelve, separate from them, flitting among the shadowy trees on the fringes of the gathering like an innocent sprite.[10] But what is the significance of the linen cloth? What is the significance of him, on being seized by other young men, fleeing naked, leaving the cloth in their hands?

At this point in the narrative, we may be, at the most, alert to his presence, and aware that it may signal forward.[11]

After the Last Supper the teacher tells the twelve that they will all stumble. Gethsemane follows. There, it is he who is scandalised, collapsing to the ground. It is night, close to Passover full moon. We are not told directly by Mark whether the moon has risen. During his *watch* cantata, however, he had predicted the kairos time when the moon would give no light, which we can assume means now. What will come to be known as 'the agony in the garden' takes place in darkness.

The silhouettes of olive trees ghosting their way, he leaves eight of them behind, with whomever else, including the young man who has followed, to sit in one clearing. He moves further ahead, leading the preferred three into the depths of the olive grove, accompanied by the black anger that is *melancholia*[12] rising within, agitating him, filling him with dread. He can barely speak: 'My soul is exceeding sorrowful unto death.' He leaves the three behind, like a man staggering along lost in a desert who ditches his last encumbering possessions. Luke will specify him as moving a stone's-throw distance beyond.

Alone, he stumbles, pitching down. Emptied, flat on the earth, he prays that the hour may pass from him. He prays for a change of destiny. He prays for relief. *Let me not be who I am. Lead my path elsewhere. Take my cup away from me.* He wants to throw the cup away, spilling its contents. He who filled the cup wants not to be. This is the ultimate profanity. He himself is close to pneumaphobia.

The site he has chosen is a garden—an olive grove—and outside the city walls.[13] It is not the wilderness of the moral preacher, John the Baptist; not the sea for crossing over; not the high mountain of the Shining; not the city of the Temple. It is the garden of the second fall. Adam and Eve in the paradise garden were the first fallen. Theirs was a moral fall. They lost their innocence, and were cast out. Their defining act was one of disobedience, making them ashamed. This gave birth to the need for moral order, and for preachers to defend commandments. It gave birth to the culture of the Old Testament, the Hebrew Bible.

The second fall is into an utterly different domain.

What has it all been for? For him, looking back loads sorrow with bewilderment. He sees the nothing that he has achieved. He has failed in everything he set out to do, stage by stage, apart from the wayward, unintended process of learning what his mission was not, and thereby gaining a sense of who he is. He quickly came to begrudge healing the sick, as with the Greek woman. He was not a miracle worker. He withdrew from teaching the crowds. And he forsook the role of good shepherd—of servant to children, the poor, and the afflicted.

What were his gifts for? He chose and trained followers, only to leave them behind. Why did he continue teaching? He did so fitfully. Maybe the only reason was that he was a teacher; teachers teach. Whether in the Temple, by the sea, or in the wilderness, no edification came. Not one person taught by him, learnt. The ones who did learn—notably Legion, the mad boy, and the woman in Bethany—simply came to know what they know. His only role for them was to be present. Otherwise his vocation has been no more than a talking to himself: one sporadic, long, agonised monologue, for his own ears only. That it has been for the sake of the Story is another issue.

No more does he trust his god. If there is a higher guide to the way his life has been cast, he, now, in the moonless garden, turns away from him. Since the voice spoke out of the dark cloud, after the Shining on the high mountain, there has been virtually no sign of a godly father. God has gone from the Story.

Gethsemane is not a prayer to some power above, but a lament and an agony, a suffering within that has choked his will to go on. His groans have given way to a gentle, exhausted curse. The exceeding sorrow unto death intimates his longing for the dark peace of *no more*, the endless sleep that is on his mind. Without support from above, without human aid, his final concession,

'Nevertheless, not my will, but yours', is a mere reflexive acknowledgement of the hour.

The absence of divine support is not the heaviest burden—not what pitches him to the ground. His story has been one of switching from God above, and the Law, to his own *I am*, here and now. He proclaims, before the Jewish assembly, '*I am. And you will see the son of man sitting on the right hand of the power.*' This is the only positive, potentially redemptive phrase he has uttered since his entry into Jerusalem four days earlier. His lament in the night garden focuses on whether he is strong enough to carry what he is about to suffer. Yet again, he is unsure of who he is, unsure whether he has the power.

He is the chosen or anointed one—the Christ—only in the sense recognised by the woman in Bethany. He is living *being*. In Gethsemane, that is not enough.

First thing in the morning, the chief priests conferred with the elders, intellectuals, and full council. They bound him, led him away, and delivered him to the Roman governor, Pilate.

Pilate asked him, 'You are the King of the Jews?'

He answered, 'You say.'

The chief priests piled on their accusations. Pilate asked him again, 'Do you answer nothing? See how many things they charge you with?' He still answered nothing. Pilate was in awe.

At the Passover festival Pilate was accustomed to release one prisoner to them, whomever they requested. There was one called Barabbas, imprisoned with fellow rioters who had committed murder during an insurrection. The mob began yelling out that Pilate should do what he always did for them. He responded, 'Do you want me to release the King of the Jews to you?' He knew the chief priests were acting out of envy.

But the chief priests stirred up the mob to demand he release Barabbas. Pilate responded, 'What then do you want me to do with he whom you call King of the Jews?'

They howled out again, 'Crucify him!' Pilate questioned, 'Why, what evil has he done?' To which they yelled all the more violently, 'Crucify him!'

So Pilate, wanting to satisfy the crowd, released Barabbas, and handed the teacher over, after flogging, to be crucified.

Soldiers led him away into the Praetorium courtyard, where they assembled the whole garrison. They clothed him in purple and wound a wreath of thorns they had plaited around his head. They saluted him, 'Hail, King of the Jews!' Caning his head and spitting on him, they knelt in worship before him.

When they had mocked him they stripped the purple, put his own clothes back on, and led him out to crucify him. They commandeered a certain man passing through from the country — Simon, a Cyrenian, father of Alexander and Rufus — to carry his cross. They then brought him to Golgotha, which means 'Skull Place'. There they offered him wine mixed with myrrh, but he did not take it.

It was the third hour when they crucified him. They divided his clothes among themselves by lot. The charge against him was inscribed above, THE KING OF THE JEWS. They also crucified two robbers with him, one on his left, one on his right.

Those who passed by vilified him, shaking their heads and mocking, 'Aha, you who destroy the Temple and rebuild it in three days, save yourself! Come down from the cross!'

Likewise, the chief priests scorned him among themselves and the intellectuals, 'He saved others, himself he cannot save. Let the Christ, King of Israel, come down from the cross, so that we may see and believe.' Even those crucified with him jeered at him.

At the sixth hour, darkness came over the whole land, until the ninth hour. And at the ninth hour he screamed out with a great voice, *Eloi, Eloi, lima sabachthani?* which translates as, 'My God, my God, why have you forsaken me?'

Some standing by, when they heard, exclaimed, 'Look, he is calling for Elias!' Then someone ran to soak a sponge in vinegar, and lifted it up on a reed stalk, to offer him to drink, saying, 'Leave him alone, and let us see if Elias is coming to take him down.'

Letting off a great voice, he expired [*exepneuse*].

The veil of the Temple sanctuary was ripped in two, from top to bottom. And the centurion standing opposite him, seeing how he breathed his last, exclaimed, 'Truly, this man was the son of God.'

There were women looking on from afar. Among them were Mary Magdalene, Mary the mother of James the Less and Joses, and Salomé—who had all followed him in Galilee—and also many other women who had accompanied him to Jerusalem.

When it was evening, being Preparation Day, the day before the Sabbath, Joseph of Arimathea came, a prominent council member who was also awaiting the divine kingdom. He took courage and went to Pilate to ask for the body. Pilate was amazed that he was already dead, so he summoned the centurion to ask whether he had been dead long. Once knowing, from the centurion, he granted the body to Joseph.

Having taken him down, Joseph wrapped his body in a linen cloth he had bought and placed it in a tomb that had been cut out of the rock. He rolled a stone across the door of the tomb. Mary Magdalene and Mary the mother of Joses observed where he was put.

What is puzzling in Mark's account of the Roman trial and crucifixion is the reticence of the central figure. During the trial he remains silent, apart from two words he utters enigmatically in response to Pilate: 'You say.' The crucifixion is reported indirectly; almost all attention is on surrounding events, many of which are trivial. Nothing is said of the nailing to the cross, nor the erection of it, nor the six hours of physical torture suffered on it.

Most of the narrative is taken up with mockery. His experience of suffering is more of the psyche than the body. Scorn drowns out the physical pain. Those who haven't abandoned him, betrayed him, or disowned him gather around, like black crows, to scream their abuse. It starts with the chief priests snapping out accusation after accusation to Pilate, whom he stands before, bound in silence. They have induced the governor to question whether he makes the blasphemous and treasonous claim of being King of the Jews. Then the mob begins its chant, 'Crucify him! Crucify him!' Those who flocked to his teaching two days earlier in the Temple, listening with rapt attention, now howl for his blood. Waves of hatred roll up from the crowd and over him, a collective euphoric fury. 'Crucify him! Crucify him!' Under this onslaught, Pilate capitulates.

Next, it is the turn of the Roman soldiers. They can bear no grudge against him. For them it is an ordinary working day, and he is a Jewish nobody whom they have been ordered to crucify. Presumably, he is dignified in spite of being bound—his bearing contrasting with that of a common crook, or a rabid rioter like Barabbas. Yet they take elaborate care in their mockery, turning it into a sadistic play. They clothe him in purple, the colour worn by the Roman emperor, thus ridiculing his kingship. They plait a wreath of thorns and crown him with it—the golden aura of the royal symbol inverted into a barbed assault on the head, which draws rivulets of blood. They parade around him with derisive saluting, hailing the King of the Jews. They slash him across the head with canes. They come up close, leer in his face, and spit at him. They get down on one knee before him, smirking and cajoling.

They nail the satirical epigraph, 'King of the Jews', to the upper section of the cross above his head. It induces those who pass by, during the six-hour ordeal, to heckle him over his professed power to destroy and rebuild temples. Why doesn't he save himself? He is merely an idle braggart, for he can't even get himself off the cross! The chief priests use similar terms to scoff at him. Even the wretched creatures crucified alongside him join in the jeering—that they are bandits, and he innocent, underscores the humiliation. Rancour licks its lips at the binding of the power, frothing up among the mobs of cowards.

At the same time, the vast scope and intensity of the mocking indicates the force of his authority. Mark the storyteller displays his immensity through the portrayal of negation. The reaction of the Roman soldiers is particularly telling, for they have no personal, political, or religious interest in his fate. What is it that possesses them to reduce him to a pathetic object, a nothing, fit only for scorn? What vastness and intensity of presence must this lonely stranger now have, to trigger such a mania of derision? They must hate him instinctively, viscerally, for what he is.

Relentless is the world that now surrounds him, brutal and without pity. He remains silent. What of the source of his might — *I am*? Is it in recess? Is it winded and bruised? Is it taking stock? Or is this the soul's exceeding sorrow, its sickness unto death? That he needs help carrying the cross implies the profundity of his weakness, as does the speed of his death. Passion (deriving from the Greek verb, *paschō*) means *pathos* — that is, living and suffering, each innate to the other.[14] The Passion is now, and these are the terms in which it will resonate forward, word and story, to become the core of the culture of the West.

Soldiers offer him wine mixed with myrrh, suggesting some mercy — an anaesthetic to numb the pain. He rejects it, implying perhaps that he feels he is being tested for weakness. Equally, it may indicate that he has had enough, and wants to get it over with — as John will report him saying to Judas at the Last Supper, 'What you do, do quickly!'

The Roman governor does not mock him. He is the single exception, apart from the women looking on from afar. How much does Pilate know? He has seen through the chief priests: they are motivated by envy. Pilate seems curious about what authority this man has to induce the entire Jewish elite to conspire against him. Pilate is in awe of his silence, his contempt for the priests, his indifference to their charges, his lack of interest in defending himself. He hears two words, spoken directly to him — that is all — and they are tauntingly ambiguous. The prisoner treats the question, 'You are the King of the Jews?' as rhetorical, responding with the non-committal, 'You say.'

Pilate is not to know that he has put a *Who am I* question, one which always elicits a response. But he has understood that the title 'King of the Jews' is merely thrust upon this man by his accusers. He knows this man has done no evil.

The principal responsibility of the Roman governor is to keep the peace. He is not running a police state — he has too few soldiers for that. So his rule depends on good relations with the local populace, which means good relations with its leaders. Those leaders now threaten to induce the mob to riot if Pilate does not give them what they want. Rioting in Jerusalem will be reported back to Emperor Tiberius in distant Rome as an insurrection, with the risk that the governor will be dismissed for not maintaining order.

Pilate has no choice but to give the mob what it wants. His obligation to his office, his Roman duty under oath, supersedes what is just. He is in a terrible position, and feels it. When Joseph of Arimathea asks him for the body, he is surprised that the man he condemned is already dead — six hours being a short time for death by crucifixion. He calls the centurion to him. It is the same centurion who has just exclaimed, as witness, 'Truly, this man was the son of God.' Mark cryptically describes Pilate's response to what the centurion tells him as 'knowing'. The word is *gnosis*, from the verb *gignōskō*, just as Pilate's state of amazement at news of the death suggests a grander awe. *Gnosis* will come to mean, in later Western usage, special knowledge.

Pilate represents the man in high political office confronted with an impossible moral dilemma. He does what he has to do, which in this case is to condemn an innocent man to death. He acts wittingly, and responsibly. Not only is the man innocent, but Pilate suspects that he is the key to the mystery — he more than suspects, for by the end he is close to the centurion in what he knows.

Skull Place is the site. Although Mark may simply be translating 'Golgotha', which is Hebrew for 'skull', the term seems loaded. The mockery deepens into metaphysics. Death and oblivion sneer in wait for him. The place was probably, in reality, a hill or knoll just outside the city walls used for executions, including crucifixions. Whether it bore the topographical form of a skull, or its ground was dug in with skeletons, is beside the point. It is Death's place. The sinister chill presiding on this rocky waste where nothing grows is that of the skull. The Master staggers up the hill to meet the leering, black-socketed, toothy, human cranium — challenging him whether there is more meaning than its vacant eternity, more than the big sleep.[15]

On arrival at Skull Place, it is himself he faces. He is in a state of utter psychic exhaustion. He has been surrounded by milling and jostling thousands who hate him — jeering, yelling, whipping, beating, spitting. He has the mob chant of 'Crucify him! Crucify him!' throbbing in his ears. Abandoned by all who have been close to him — from his family, to the twelve, to the multitudes of other followers — what is there left but death? And he is about to endure one of the worst deaths that humans have ever inflicted on one another. Indeed, what is there to differentiate him from the crudely buried human bones, stuck with the partly decomposed flesh that the dogs and vultures have left, the source of the faint stench of ultimate nothing wafting over this Jerusalem hill?

Hell is manifest here, at Skull Place, the end of the road that began with the heavens opening above the River Jordan, and the sacred pneuma descending over his head. His head, twice anointed, is now bleeding and stripped of flesh, of pneuma, of identity.[16] Is this his path, the cycle that the furies have mapped out for him? Is this his cup, from which came the precious fragrance in the Bethany room, and now vinegar dripping from a sponge?

Time is counted off — the third hour, the sixth hour, the ninth hour — like a ship's watch sounding, or a royal funeral where the doleful tenor bell tolls once every minute as the gun carriage rumbles along, bearing the casket. The regular pace is set as a limit against the boundless horror of what is taking place. Chronos time tolls. Meanwhile, it is silent at the kairos centre, with the quakings displaced into the surrounds. Nature begins to rage. The darkness comes at noon. Men are like trees walking, three withered trees glimmering in the gloom. The black stump stands centre-stage with a man nailed to it.

What was the actual chronology? First thing, early on the Friday morning, he is taken to Pilate. At nine o'clock, they crucify him. At midday, a darkness comes over the whole land. At three in the afternoon, he dies. In the evening, he is buried. But, according to this strict, almost obsessional chronos tolling, the sun should rise in the morning and set in the evening. Here it disappears at noon, as kairos asserts its higher authority. Whereas the fig was unable to fruit out of season, the sun goes into eclipse at will.

Of him, we are told little. Such is Mark's tact. We know the agony in the garden, so what must this six-hour magnification of the soul's exceeding sorrow unto death have been like? He has time up there to reflect, through the waves of pain crashing over him driving him into unconsciousness, then back into consciousness. The suffering is not to conceive. He is like the fig: one day, verdantly flourishing; the next, withered from the roots up. We are left to try to imagine the in-between state. Indeed, Mark has displaced some of the impact onto the black stump.

When the Master looks down he can see no one whom he cherished, for they have all fled, scandalised by him. The centurion stands opposite, alone, watching.

The silence at the centre is amplified in lurid purple — by irony. Attention is deflected onto trivial events at the margin. The soldiers cast lots for his clothes. Passers-by call out mindless insults. The bandits crucified on either side of him jeer. Others mishear his final 'Eloi, Eloi' as a call to the Hebrew prophet Elias. As if he would care about any of this! Except that it provides him with a last reminder of what he was called to take on — the chronic banality, nastiness, and folly of much of the human condition. Even the kairos mocks.

Forsakenness, as the text makes clear, was the condition of the cross. At the climax of his sixth hour upon it, he cries out with a great voice his last words, 'My God, my God, why have you forsaken me?' The words quote the opening line of Psalm 22, and Mark writes them in the original Aramaic, then translates them into Greek.

As his story had opened with a voice coming down from the heavens, so it ends with his reply. It is a screamed-out, bitter, rhetorical question, quite unlike the long, mournful prayer that is Psalm 22. The intimacy of the Hebrew Bible has given way to divine absence. This is not a call, direct and personal, to some power up above, but a cry against existence, against being, and against fate.

It is three in the Friday afternoon. The black, shadowy expanse echoes with the vast silence. An unnatural darkness sits dankly over Skull Place. As if out of nowhere, as if out of some *daimonic*, obscure beyond, his voice trumpets. Until now, through the many hours since his Jewish trial the preceding night, he has spoken but two words. Only two words! Uttered eight-or-so hours earlier, responding directly to Pilate during his Roman trial, 'You say' echoes now as a mere melancholy sigh that he was even then past caring.

Such is his withdrawal, his 'I have had enough.'[17] The outer man has been in hiding since Gethsemane. His final words to the divinity above might just as well have been, 'You say.'

Dark for three hours since noon, the sun is in eclipse, as if to blinker its eyes from the human *abomination of desolation* being enacted below. Out of this dark, out of this ghostly quiet, 'Why have you forsaken me?' sounds across Skull Place and out over the Jerusalem hills. The centurion watches.

Again there is silence. Then the *mega phonē* bursts forth as a second great scream, with no words this time. It is an apocalyptic war cry, an explosion of repressed fury, a wail of cosmic pain as he lets go after all his pent-up silence and suffering. So he howls against existence — the supreme lament — and the cry is dispirited to the point of pneumaphobia. So he smashes the cup. The precious oil dribbles away. There is no god. There is only him; and, at this ultimate moment, he despairs. As he breathes out, the pneuma escapes his lips.

He is dead.

The centurion watches.

On the instant, a great calm settles over the wasteland. All is breathless and silent, but only for a moment. The exhaled pneuma returns, transformed into a raging gale, as it was when it drove him into the wilderness for forty days. It eddies over the three crosses on Skull Place, wheeling, rising, before descending back into the Jerusalem gloom. Or is it now light, just as God in the Old Testament's beginning had created light out of the primeval darkness?

Violence is upon the city. The pneuma whirlwind whips through the Temple, ripping the sacred veil apart — rent from top to bottom, exposing the holy of holies in all its profanity. The old order lies in shreds. Pilate, sitting a few hundred metres away to the west, in the Palace of Herod the Great, is inexplicably and unwittingly struck with awe.

The heavens had parted in the beginning, as if giving birth to pneuma, which descended over his head. Now it is the same Greek verb for parting — *schizō* — that describes the schism in the holy veil, as pneuma the god strikes again. The wind bloweth where it wills, and thou hearest its sound, but canst not tell whence it cometh, and whither it goeth. It drives sometimes violently, the Power.

Back on Skull Place, the centurion speaks out. Mark is precise as to the timing. It is in direct response to seeing the pneuma leave, the last breath. As the Jewish woman in Bethany watched, so has this Roman officer. Both have witnessed *I am*. Truly, the centurion exclaims, this man was the *mystery*.

CHAPTER SIX

THE EMPTY TOMB

When the Sabbath was over, Mary Magdalene, Mary the mother of James, and Salomé bought spices so they might anoint him. Very early, at sunrise on the Sunday, they came to the tomb. They said to one another, 'Who will roll the stone away from the entrance for us?' But when they looked they saw that the stone had been rolled away — it was huge.

When they entered the tomb they saw a young man sitting on the right, clothed in a white robe. They were alarmed.

He said to them, 'Don't be alarmed. The Nazarene you seek, the one who was crucified, he has arisen. He is not here. See, the place where they put him! But go and tell his followers, and Peter, that he is going ahead of you into Galilee. There you will see him, just as he said.'

They fled from the tomb, quivering in ecstatic fear. They said nothing to no one, for they were terrified.

S o it ends. Mark opened with genesis, at the foundation of all that is. He closes the Story with three terrified women fleeing an empty tomb. The finale is deeply encrypted. Dawn on Sunday. It is women who have been watching, first from afar then up close—on the Friday evening, the two Marys had approached Skull Place to observe where he was laid.[1] After the burial comes a pause, a one-day interregnum, while the Jewish holy Sabbath, Saturday, passes. It is as if everything has gone into hibernation for thirty-six hours—nature, physical human, psychic human, and metaphysical.

Is Easter Sunday a new dawn? The Temple has indeed been destroyed, as he predicted—on the Friday, with the veil ripped from top to bottom. Raging pneuma wreaked its will. The women are about to find out that on this, the third day, he has left. Has the Temple been rebuilt without hands, as he foretold, in three days?

The women have brought spices, but there is no body to anoint. And we already know, from the beautiful thing done by the woman in Bethany, that these three have got it wrong. They are still acting from within the framework of the old religion, but this is not about resurrection from the dead. They have not watched in the way that sees. To quote his *mystery* monologue, it is rather a case of 'seeing they may see, and not perceive'. It was the living *I am* that bore the mystery. The implication is that now is too late. He has gone. Hence their withering, ecstatic fear—quivering in terror, as if, in a demonised, trembling state, choked up, they cannot speak. Male seed on stony ground is now female seed inside a gloomy rock cavern. Without courage, like the twelve minus one, dumb with fear, they flee.[2]

Some power has moved the boulder. We are told it was huge. The place is bare where they put him, inside this tomb carved into the rock face. He has risen, like the paralysed man, and Jairus' daughter, like men like trees walking. The Greek verb for arisen, *egeirō*, also means to awaken, and to keep watch. Here is the counterpoint to the night stumble in the garden. Furthermore, if we are to believe the young man inside the tomb, the Master has gone ahead, into Galilee. Only we, the readers, know this, for the women say nothing to anyone. The eleven are left in the dark. Peter, who is singled out by name, remains where he was when the cock crowed, weeping.

Inside the tomb there sits a young man clothed in a white robe. He is calm, and tries to settle the women. His soft imperative, 'Don't be alarmed' echoes the earlier command, 'Don't fear!' And, as before, it has the opposite effect. What is he doing here? Who is he, and what is his role? He is not an angel, as some have speculated; if he were, Mark would have said so.

The narrative has returned to its underlying dualism of insiders and outsiders. The women try to watch, seeking to know the mystery — but they are outsiders. They depart the scene confounded and terrified. The young man has the last important word in the Story. He sits on the right, the position of authority — his words are endowed with exclusive legitimacy. To whom does he address himself? It can only be that he speaks from inside the tomb directly out — to the reader, to you and me.

By now we are familiar with Mark's habit of leaving key characters without a name. This one is, simply, the young man robed in white. By using this tactic of anonymity, Mark creates character types rather than individuals — *archetypes*. The 'young man' is a composite — in the way that types may be compounds.

The implication may be that it is the very same 'young man' (Greek word: *neaniskos*), likewise dressed plainly, in linen, who fled naked in Gethsemane.[3] Once the sub-textual logic is traced through, the two appearances complement each other. The first appearance created the anticipation of something to come. Together they make Mark's puzzle clearer, but far from complete.

Legion was the one instructed to go forth and tell the

story — at the same time as others, who were made whole, were ordered to speak to nobody. Might the 'young man' also be Legion?

Legion was the first candidate for insider status. In his deranged state, before his metamorphosis, he dwelt among the graves, screaming out day and night in the mountains and among the tombs. He was at home among the tombs. It was as if he knew instinctively where he should reappear, that here was where he belonged — his kairos place. There is also the implication in the description of him sitting calmly and clothed that, in his earlier demented state, Legion was naked. The young man fleeing naked in Gethsemane was demented with fear.

The associations multiply. This time it is the young man sitting calmly and clothed inside the tomb. He speaks the final word from *inside*. He now completes the Story. When the people saw Legion of sound mind, calm and robed, they were afraid. So are the three women in the presence of the young man.

Legion has prodigious strength — he has torn shackles apart, and pulled chains to bits. He was untameable. Mark had taken care with these details. Was it in preparation for a later development in the story? Now, at the end, he plants the beguiling query of how the boulder over the entrance to the tomb was rolled aside. It has generally been assumed that the power of the one buried inside had moved the huge rock. Matthew will alternatively give the role to an 'angel of the Lord coming down from heaven', but this is not in keeping with Mark, for whom the power is among the living. Moreover, Legion had a deranged attraction to rocks, a skewed affinity — he would hack at himself with stones. Now, in his Shining state, he can move mountains; indeed, he is the one who brings this lingering saying of the Master, uttered in the shadow of the withered fig, to fulfilment.

Dunamis — meaning 'force', 'energy', or 'power', the root of the modern English word 'dynamic'—is an important category. In the Master's final *I am* proclamation he refers to himself sitting on the right hand of the force. When the haemorrhaging woman touched his robe, he felt the energy go out of him. The implication is that the power is now with Legion.

The linen burial cloth (Greek: *sindona*) used by Joseph of Arimathea is not to be found in the tomb. The young man, in his first manifestation in Gethsemane, had worn a linen cloth (the same Greek word, *sindona*); now he wears a white robe (*stolē leukē*). This Story is about the living, not the resurrected dead. Is it not almost incidental that the Master has awakened—or simply gone?[4]

Legion's name, which is not a name, here gains deeper resonance. He is indeed *many*. The probable source, the Roman legion, contained several thousand soldiers. Legion in his beginning loses his many *daimones*, two thousand of them—the 'legion' of his original identities—which find their home, care of the drowned pigs, in the Sea of Galilee. The teacher, who as a phantasm had once danced across that sea, with them beneath his feet, now returns in his own differently transformed state to the region, in a sort of parallel homecoming. We know that the going ahead to Galilee was not to meet his followers, for they are in the dark. The final impression of the twelve, minus one, is that they are left forever, like the three women, in a state of fearful flight—and endless sleep.

Legion's first appearance was running down to meet the Master by the Sea of Galilee, addressing him with a great voice. The *mega phōnē* is another affinity—to the profoundly disturbed *daimōn* on Skull Place that screamed out from the cross.

Legion reborn has a range of personae—the legion of his new identities. Apart from himself, he is the young man (*neaniskos* means 'new one') who makes two appearances.

The young man's flight in the garden was a denial, a baptism of fear. The teacher, we know, found himself forced from early on in his mission to teach by inducing fear. The initiation, true to form, has stripped the neophyte naked. He has left his old self behind, like a lizard shedding a skin. This was the time of his derangement, his pneuma berserk and homeless, like Legion's *daimones*. However, the young man is not Peter—he returns. He returns wearing a white robe. White is the colour of transfiguration, from out of the crucible of fire on the mountain, 'white like snow, such as no earthly bleaching could achieve'.

Mark closes his story with the bewildering and arresting image of the empty tomb. There is no God inside. There is no hint of his presence in the near vicinity, or beyond. This is an anti-Christian ending—anathema to those churches founded in his name that would pivot belief on the pre-eminence of Lord God the Father up above, and human salvation via some kind of Resurrection from the dead. What is inside the tomb is the living Legion—Shining in his *I am*—reassuring the reader that all is well.

Legion has a fourth identity. If he tells the story, he is Mark. Nietzsche provides a helpful key:

> Whatever is profound loves masks ... Every profound spirit needs a mask. Even more, around every profound spirit a mask grows continually, thanks to the constantly false, namely shallow, interpretation of every word, every step, every sign of life that he gives.[5]

Mark is profound, and subtle. In his shadowy, incognito presence, he follows his own prescription of leaving strategic characters nameless. He plants several clues. The early phase of the story, its foundation, turns on the sower parable.[6] The climax to its telling is the delivery of the mystery monologue—this is where the teacher introduces the contrast between insiders and outsiders. Mark specifies that others were present apart from the twelve. In Gethsemane, we are told that the young man has been following along; by implication, he has witnessed from the fringe most of the happenings since the triumphal entry into Jerusalem. He has been present at the Last Supper—how else would he know where to go, and when? Inside the tomb, sitting on the right, clothed in a white robe, and of sound mind, two powerful things are signalled. This is the authoritative teaching, and the young man has grown up to be in full command of who he is.[7]

We are left with an intricately coded outline of the identity of the storyteller. Mark worked with what he had seen first hand. He judged 'on the mark' the governing sense and feel of what he had experienced. He complemented that with fragments and episodes reported to him personally by others. He quite likely wrote down his narrative later, after a long period of digesting what he knew—three or so decades on, if we are to accept the modern scholarly consensus.[8] What he did, he did with a virtuosity never to be matched.

Watch! Watch! Watch!—the apocalypse cantata—has its climax in the tomb, with the one who has eyes to see. Mark is the true follower: he was the last to flee, and he recovered from his flagellating humiliation. Then he returned. The three women who followed the teacher in Galilee and observed the crucifixion from afar were also present, but they did not know the secret of how to watch.

For Mark, 'pray' means to get inside the story in order to tell it. 'Worship' has no other meaning. Mark's story is the vehicle for the mystery that insiders know. Yet it is an *enigma*—one long and complete *dark saying*. It warns to beware of clarity, and of detachment.

Mark's own enigmatic, elliptical presence even stretches to the storyteller personifying himself as universal *being*. This might appear arrogant; but it is, rather, a form of devotion, and a method of teaching. Through initiation, through his own Passion, Mark has become the representative, archetypal *insider*.

Apart from the Master, Mark's insiders are anonymous composites. The reader is being taught that he or she, too, is an anonymous composite. The *I* is Legion—many. It is, in essence, nameless. The individual person is compounded with the archetypes into whose beings he or she merges, including pneuma forms. The Story provides the archetypes that matter, starting from insiders and outsiders. They all orbit around the Master.

The image of the calm young man in white, who presides inside the dark tomb at sunrise, is like that of a spectre. Little wonder that the women quiver in ecstatic fear. Two nights before in Gethsemane, from flitting about sprite-like on the fringes of the drama, clad merely in a white linen shift, he had, once caught, sped off naked through the shadowy gloom of the olive grove. That scene is wild and strange, uncanny. The Story, with shades of a midsummer night's dream, or midwinter nightmare, insinuates a ghostly, magical dimension to *I am*.

As Legion, the young man must have come, late on the Saturday night, early on the Sunday morning, to use his prodigious strength to roll the huge boulder aside. We are not told what followed—who or what came out of the opened tomb. We do know what went in—or, at least, who it is dwelling within at early light. At the *daimonic* hour of in-between, neither night nor day, the mercurial man in white, sitting in wait, is as much a pneuma-conjured apparition.

We can now make sense of the opening: 'In the beginning was the Story.' These words carried the implication, 'as I shall tell it'. The cycle is closed with the narrator appearing in person inside the tomb to address the reader directly. His Story is told.[9] In effect, he confirms that from the outset it has been the reader to whom the teaching monologue has been directed, not the twelve. Hence the young man's closing intimacy of manner. It is the archetypal insider welcoming the initiate.[10] 'Don't be alarmed,' he encourages. He sits calmly, robed in white, gesturing to the future: 'he has gone ahead.'

The storyteller is as significant as the Master, although his role is clearly different. The physical location is arbitrary. Jerusalem is merely the profane city. Galilee just happens to be the serenely beautiful spot in which the Master chose to base himself. There is no sacred site. There is no place on earth for pilgrims to visit, where they can sense what it might have been like, then. There is no altar to kneel at; no holy grail to unearth. Mark, the man, with his *dark saying*, is all.

That dark saying is about Transfiguration — what the sower sows. For one and all, the common everyday self is a mad boy desperate for metamorphosis. Here is that self's deepest desire, driving all its clumsy groping for truth. The boy's furious *daimōn* tries to fling him into water and fire, the mediums for initiation — seeking annihilation, seeking rebirth. His *I* remains demented until he looks up and sees the Shining.

At this point, the ordinary self conjoins with the mythic form, turning into much more than it ever was. As it becomes the Shining, ordinary time is obliterated. Chronos melts into kairos, the puny life of the individual now flung out of its normal being into something grand and timeless.[11]

Shadowing the journey, as directing spectral forms, are the withered fig, the night suffering unto death in the garden, and the great cry from the cross. The life of that ordinary individual, here and now, has become possessed by the Story — and thus itself, enshrouded in pneuma, reappears like a phantasm. Having descended from the mountain, it now crosses the disturbed, dark water in the middle of the night, on the long way to the unholy city.

The Story is *his* existential journey. Yet once it becomes a Shining for the reader, perfume fills the room.

PART TWO

They Who Follow

CHAPTER SEVEN

PETER THE OUTSIDER AND THE CHURCHES

Peter is Icarus. Impulsive with enthusiasm, he flies closer to the sun than his frame can support; the wax attaching his wings to his body melts, and he plunges to his death. He is the man whose chosen path puts him under a pressure he cannot bear. He is the one welcomed inside who finds he does not belong. So he skulks around at night on the fringe of the drama. He becomes Peter the fearful. He founds a church.

Peter is not present at the crucifixion. The Story left him in the courtyard of the high priest at Friday pre-dawn, with the cock crowing and him weeping. He has just confessed before the outraged young woman that he does not know. He has just denied his recent past. He has just cursed his Master.[1] Where does he go that Friday morning?

He had started off as a simple fisherman on the Sea of Galilee, married and with a mother-in-law — this much, Mark tells us. His origins were ordinary. Then he responded to the call from this man, as did his brother, Andrew. He thought he had found the Messiah anticipated by his people, the Saviour, the anointed one who would deliver him from who he was. He left his home and livelihood — everything from his life before — to follow. Present at all the miracles, hearing all the teaching, the first among the favoured three, he continued to see him as the Saviour, in spite of an angry rebuke.

137

Nicknamed the rock, the reader is left to assume that he will be the foundation stone for something: Matthew will make this explicit, with Peter the rock on which the church is to be built. Alternatively read, the path he chooses is hard, like rock, giving up ordinary securities—he will plausibly contrast himself with a rich man who refuses to give up all his possessions to follow. And Peter needs courage, even if it is foolish courage, a certain hardness of spirit and purpose, to act as decisively as he does. The *Petros* we meet in the story tries hard.

Will he learn? Will he come to understand? One of the many cruelties in the Peter story is that it is very early on when the answer is provided. The first and most decisive parable, of the sower, bewilders him. Nor can he make any sense of the accompanying teaching about the *mystery*—and about insiders and outsiders. The parable reveals the nature of the rock. It is *petrōdes*—stony ground. With him, the word has fallen on rocks. He had responded with enthusiasm and joy to the call to become a fisher of men; but, as he has no roots, once the sun rises, he withers. He exemplifies what it is to have no roots. Weak characters wilt under pressure. Boldness is not enough, if there is no anchor.

Following the sower parable, the test continues. He is taken into a boat to cross over—over his own Sea of Galilee. At night, when a storm strikes, his boat begins to sink. Frightened for his life, he wakes the Master. From this moment he begins to cling. Fear has possessed him; he has lost confidence. By the time of the second boat crossing at night, he is so unnerved that a slight headwind makes him panic. As if spooked in his deepest being, he then visualises his teacher dancing across the waters as a phantasm. His courage leaves him, and simultaneously his signature word-seed is planted—*I am not* or, as he puts it at the Last Supper, *Not I*.

At the outset of the next phase, after the two-stage healing of the blind man, he will rebuke the teacher when told of his imminent death. Peter does not want to be left alone.

The withering sun that rises in the story over stony ground is the Shining. Peter, who is taken up on the high mountain as witness, cannot look on the Shining. It terrifies him. He stumbles, collapsing to the ground. On stony ground, men stumble. Peter sinks into pneumaphobia, and in his holy terror of pneuma he misreads the divinity hovering over the mountain as a black cloud. Pneumaphobia profanes—that is, it makes dirty and low what was high. From this moment, midway through the Story, out of his mind, terrorised by confusion, he begins to enact his own future—building temples. Whenever anxiety will stoke his obsession, his reflex will be to do something; and his nervous fidget, his 'doing something', will be church building. To cure a withered hand, a man must be drawn outside the church; to nurse withered being, a man must retreat inside a church. Mark is uncompromising.

The climactic withering is that of the fig. In the morning, on the road up to the city of Jerusalem, Peter is stopped in his tracks by what he sees. In shock, he reads the black stump as himself. He is right, and not right. His own black stump is lethal *no-truth*, the cancelled initiation as he reverts back to Simon. For the one he follows, in contrast, it is part of a larger whole, the whole that matters, one with which Peter has failed to gain contact. The episode of the fig for the Master himself involves the stripping back to ultimate nothing, before the next stage, which is the beautiful oiling of his head. For Peter, there will be no next stage.

Peter is dazed in the aftermath of the fig. All he can do is stand by during two days of teaching, looking on with blurred vision. These two days are of no consequence for him—they are the passing of chronos time. Then his story recommences, with him attending the dinner in Bethany. He fails to register the example of the woman, and he is blind to the response of Judas—the beginning of the betrayer's evil. On the next evening, Thursday, he stumbles into the Last Supper.

This gathering is different from earlier meetings. The Master has organised it, sending followers ahead to enact a preordained script. The portentousness must weigh on all present. The Master presides at the supper. He opens not with a welcome; he makes no reference to the Passover, the Jewish festival they have gathered to celebrate; nor is there a convivial breaking of bread. He makes no attempt to bind the twelve into a cohesive band. This is no sacred brotherhood of inspired disciples. The Master starts with the announcement that one of them will betray him—to which they all, every one, including Peter, respond, 'Not I.'

Peter, leading the others in a chorus of non-entity, has identified himself. Now the bread is broken and wine shared. In their confessed state of *not-being* they are told that the bread is his body; the wine, his blood. He invites them to new life, with the heavy hint that this invitation is no more than a mockery, given their unteachable natures. They sing a hymn, then depart.

On the way down to Gethsemane, in the dark, the Master tells them that they will stumble. Peter protests that he will die for the Master rather than disown him. Whenever on edge, he is the person who tends to act rashly, or to jabber incoherently. This preposterous boast, as he fights down an intuitive knowledge of his imminent cowardice, saps his remaining energy. Now exhausted, he falls asleep at the first opportunity, in the garden, and three times. The final words, his last judgment, are then spoken to him: 'Endless sleep!'

During the arrest in the garden he flees, but returns, and

follows along behind the mob at a distance. He slinks into the High Priest's courtyard, still seeking the light. He finds a profane fire, at which he warms himself, before the young woman exposes him to existential ridicule.

The cock wakes him up. It crows out his shame. He weeps tears of humiliation, for on this very same evening he had sworn such an oath that a man makes once in a lifetime — at most, an oath to the death. He has become the breathing negation of the ultimate command, 'Courage! *I am.* Don't fear.'

Is he still afraid? He had hesitantly overcome his earliest fear, and tagged along into the courtyard, before flaring up in denial. Recognised as a follower, he has new reason to fear. And he has also been confronted by the magnitude of his own weakness, which he can no longer deny. Shame now spikes his endemic fearfulness.

Where does he go on crucifixion Friday? It is unlikely that he would retreat down the mount, to Bethany — humiliating memories would haunt him there. Maybe he sleeps in some Jerusalem alley. Perhaps he has gone home, back to Galilee.

Peter the Fearful is in the clutches of his fate — *either-or.* Either profane fear will rule, driving him back to his former life in the hope of regaining his old self. This is fear for his mortal life. The result, at best, to draw on one of Mark's categories, will be a benign form of endless sleep. Or he will fear the great fear — the higher fear — of pneuma.

The power of pneuma rules the crucifixion. Its force presides over Skull Place, radiating out across Jerusalem and its hills. When the human head finds itself bowing in shame, eyes lowered, the face flushes at judgement from on high, and the nape of the neck bristles as if branded from above. Shame is sacred dread, the holy emotion, carried in the breath of pneuma. The same gale that tears the Temple veil from top to bottom burns Peter's face crimson. The angel of death is accompanied by the angel of sacred shame. Peter has gone missing out of pneumaphobia.[2]

Mark leaves Peter weeping in the courtyard. It is not the rock standing as witness, on Skull Place, but the centurion. The centurion hears the great scream.

John's Life of Jesus will take up Peter's story and continue it on after the crucifixion. Some of the content is new; some, a midrash of Mark. Mark had hinted that more might be to come, by having the young man inside the empty tomb charging the three women to tell Peter that the one they seek will reappear in Galilee. The women don't pass on the message.

According to John's account, Mary Magdalene, early on the Sunday morning, fetches Peter and John to the empty tomb. She has seen that the stone had been rolled away from the entrance. They follow, running. John gets to the tomb first, stoops down, and looks inside. He sees the linen burial cloths lying there. Peter arrives, and he enters the tomb. He observes the linen cloths, and a smaller cloth that had wrapped the head, rolled up by itself. John then follows Peter inside. He sees and believes.

Both followers then go home. Magdalene remains, and she now discovers two angels in white inside the tomb. She has known where and when, in contrast with Peter and John. Peter, in particular, is depicted as being out of tune with these kairos moments.

Peter then returns to fishing on the Sea of Galilee. One night he takes six of the twelve out in a small boat with him, but by morning their nets remain empty. The Master stands on the shore, with the seven failing to recognise him. He tells them to cast on the right side of the boat, and they find there are so many fish that they cannot draw in the nets:

> The beloved follower said to Peter, 'It is the Master!' Peter
> responded by putting on his outer garment and plunging
> into the water. When the others reached land they saw a
> fire of coals there, with fish on it, and bread.
>
> The Master requested them to bring some of the fish.
> Simon Peter dragged the net to land, full of a hundred and
> fifty-three large fish, the net unbroken. They were then
> told to come and eat breakfast. None dared question,
> 'Who are you?' They knew it was the Master.
>
> When they had eaten, the Master asked Peter, 'Simon,
> son of Jonah, do you love [*agapē*] me more than these?' He
> replied, 'Yes, master, you know that I love [*philia*] you.' At
> which he was told, 'Feed my lambs.'
>
> He asked him a second time, 'Simon, son of Jonah, do
> you love [*agapē*] me?' He replied, 'Yes, Master, You know
> that I love [*philia*] you.' At which he was told, 'Tend my
> sheep.'
>
> He asked him a third time, 'Simon, son of Jonah, do
> you love [*philia*] me?' Peter was upset that he had been
> questioned three times, 'Do you love me?' He replied,
> 'Master, you know all things. You know that I love you.'
> To which he was told, 'Feed my sheep.'
>
> 'Surely, I say to you, when you were younger, you
> dressed yourself, and walked wherever you chose. When
> you are old, you will stretch out your hands, and another
> will dress you, and carry you where you do not want to
> go. Follow me!'

This is a tender scene, in mood quite unlike Mark. Peter is
again eager, plunging into the water to rush to his Master. The

context is the return to ordinary fishing, a quiet night on the Sea of Galilee labouring with some of those who were once chosen. The labour is barren. Then the seven are fed like lambs.

The reader learns four distinct things about Peter in these scenes. First, he is distinguished from Mary Magdalene, the insider whose story I shall explore in the next chapter. Second, he is distinguished from John — the beloved follower and author of this Life of Jesus — whose story will be taken up in Chapter 11. The Master had commanded, during his apocalyptic teaching, that the followers should tell his story. Here it is underlined that Peter will not have this role, the task being carried out by Mark and John.

Third, Peter is demoted from agapē to philia. He is questioned three times — in his previous encounter he had uttered denials three times. He is addressed by his profane *I am not* name — Simon, son of Jonah. Each time he is thus addressed.

The first question is about sacred love — agapē — and it is comparative. Does he love the Master more than these? Peter answers that, as the Master knows, he loves him. However, Peter uses the Greek word for friendly or brotherly love — philia.

The question is repeated, indicating that the answer is not satisfactory. And the question is simplified down to: 'Do you love me?' Again, the Master uses agapē; again, Peter replies with philia.

This seals the matter. In the third questioning the Master himself switches to philia. He accepts that philia is the most that Peter can give. Peter is upset that it has been necessary to query him three times. The subtext is that what really upsets him is that his attachment is confirmed as one of philia. He does not know the meaning of agapē — it will only be in the Magdalene story, as completed in John's narrative, that its deeper sense will be signalled.

The scene is designed to humiliate Peter, once again. He is questioned three times in front of the other six, and with a portentous theatricality, 'Simon, son of Jonah …' Three denials; three rhetorical questions. Then there is the ambiguity of the comparative, 'Do you love me more than these?' Are 'these' the hundred and fifty-three large fish, or the other men? And, if the latter, does the question refer to Peter loving six followers more than he loves the Master, or to them loving the Master more than Peter does? Or does John deliberately leave the reference cryptically opaque, to allow all three interpretations?

Peter has returned to his upbringing, of fishing, and to his fishing community. His strongest love is for fish and for other men — out of fear of the consequences of higher love. So the teacher uses the humiliating image of large fish to brand into Peter the will to carry through his calling, whatever it may require of him. An end is foretold which will test his courage.

The distinguishing of Peter from Magdalene and John, and his demotion to friendship, are extensions of Mark. This is the same outsider portrayed in the first Gospel. There is yet a fourth distinct thing the reader learns about Peter in John's account, and it is new. Peter is given a role: Simon the fisherman, son of Jonah, is commanded to 'Follow!'

The Master repeats the first call, also given by the Sea of Galilee, early in Mark's account, *Follow me, and I shall make you fishers of men.* Now the intention is more specific, and different.

There has been a change of direction on the question of churches. It is as if John has digested Mark's uncompromising picture of churches as the domain of the withered, where no truth breathes. He gestures towards a middle ground, on which there is a legitimate and necessary role for sacred community.

John includes in his reporting of the Master's teaching in

Jerusalem, during the last week, the obscure command, '*If anyone serves me, let him follow.*'[3] *Follow* is equated with giving service. During the Last Supper, the Master begins to wash the feet of the twelve. Peter protests, '*You shall never wash my feet.*' He receives the reply, '*If I do not wash you, you have no part with me.*'[4] The lesson is about selfless service.

Peter is capable of brotherly love, or friendship, and mateship. After he has received the shadowy warning that when he is old another will control his destiny, he is told to follow. At this, Peter, turning around, notices the beloved follower, and queries, '*But Master, this one, what about him?*' He receives the curt reply, '*If I want him to abide until I come, what's that to you? You follow me.*'[5]

These are the final words, in John's account, that the teacher speaks to Peter. They are sharp, irritable, and dictatorial: 'You, follow me!' They are preceded by, 'Feed my lambs!' and 'Tend my sheep!'

We know from Mark that Peter, following his given nature, will build churches. Here, those churches are provided with a function—that of worthy service. Peter is to diffuse his brotherly love into care for the sheep. The sheep are the human multitudes in need of a shepherd, those unable to find a way on their own. Peter is to be the Good Shepherd. His churches are to guide and protect the weak.

There is one remaining problem in the Peter story—that of why the last encounter takes the form of a post-resurrection meeting. After the crucifixion, Peter has returned to his former life, as a fisherman on the Sea of Galilee. He has responded simply to the question that confronts him—how are you to live now? He retreats into what he knows, attempting to become what he was.

The final encounter tears him out of this oblivion of his own choosing. The first time that he had seen his Master as a phantasm, on the Sea of Galilee, he had been struck dumb with terror. This time, he himself plunges into the sea, rushing fully robed into following—again, the seed on stony ground, springing up, hearing the word with joy. The instruction he receives once he reaches land, and has been fed, reminds him of his own limitations. He is thrown off balance by the teacher, with the thrice-charged question grilling him about who he is. A scene that had opened in a gracious, even lyrical, mood now tenses. Made fearful, and shamed in front of the others, Peter appears foolish.[6] He is then told, in effect, and brusquely, 'You are on your own. Go and be true to yourself. Build churches and tend my sheep!'

John ends his Life of Jesus with the order to Peter, 'You, follow me!' At the beginning of his Story, the first two events he recounts, after some followers have been called, are a marriage—at Cana in Galilee—and the cleansing of the Temple in Jerusalem.

Why does he shift the Temple-destruction scene from the climactic last week, where Mark had placed it, to the start of his story—during an earlier Passover festival? It seems significant that he opens with a wedding and a church.

The Marriage at Cana is perplexing as a beginning story. Jesus is there at the feast, at a small town near Nazareth, with his mother and some followers. There is no mention of who is being married—the story is clearly not about them. Wine runs out, so the mother of Jesus says to him, 'They have no wine.' He turns on her, 'Woman, what have I to do with you? My hour has not yet come.' The mother is unshaken. She tells servants to do whatever he says. He then obliges her by turning water—six large stone pots of it—into wine.

That is the end of the episode, apart from the master of ceremonies noting that the best wine has come last. The facts are few and spare. Indeed, the story reads as frustratingly incomplete, perhaps a fragment, as if the main part has been lost or remains to be told.

He is cold, impersonally hostile to his own mother. His detachment has to do with his hour not yet having come. But he obeys her anyway, providing wine for the marriage gathering.

The Peter story and its finale have been prefigured—set up in anticipation. His barbed snapping at Peter about the beloved follower, 'If I want him to abide until I come, what's that to you?' echoes the early rebuke to his mother, 'Woman, what have I to do with you?' The Master's first decisive act in his mission is to destroy the old church. He abolishes the religious past. What matters is kairos: his hour. In the kairos context, in the context of *mythos* order, nothing else is of consequence, including his own family—his mother is merely some intrusive woman. Peter's clumsy questioning is similarly intrusive, by someone who has no sense of kairos.

At the Cana wedding feast, in the next breath, he refocuses his attention back onto the common human plane, and concedes to a lower order of truth. He respects his mother's wish, although we can hear him groaning inwardly as he turns water into wine. He will, half-heartedly, provide some good cheer—wine—for such human communities as families. As he has followed his mother, Peter shall follow him.

The story notes in passing that the water had been for Jewish ceremonial purification. So there is the further signal that the human communities he endorses will be bound, not by pious ritual, but by merry conviviality, even drunken release. In the next 'impression point' episode told by John, after the cleansing of the Temple, the Master meets a Samaritan woman alone at a well. He is not the least concerned that she has had five husbands and currently lives with another man out of wedlock. If the churches founded in his name are to be ethical institutions, they are not to be petty in their morality.

Another possible reading of the Cana marriage is that his mother knows his future, and indicates to him that it is time to start his mission. Raphael, in his painting of the *Sistine Madonna*, has the Pope urging a reluctant Mary out into the world, so she can deliver her infant son to his tragic destiny. In the Marriage at Cana, it is the son who is reluctant.

Mary reappears in John's Life of Jesus at the end. She is present at the crucifixion, where Jesus from the cross nominates the beloved follower as her new son, and she as his mother. John may have given her a role at the beginning of his narrative as some form of acknowledgement of her status. She becomes *his* new family.

Either or both of these readings complement the main message that kairos is what counts. His mother's part is to remind him that, nevertheless, he has some responsibility to families and churches. And he does contribute something of his own presence, as symbolised in the wine.

The quiet confidence the mother exhibits at Cana gives a warmth and dignity to the sense of family—his family. These are qualities that are entirely lacking in Mark's story. In return, her son acknowledges her at the end, from the cross, recreating a family. In what is to come, neither Mary nor John will be alone.

'You, follow me!' provides Peter with a role. However, from the outset, at Cana, the Master has made it clear that building churches is marginal, if necessary. It has little to do with the *mystery*.

We are left with two inflections to the Peter story. Mark's narrative is one of tragic failure, compelling the reader to swing confusedly between disdain for Peter's obtuseness and pity for his folly. This Peter is lost, and devastated—out of his mind and senses with fear. He exits without redemption, disappearing into a night fog of pneumaphobia. John's Peter, in contrast, is a prosaic figure, almost a buffoon at the end, but one with a role: founding churches.

The symmetry of opening and closing with marriages and churches is, perhaps, to signal their resonance beyond the boundaries of the story proper. The Story is *mythos*—tightly contained and complete within itself. Human life, however, must go on in chronos time, and for that there shall be churches and families—helped along their way by some infusion from the *mythos* core. This, the Master reluctantly authorises.

CHAPTER EIGHT

MAGDALENE THE INSIDER

Magdalene is the most pervasive *mythos* archetype from the Jesus Story—apart from Jesus himself. She is hamartia as story. From the time of the Renaissance, she has been irrepressible in the culture of the West. She is there, wherever the dual movement occurs, of a life that has lost its way—due to a damaged or out-of-balance character, or a savage fate—followed by transformation. She is there, in fiction and in real life, in stories of redeemed hamartia. She is the mad boy seeing the Shining. She is Legion sitting calmly clothed. The recent world best-selling book phenomenon, *The Da Vinci Code*, is but one projection of the archetype.[1]

Her story reaches its climax in the garden outside the empty tomb at dawn on Sunday. From her will flower the rebirth. Here is the new Genesis, replacing Adam and Eve in the first garden, that of Paradise. The first Genesis saw the birth of knowledge—of the moral law—and of transgression, and the banishment of humanity from primal innocence. This time it is the birth of *being*.

Magdalene's story, as a story, is lush with fertility. It demonstrates the potential of midrash. Mark provides the fragments, enough to generate the archetype—like a body cell that can reveal to the modern scientist the genetic coding for the whole person. It is as if the archetype was created in the beginning, before any humans started telling the story. It lodged in some cosmic womb of consciousness. Once seeded, it then manifested itself, growing prodigiously. It seems to press from within itself for completion, for fulfilment.[2] To be specific, this particular seed generated three virtuoso pieces of narrative—one in Luke's Life of Jesus, two in John's.

So who was she? What do the texts have to say? And here I shall stick to the foundation texts—although this story might just as well be communicated through many of its thousands of later midrashes.

The seed of the story is sown by Mark, with the woman in Bethany. Then his cryptic suggestiveness progressively gives way, in the later retellings, to a fuller exposition.

Mark tells us that the Master was reclining for a meal at the house of Simon the Leper, in Bethany. An unnamed woman arrives with an alabaster flask of very expensive perfume, worth three hundred denarii. She breaks the flask and pours the perfume over his head. Some of those present are indignant at the waste, and castigate her—the proceeds from sale of the perfume could have been given to the poor. The Master intervenes, telling them to let her be, for she has done a beautiful thing. They will always have the poor. She has done everything, anointing his body for burial before the time. Henceforth, wherever his story is told, what this woman did will also be known.

The story is linked by sequence to Judas' betrayal, with the inference being that he is the rancorous one protesting at the waste of precious perfume. Chronologically, it is placed late in the final week, after the withering of the fig and the apocalyptic teaching, and immediately preceding the Last Supper.

L uke is the first to elaborate:[3]

Now the Master was invited by a certain Pharisee to dine with him. On entering the house, he reclined, in order to eat. And behold, a woman from the city who had lost her way [*hamartia*], found out that he was dining at the house of the Pharisee. She came, bringing an alabaster flask of perfume.

Standing close behind him she wept, and began to wash his feet with her tears, and wipe them with her hair, kissing them, then anointing them with the perfume. Seeing this, the Pharisee host thought to himself, 'This man, if he were a prophet, would know who — what sort of woman — touches him. She is a sinner [*hamartia*].'

The Master answered him, 'Simon, I have something to say to you.' He replied, 'Teacher, speak.'

'There was a certain creditor who had two debtors. One owed five hundred denarii, and the other fifty. When neither had any means of repaying him, he freely forgave both. Tell me, which of them will love him more?'

Simon answered, 'I suppose, the one he forgave more.' The reply came, 'You have judged rightly.'

He then turned to the woman and said to Simon, 'Do you see this woman? I entered your house. You gave me no water for my feet; but she has washed them with her tears and wiped them with her hair. You gave me no kiss; but this woman has not ceased kissing my feet since I came in. You did not anoint my head with oil; but this woman has anointed my feet with precious perfume. Therefore, I say to you, her waywardness, which is great, has been forgiven — because she loved much. The one to whom little is forgiven, loves little.'

To her, he said, 'You have found your way.' Those reclining to eat with him at the table began to think to themselves, 'Who is this who even forgives sins?'

He finished, to the woman, 'Your trust has saved you. Go in peace.'[4]

The woman is not named, but in the next episode recounted by Luke the teacher tells the parable of the sower. The parable is preceded by the reader being informed that among those present are a group of women who had been healed of unsound pneuma and sickness. The first is Mary, called Magdalene—out of whom seven *daimonia* had come.[5]

Luke has extracted the anointing story from the last week in Jerusalem; he does not report any happenings in Bethany. He has placed it early in the ministry, and shifted the site to Galilee; the host is now Simon the Pharisee, not Simon the Leper.

Luke makes it virtually explicit that the woman is a prostitute. As in Mark, we have both an extravagant sum of money—here registered obliquely as five hundred denarii, more than a year's wages—and the perfume. Luke accentuates the lush sensuality with the flooding tears, and the use of her hair (which must be long) for wiping the Master's feet. She kisses his feet throughout the scene, in another evocation of gushing emotion.

Moreover, Simon calls her a sinner, a woman with a known reputation in the town—with the particular slant that it is polluting to be touched by her. She is nameless, 'that woman'. The scene highlights *touch* and *transgression*. Prostitution is the living that most blatantly transgresses the law governing inappropriate human contact: Thou Shalt Not Touch!

The location may be Magdala, a resort town on the Sea of Galilee, not far from Capernaum, where Romans and wealthy Jews owned villas—as the Mary, who appears in the adjacent scene, is from Magdala. Simon is a prosperous Jew who has invited Jesus to dine with him, presumably so that friends, and perhaps leading citizens, can meet the esteemed teacher and miracle worker. Jesus must also have had a reputation as a prophet, which Simon now questions: a prophet would recognise a whore, and have nothing to do with her.

Simon is a Pharisee — a Jew strict in his obedience of the moral law and in his observance of religious ritual. He is outraged that a woman should enter his house, and that she should do so uninvited, intruding on an all-male gathering. And she is a scarlet woman. Jesus, sensing the host's indignation, toys with him. He sets him a riddle that is child's-play to solve. It concerns debts — the inference being that money is important to Simon, who is proud of his wealth, and of his social soundness and reputation.

Simon hesitates in reply: 'I suppose, the one he forgave more.' He dimly suspects that the obvious solution misses the point, but Jesus then tells him he has answered correctly. This is a temporary reprieve, for it leads directly into a highly charged public rebuke of Simon in front of his guests. The Master is teaching by shaming: setting Simon up with a simple trap, then relentlessly exposing his lack of hospitality and his letter-of-the-law meanness of spirit.

Hamartia is at issue. The story hinges on its double meaning. From the traditional perspective, represented by Simon and those who dine with him, the woman is a sinner. She is guilty of serious moral turpitude, to the point that her presence endangers all in her vicinity with pollution. The ethical way of thinking produces a moral calculus for weighing up the gravity of different types of transgression. This, Jesus plays upon, with his contrast of two debtors: one owing five hundred denarii; the other, fifty. Moral thinking computes, and it equates units of sin with units of repentance, punishment, and forgiveness. Such is its nature.

Jesus has to humiliate Simon publicly in order to snap him out of this one-dimensional way of seeing and judging. Or perhaps the point is being directed at the reader, with the assumption that the Simons of the world will not change their ways. Their righteous indignation is like a snug blanket that keeps them warm at night.

Jesus uses the wayward woman to teach hamartia — as missing the mark, because of imbalance, or loss of direction. He tells Simon he has judged correctly, which he has from within the ethical frame of reference. The teaching then switches abruptly into the *being* perspective. In the story, Jesus literally turns around, towards the woman. From that altered line of sight, he berates Simon for his petty character and his blindness. Simon is tight whereas the woman is generous, giving prodigiously and without cease.

Most importantly, she is not forgiven according to the ethical logic of the riddle — which would have Jesus manipulating compassion for tactical reasons, calculating that she is such a great sinner that, if he releases her, she will be so heavily in his debt she will love him accordingly. She is forgiven quite simply, as the text puts it, 'because she loved much'. Jesus has, in the instant, observed her character. She has seen the truth about herself and, wretched with shame and remorse, cast herself at his feet. What is there left to forgive? Her finding her way has come from within, through finding recognition of him.

'The one to whom little is forgiven, loves little.' With these closing words in the address to Simon, it seems that Jesus has switched back into the ethical reasoning of the riddle. Except, the Greek verb translated as 'forgive' might alternatively be rendered as 'set free'. A pneuma equation would stipulate that one who is unfree in herself will not be able to love much. John's

Jesus puts it, 'The truth will set you free.'

Jesus' signal to the reader is to switch focus, as he does, from Simon to the woman, from moral consciousness to *being*. So what can we make of *her* story? Like Mark's woman in Bethany, she appears from nowhere. Nor does he know her. She must have seen him some place or other — on the street, amongst the crowds listening to his teaching, or observing miracle healings. The particulars do not matter: neither Mark nor Luke bother to record them. She is struck by the Shining.

Luke merges Mark's episode of the metamorphosis of the mad boy.[6] In the kairos instant in which she sees him, her eyes are opened. It is as if her *daimōn* is magnetised by him. However, what she sees is not his radiance, but her own degradation. He serves as mirror. Her illumination is about herself and her past life. She has been sleepwalking through her days; but now, in the moment that changes everything, she wakes up. What appears before her clearly and distinctly revealed in the mirror is the great fear — in her case, the Horror. It is herself.

She sinks to the ground. The reader is left to imagine her thoughts: all those sordid evenings she has spent, the shame of her nakedness, the ugly, sweaty men leering lecherously, groping all over her. Her body filthy, contaminated, utterly profaned — she just wants it to burn away. Then there are the wages of sin, the guilt money. There is a lot of money, her rationalisation to herself, and even pride: the gorgeous silks, the comfortable house, maybe even support for poor and sickly parents. She was a high-class courtesan.

Or maybe she was just testing the limits, out of loathing for the self-righteous Simons of the world and their hypocritical social order. So she played the temptress, finding out how much they desired her; the more frenzied their lust, the more virulent their ostracism of her. No one understood her. This was a girlish rebellion, heedless of the consequences — one that got out of control. Suddenly, the consequences are upon her.[7]

Her wretchedness pours out in tears that will not stop. She caresses his feet, and then loosens her hair. As it cascades down, she takes it in her hands, to wipe his feet. Head down, her face lost in her abundant hair — now damp and grimy — her tears gushing over the dusty feet, she kisses them, and continues to kiss and caress them, oblivious of the exchange going on between the Master and Simon. Her actions would be excessive in someone who did not 'love much'.[8]

There has been some method to her visit. She has brought with her an alabaster flask of perfume. The precious fragrance was, before, a signal of her vanity. Now, in its transmuted, sublime state, it is everything she fears she is not. It is her very spirit that she gives away, lavishing it on his feet to the last drop. Soiled feet, coated in the dirt of life, are the profanity which has been her, transmuted here by holy oil. As the fragrance fills the room — uplifting, enchanting — it is the sacred pneuma drifting out above the reclining diners.

In Mark's account, the woman breaks the flask. Alabaster is translucent, snow-white gypsum.[9] To snap the neck off this fine and delicate object is a violation. There is something shockingly assertive and decisive in her act — she has not completely crumpled. With the crack echoing through the stunned silence, a trace of fragrance reaches the nostrils of Simon and his guests.

She is dying as she sinks down, her life draining away with her sobs. Withering towards nothing, she is so wretched that she wishes only not to be. If only she could declare, 'I am not!' Then, out of the depths of the great fear, she begins to sense the Master's acceptance, hearing the muffled drift of his words as he frames her acts in his irritable targeting of Simon. His presence now steadies her, arresting the downward motion. She feels obscurely that she has been recognised, for the first time in her life — and freed from the loneliness that precipitated her into selling herself. Maybe she is not Simon the Pharisee's sinner, but the wayward woman who loves much.

Agapē is inborn. It is of her nature. All that needs to be known about her is, simply, that she is the woman who loves much. Her character is given. What she undergoes is not metamorphosis. According to his hamartia teaching, it is rather a finding of the mark. Her second life, which begins at Simon's house, develops out of the first. It will be directed by the power of touch — her transgressive medium — henceforth having found its right order, guided by agapē.

The role of the Master has been twofold. His presence shocked her into waking, placing the mirror before her. In Simon's house, he is the midwife, delivering her into her second life.

His is the power of *being*. In his presence, she is reduced to a non-entity, finding that her old self was a bundle of flailing-around notoriety — hitting out, pretending, dressing up, driven to scandalise, gaining a kind of anti-identity as a scarlet untouchable. From an angry, hollow mannequin, she is reborn into being. She has herself become a presence.

John chooses a different point of entry in order to tell the same story:

> Now a certain man was sick, named Lazarus, of Bethany. His sisters, Mary and Martha, sent word to the Master.
>
> When the Master heard, he said, 'This sickness is not unto death, but for the glory of God, that the son of God may be glorified thereby.'

Now he loved Martha, and her sister, and Lazarus. When he heard of the sickness he remained two days where he was. Then he said to his followers, 'Let us go again into Judea.'

They said, 'Master, the Jews of late sought to stone you. And you want to go there again?' He answered, 'Are there not twelve hours in the day? If any man walk in the day, he does not stumble, because he sees the light of this world. But if he walks in the night, he stumbles, because there is no light in him. Our friend Lazarus sleeps, and I go so as to wake him.'

The followers responded, 'Master, if he sleeps, he shall be well.' To which the teacher replied aggressively, 'Lazarus died. And I am glad for your sakes that I was not there, so that you may trust. Nevertheless, let us go to him.'

Thomas, called Didymus, said to the others, 'Let us go, that we may die with him.'

When the Master arrived, he found that Lazarus had already been four days in the grave. As Bethany was only three kilometres from Jerusalem, many Jews came to comfort Martha and Mary. As soon as Martha heard the Master was coming she went to meet him. Mary still sat in the house.

Martha addressed him, 'Master, if you had been here, my brother would not have died. But I know that even now, whatever you ask God, will be given you.'

The Master told her, 'Your brother will rise again.' She retorted, 'I know he will rise again in the resurrection on the last day.' He continued, '**I am**—the rising up, and the life. Whoever trusts in me, even though he die, will live. And whoever lives, and trusts in me, shall never ever die.

Do you believe this?'

She replied, 'Yes, Master, I believe you are the Christ, the son of God, the one coming into the world.' Then she left and told her sister, Mary, in secret, that the Master had come and was asking for her.

When Mary heard, she rose quickly and went to him.

Now the Master had not yet entered the village. The Jews who were in the house comforting Mary, when they saw her rise quickly and go out, followed her, saying, 'She is going to the tomb so she can weep there.'

Mary came to where the teacher was. She saw him, and fell at his feet, complaining, 'Master, if you were here, my brother would not have died.' When he saw her weeping, and the Jews weeping who had accompanied her, he snorted angrily, and shuddered.

'Where have you put him?' They responded, 'Master, come and see.' He wept.

So the Jews observed, 'Look, how he loved him!' Some of them said, 'Could not he who opened the eyes of the blind, have kept this man from dying?'

The Master, snorting angrily again within himself, came to the tomb. It was a cave, with a stone against it. He commanded, 'Remove the stone!'

Martha warned, 'Master, he already stinks, for it is the fourth day.' He responded, 'Did I not say to you that if you trust, you will see the glory of God?'

They took away the stone. The teacher lifted his eyes upward, and said, 'Father, I thank you because you heard me. I know you always hear me, but I said this so that the crowd standing around may believe that you sent me.'

Then he shouted with a great voice, 'Lazarus, come forth!'

The dead man came out, bound hand and foot with
grave cloths, his face also wrapped. The Master instructed,
'Loose him, and let him go.'

The Raising of Lazarus is told in John 11: 1–44. John, opens
his next chapter (12) with Mary anointing Jesus.[10] In narrative
terms, it follows on directly from the Raising of Lazarus — and
both occur in Bethany. It takes place on a later occasion — that of
the crucifixion Passover. John then proceeds directly from Mary's
anointing to the triumphal entry into Jerusalem. So the second
Bethany scene occurs on the eve of the final week:

> Six days before the Passover, the Master came to Bethany.
> There they made him dinner, with Martha serving.
> Lazarus was one of the company who reclined to eat with
> him. Mary took twelve ounces of very expensive, pure
> nard perfume and anointed the feet of the Master, and
> wiped his feet with her hair. The house was filled with the
> fragrance.
>
> One of the followers, Judas Iscariot, Simon's son, who
> would betray him, protested, 'Why was this perfume not
> sold for three hundred denarii, and given to the poor?'
> This he said not out of care for the poor, but because he
> was a thief, and had the money-bag. He used to filch from
> it.
>
> The Master replied, 'Let her be! She has kept it for the
> day of my burial. You have the poor with you always. Me,
> you do not have.'

The anointing scene has been shifted back to Bethany, but at
the opening of the final week, not on the Wednesday. The
woman is now identified as Mary of Bethany, sister of Martha

and Lazarus—a family that Jesus knows and loves. The scene is recast as the conclusion to a bigger story: the Raising of Lazarus. John expands the archetype so as to make it the central episode in the Master's teaching.

The opening of the story makes clear that its purpose is not to show Jesus acting out of compassion for the sick Lazarus. He deliberately delays setting out for two days—till Lazarus is dead. When his followers take literally the comment, 'our friend Lazarus sleeps', he snaps back angrily that he died, adding, 'I am glad for your sakes that I was not there, so that you may trust.' In other words, Jesus is engineering this story into a device for teaching his obtuse followers. That is its point.

The story then presents a hierarchy of human types, rising from rank outsiders up to the one insider—Mary. This unfolds in sequence, with the exception of 'the Jews', who are at the bottom of the scale but only appear in the middle of the narrative. The Jews are characterised as getting everything wrong. The cue for this is their assumption that when Mary leaves quickly she is going to the tomb, so she can weep there. They then misread Jesus' weeping as grief over the death of Lazarus.

The twelve followers occupy the second-from-bottom rank of the outsider hierarchy. They are blind to the fact that 'sleeping' means death—John may be alluding to Mark's use of 'endless sleep'. They are identified with those who stumble at night because they have no light within. They are fearful of returning to Jerusalem. Then they suddenly switch into false bravado, represented by Thomas', 'Let us go, that we may die with him.' Thomas is singled out here because John will later record the episode of Doubting Thomas—it is he who will refuse to believe that the Master has reappeared after his death. While Jesus sets up the death of Lazarus as a means of teaching his followers, none of them learn from it.

Martha represents the next-higher rank in the outsider hierarchy. She credits that whatever the Master asks is given by God. But she interprets the reassurance that her brother will rise in terms of stock Jewish doctrine: 'I know he will rise again in the resurrection on the last day.' Moreover, her understanding is like that of Peter in Mark's narrative, that Jesus is the Messiah anticipated in Jewish circles.

As one who does no more than parrot doctrine, she remains blank to his pivotal teaching, 'I am — the rising up, and the life.' The surprise is that he addresses it to her — a paradox planted in the middle of the story. Her lack of trust is highlighted later in her fear that the corpse of Lazarus will be stinking after four days. Martha is ruled by profane fears, and secured by empty pieties.[11]

There is no great difference between the Jews, the followers, and Martha — all outsiders.

We meet Mary devastated by the death of her brother. She weeps profusely. When she hears that the Master has arrived, she rushes to him, falls at his feet, then blames him for Lazarus' death. Why, she asks, was he so slow in coming?

He responds to her weeping, and that of the Jews who follow on her heels, with an angry snort. He shows no sympathy for human grief — and at the untimely death of a brother. Indeed, his reaction is perplexingly extreme: so angry is he with Mary that he shudders.

The standard Christian interpretation of the Raising of Lazarus has been that its purpose is to show Jesus' compassion. This is a Good Shepherd story, of agapē — hence the well-known words, 'Jesus wept.' The churches have acted like the Jews in the story, misunderstanding his agitation as sympathetic grief. It is out of heartfelt pity, they have taught, that he then brings Lazarus back to life.

This reading is doctrine-driven, depending on blindness to the detail of the events and, above all, to Jesus' own words. That he responds to Mary's tears with an angry snort and a shudder, rather than with empathy, is especially problematic.

The Greek is *enebrimēsato tō pneumati kai etaraxen eauton*. This brief passage has troubled translators ever since. William Tyndale rendered it as 'He groaned in the spirit, and was troubled in himself.' The King James translators copied Tyndale, but deleted 'in himself'. The New Revised Standard Version softens the words to 'He was greatly disturbed in spirit and deeply moved.' The New English Bible goes further: 'He sighed heavily and was deeply moved.' The Catholic, New Jerusalem Bible continues the trend of changing the meaning: 'Jesus was greatly distressed, and with a profound sigh he said, "Where have you put him?"' And the Good News Bible even replaces the phrase with its own invention: 'His heart was touched, and he was deeply moved.'

The principal verb means 'to snort with rage', and carries the inflection of 'indignation'. We can see how the various translators have struggled to twist the words to fit the model of Jesus that they want. And the fabrication is worst in recent translations. Raymond E. Brown notes that the basic meaning of the verb implies 'an articulate expression of anger', including 'a display of indignation'; but then, he assumes, 'it does not seem that Jesus would have been angry at the afflicted'.[12]

The second verb, *etaraxen*, means 'troubled', 'stirred up', 'alarmed', 'disquieted'. It is followed by the word *eauton*, meaning 'himself'. Tyndale plausibly rendered the whole as 'troubled in himself'. The first three words—*enebrimēsato tō pneumati*—mean literally 'snorted angrily in pneuma'. The concept of pneuma is electrically charged in John's story, more so even than in Mark's. The evocation here is of violent disturbance and indignation in the domain of pneuma. In my translation of the whole line—'he snorted angrily, and shuddered'—I have strengthened the latter verb to catch some of the feeling of an inward wrenching of spirit.[13]

Why this furious disquiet? The Master's next move is to question where Lazarus has been put. He follows with two further strong emotional reactions (first weeping, then snorting angrily again within himself) as he approaches the tomb. In general, John's Jesus is magisterial, and in calm control of his destiny—highlighting just how extraordinary is the pitch of emotion in this scene.

He orders that the stone covering the cave entrance be removed, then lifts his eyes and says, 'Father, I thank you because you heard me.' He makes it clear that the only reason he speaks these words is so that those present will hear, and believe in his divine parentage.

He shouts with a great voice—*mega phōnē*—into the cave, 'Lazarus, come forth!' The corpse appears, swathed from foot to head in white burial-cloths, presumably hobbling blindly forth out of the dark cavern.

This is a ludicrous scene, comic in its detailing, with an apparition bound like an Egyptian mummy reeling out to join the living. The teacher's great shout is in part in anger at what he has to do—anger that it will be misunderstood as love for Lazarus. Above all, he rages against Mary, signalling that *I am doing this for you, although I am so fed up. You don't deserve it.*

What is going on? The next scene provides the key to the entire story. We know from Mark that the woman in Bethany who anoints the Master is the true insider—'She has done everything.' Mary of Bethany is given that role here. She has realised it is the living Master who counts, so she brings out the perfume she had stored for his death. The anointing of the corpse was a Jewish custom, to do with the resurrection on the last day—referred to by Martha. In other words, Mary had occupied the same spiritual universe as her sister. By the time of the second scene in Bethany, she has changed. It is the same switch as in Luke's story, from Simon to the wayward woman. Whereas Martha falsely calls the Master the anointed one—Christ—her sister enacts the true anointing. This is another hamartia teaching.

Further, Mary's weeping over her dead brother was all-too-human grief. It was of the same metaphysical order as Peter clinging to Jesus: not wanting him to die for the selfish reason that he, Peter, would be left alone. The Master had expected more from Mary. She has proved no better than the foolish Jews who get everything wrong.[14] This scene makes sense of why Mark's Jesus had disparaged 'knowing in your heart'.

The text makes it clear that the Master is putting on a show in front of Lazarus' tomb. He addresses his father up above ostentatiously, so the assembled throng will associate him with divinity. But Mary has been singled out as the target of his teaching. The angry snort was directed at her—he has no interest in 'the Jews', their role in the story being merely to represent the wrong way.

Mary must, by now, be deeply mortified: by his fury, his shuddering in indignation before her, and his weeping at the naive enthusiasm of the crowd—which includes her. Now he commands that the stone be removed, and with a huge shout he bellows at the four-day-dead Lazarus. Her brother appears.

Mary is shocked out of the ordinary plane of consciousness. In a vulnerable state, bleak and low with mourning, she finds that the man she admires above all others—her Master—is beside himself with uncontrolled rage at her. She does not know what she has done wrong. In rushing out to meet him, she had fallen at his feet—this was her stumble. Then he conjures her brother back to life, at the same time as satirising that life — the one she has lamented profusely with her tears — as a clumsy wobbling out of the dark, tightly swaddled from head to foot, in an absurd parody of the human condition.

The Lazarus mode of living is a chronos banality. Four days dead; four days of rising stink. If it were to be extended for another four years of mortal life, or forty, it would not matter. The early reference by the Master that 'Lazarus sleeps' was accurate; although the sequel, 'I go so as to wake him', turns out to be false. The rebirth of Lazarus is one without metamorphosis; that is why Jesus is indifferent as to whether he lives or dies. That Lazarus is described in the second Bethany scene, in passing, as reclining at dinner, signals the absurdity of his existence. The stench of his mortality is contrasted with the lush perfume that is about to fill the room.

The shaming of hamartia Mary has been tactical — to frighten her awake, into kairos. But for her the Shining has been replaced by black fury. She had lacked the self-awareness of the wayward woman at the house of Simon the Pharisee. So the Master, with a deep, anguished shudder, finds himself forced to seize hold of her and subject her to an extravagantly theatrical trauma. She undergoes, at his hands, a sort of psychic battering. His angry snort succeeds in breathing life into her.

The inward shudder that follows the angry, indignant snort may also reflect the Master's own disquiet. Mark orchestrated the Passion, from agony in the Garden to death scream, on a presiding mood of relentless forsakenness. John, who excludes both the garden agony and the scream, may have midrashed the forsakenness down to a single concentrated moment. The Master opened the Lazarus story by indicating that its purpose was to teach the twelve. In fact, he ends up trying to teach one person — Mary. But she is blind to what he is. If she fails to recognise him, there is no one left. He might as well enter Lazarus' tomb himself.

This story penetrates into almost all the ways that humans relate to each other. It reveals the principles that govern weakness under pressure, and the insecurities of character that shut off understanding, and drive a clinging to moral or metaphysical pieties — whether in the form of sayings, clichés, doctrine, or dogma. It exposes attempts to purge discontent through strong emotion — here, weeping and wailing. It shows why friends become false, and how life paths may diverge abruptly.

The Lazarus story is masterful in its tightness of reference and in its cryptic impression points. Planted obscurely in the middle of this episode, the Master utters the vital teaching, and he does so in an offhand manner to one whom he knows has no inkling of its meaning — Martha. One of the subtextual pointers, addressed to the reader, is not to look in the obvious places, nor to imagine that what you take to be a climax is a climax. Lazarus, and his re-entry into life, is incidental — of no interest in itself.

It is Martha's sister, at the moment of the *I am* teaching, sitting at home weeping, and not hearing the explicit words, who is the one. By the time of his next visit to Bethany, she has understood: *I am* the living presence, here and now; in me is the *mystery*. So she takes out the precious perfume, and she kneels. This time, her descent is not a stumble, for she has found the right orientation to him, person to person. She anoints his feet. She wipes them with her hair — such has been her humiliation during his last visit. Unlike the wayward woman in Luke, however, she does not shed tears; they came earlier, as a prelude to her shame. The fragrance of released pneuma fills the room.

The bitterness of Judas, son of Simon, spits forth. This is the cue to the reader that Mary has herself become *I am*. The force of envy signals, in negation, the force of her presence, and her poise. And John has continued the Simon motif, as a signal of continuity of theme. Mark's Simon the Leper dissolved by midrash into Luke's Simon the Pharisee; and they now, in turn, reappear as John's Simon, the father of Judas.[15]

The Raising of Lazarus is a story about *being*. John has taken the central teaching in Mark — 'Courage! *I am*. Don't fear.' — and given it flesh. He has provided it with a dense narrative of the teacher confronting outsiders and insiders. It focuses on a three-stage way. First, the potential insider stumbles. Second, this provokes the Master into the most engaged moment of teaching recounted in any of the four Lives. His didactic method sets the standard for any instruction into deep truths. It hinges on indignant fury, an inward pneuma shudder, and bellowing a decomposing corpse swaddled in linen cloths into motion. Third, she awakens, and comes into the right relationship to his *being*.

This Jesus spurns compassion. Yet it is his love for Mary that governs the action. Deeply disappointed by her, he strikes with high-voltage emotion. He who is otherwise masterfully in control of himself lets his rage go, deliberately targeting her. It creates a tense, anguished distance between them. The story ends, however, with a sharp swing to the opposite emotional pole — in intimacy, as she caresses his feet and celebrates their higher union with the release of precious fragrance.

Mary Magdalene is the subject of the third section of virtuoso narrative. Here is John's midrash of the Empty Tomb:

> The first day of the week, Mary Magdalene came early, when it was still dark, to the tomb. She saw that the stone over the entrance had been removed.

She ran to Simon Peter and the other follower, the one the teacher loved, and said, 'They have taken away the Master from the tomb, and we don't know where they have laid him.'

Peter and the other follower ran to the tomb. The other outran Peter, and, arriving at the tomb, stooped down and saw the linen wrappings lying inside. He did not enter. When Peter arrived he went into the tomb, and saw the linen cloths, and the one that had been around his head, rolled up by itself.

The other follower also now entered. He saw, and trusted.

They did not know the script—that he would rise again. They left and returned home.

Mary stood outside the tomb, weeping. As she wept, she stooped down and looked inside. She saw two angels in white sitting, one at the head, the other at the feet, where the body of the Master had laid. They addressed her, 'Woman, why do you weep?' She replied, 'Because they have taken away my Master, and I don't know where they have laid him.'

She turned around and saw the Master standing there, but didn't know that it was him.

He said to her, 'Woman, why do you weep? Whom do you seek?' She, supposing him to be the gardener, said, 'Sir, if you have carried him hence, tell me where you have laid him, and I shall take him away.'

He said to her, 'Mary.' She turned, and replied, 'Teacher.'

He said, 'Touch me not! For I am not yet risen to my father. Go to my brothers and tell them that I ascend to my father, and your father; to my God, and your God.'

> Mary Magdalene went to the followers and told them
> that she had seen the Master, and that he had spoken these
> things to her.

Let us consider this episode before attempting to link Mary of Magdala with Mary of Bethany. The Mary Magdalene here is in character with the wayward woman at the house of Simon the Pharisee. There is no awkwardness in identifying the two as one and the same person.

It is Sunday dawn, before light. The tomb is empty. From there, John's story diverges from Mark's. This time, Magdalene is solitary—not accompanied by two other women bringing spices. Two days earlier, she had stood beside the cross as a close witness to the crucifixion. She had watched on, with Jesus' mother and her sister, and the beloved follower.

Her insider status is underlined. She alone knows where to be, and when. It is still dark when she finds the stone rolled away, and peers inside the tomb. Trembling with fear, she runs to fetch Peter and the beloved follower—who John will later identify as himself. The two men follow, look, and leave—with the text indicating some awakening, in that John now trusts. She remains, and discovers that, for her, the tomb is no longer empty. Two angels in white sit at the head and feet of where the body lay. She is weeping profusely, as she did at the house of Simon the Pharisee. The presence of angels signals to her that she has entered into sacred order: she should jettison her normal human perceptions and feelings.

She turns around and sees a stranger, whom she takes to be the gardener. Hearing his voice, she still does not recognise him. His questions suggest that he is playing her gently along. It is only when he addresses her intimately, by name ('Mary') that she turns, and knows him. *Turning* is a metaphor for transformation.

Her word of recognition — 'Teacher' — is bountiful with love. It precipitates his immediate check, 'Touch me not!' These three words of interdiction will become the pivot — often in the Latin translation, *Noli me tangere* — for Renaissance paintings of Magdalene. They form the impression node for her story.

Why the gardener? The surface reason is the profane one that the tomb is set in a garden. If she sees a man at dawn whom she does not recognise, it is likely that he works here.

The Master is the stranger. At critical moments he is perceived as such — when he appeared as a phantasm dancing across the Sea of Galilee. Such manifestations occur in the dark. Or is it, by now, first light outside the tomb?

Her *turn* transforms fearing the great fear into intimacy. He then redirects the intimacy into *being*. These are the key formulae.

The gardener sows the seed, then fertilises and waters it. The soil in which the events outside the tomb are planted is rich. There was the original, Paradise garden — God's creation — from which the first humans, Adam and Eve, were banished. They now return, metamorphosed into Magdalene. This is the climax to the second creation.

Touch is her medium. Her earthy sensuality overwhelmed Simon the Pharisee's dinner — weeping, caressing, kissing, wiping with opulent hair, and anointing with precious perfume. Her presence filled the room. As a prostitute, the moral law that she broke was Thou Shalt Not Touch, and in its most transgressive mode, the desecration of the body.

The first stage in finding her way hinged on renouncing the flesh, and finding a new use for hands, lips, and hair — in a desolation of sorrow revering the feet of the Master. He now checks that mode. There is a second stage to her metamorphosis. *Touch me not!*

The three Greek words that William Tyndale translated so memorably into English as 'Touch me not!' — *mē mou haptou* — could be alternatively rendered as 'Don't cling to me' or 'Cease from clinging to me.' The New Revised Standard Edition Bible phrases them, 'Do not hold on to me.'

The Master characterised her as the one who loved much. Her essential being is agapē. At Sunday pre-dawn she cannot stay away, visiting the tomb in eager anticipation of first light. It is her initial motion after the trauma of crucifixion. Arriving in an unhinged state, she finds the entrance stone rolled back; he has been stolen away. In a panic of loss she disintegrates for the second time — again into a deluge of weeping. She needs him; she cannot live without him. She feels desolate like the black, cavernous, empty tomb — all is gone.

But selfless, sacred love does not cling. For the moment, she has lost her true being. Hamartia has struck. She has missed her way again. She cannot recognise him. Then he arrests her motion.

He is no longer who he was. That he returns in another guise — as a gardener — indicates the mutability of the concentrated supernatural presence. This, she cannot touch. She must learn another way to be with him.

'Gardener' has a further resonance. Is there ambiguity to the teacher's own feelings for Magdalene? A number of the Old Masters suggest as much, portraying Jesus as having to restrain himself in the presence of this beautiful woman, opulent with sensuality.[16] The interdict on *touch* becomes as much a caution to himself. At the house of Simon, her lavish caressing and kissing of his feet evoked a fuller bond, as does his impersonation of the man who furrows soil and plants seed. The low rays of first light illuminate the empty garden in which she finds herself. The words between them are intimate. She is desperate to touch him.

The Greek verb translated as 'touch' — *haptō* — had also been used by both Plato and Aristotle to mean sexual union. In the thoroughly Hellenised world in which John was writing, the work of the great Greek philosophers was well known. At the least, the garden scene is further tinged with red.

In the parallel story of the Raising of Lazarus, we found no complete explanation for why Jesus was deeply moved in Bethany — with indignant anger, and inward shuddering. The extremity of emotion was out of character. It may have been, we might now suspect, the expression of his special attachment to Mary. He was distraught that the one he loved with more than *agapē* had relapsed so foolishly.

Mary of Bethany changes in his presence as a result of his deliberate, harsh confrontation. We are told the full story. By contrast, the change in Mary Magdalene is only implied: we are told no more than that she reported to the followers what she had seen.

As the touch of God gave life to Adam, in the Paradise garden, it is the inverse — the prohibition on touch — that breathes life into Magdalene. The interdict is the power, care of pneuma. 'Touch me not' sets up a field of catalytic force. *You don't need me anymore. You are enough in yourself. It is time for you to find your own way, on your own. The power of touch — your touch — will become your singular potency. As the cloths that bound my body lie in there, inside the tomb — as you have seen — unbind yourself from me.*[17]

The next significant episode in John's story is Doubting Thomas, when the Master appears to the followers. Thomas, who was not present, remains sceptical when told of this, boasting that he will only believe it if he can put his finger into the nail holes, and his hand into the wound in the side. Eight days later the Master reappears, and invites Thomas to feel the wounds. *Touch* is again key. Touch is necessary to overcome doubt; a ban on it is necessary to overcome attachment. And Jesus is making the point that the prohibition to Magdalene is not because of his current supernatural form, whatever that might be.

Donatello, in the early Italian Renaissance, imagined the transformation in Magdalene. He carved her in wood, life-size. It is years after the crucifixion, and Donatello has drawn on the medieval legend that she lived the rest of her life as a hermit. He depicts her as hideously desiccated. Her body is sinew and bone, covered in long, matted hair to down below the knees, and in a tattered, filthy dress. She is an old hag, with teeth missing, and gaunt, harrowed eyes — although she has fine, younger hands attempting to pray. Magdalene has disowned the flesh and all worldly pleasures. She has turned into the negation of her former self.

Today, on entering the room in which she stands, in the Museo dell'Opera del Duomo in Florence, one reels back at the sight. It is, at first, a reaction to the breath-taking horror of what she has become. Untempered suffering has withered her face — with intimations of the dead stump between Bethany and Jerusalem. It is as if, after the death of her Master, her single worldly attachment, she has relentlessly narrowed her focus. Hour after hour, day after day, year after year, she has given everything to conjuring up what he meant by *I am*. She has spent decades struggling to subject herself to the storm of pneuma that swept over Skull Place on crucifixion Friday. This Magdalene is subtly physical, densely tactile — though, to the viewer, she warns, *Touch me not!*

The unbearable weight which sunk her to the floor at Simon's has lifted. There is a paradoxical lightness to this three-dimensional figure, given the ghastly surface details. In her physical presence, walking around her, it feels like she has risen above the pains of the human condition. She has, somehow, floated free.

How can this be? The clue lies in her face. It is not distinctively that of a woman, nor of a man. Indeed, she bears a striking resemblance to Donatello himself—as reflected in a contemporary portrait by Uccello. The great sculptor, aged sixty-seven, in this late *tour de force* has imagined himself into her. And through her, into the Master on the cross.

By means of the prohibition, she has managed to detach herself. His three words transfixed her in the garden, froze her, before he disappeared forever. They were his parting gift—one given in a spirit of pure agapē. Now, she must summon up from within herself an *I* that suffices unto itself.

Or perhaps a dynamic ambivalence has been set up, between attachment and detachment. Attachment—her desire to touch him—leads straight to the interdict, and from there is diverted via an immense burden of concentrated inwardness. The goal is balance through detachment. But the detachment depends on a binding engagement with primal *being*. This is the same dynamic ambivalence that the Master himself sought to live with.[18]

The result is another transformation. Her face, with time, has changed. It is her dead Master's face—possessing her own. On the threshold of *I am*, she becomes him. Such is the intensity and duration of her *Passion*. She has turned into he whom she loves.

The Master taught all you need to know—*I am*. Magdalene is the earthly, hamartia manifestation. She marks the second Creation—the power of God replaced by the fertility of being. Inside Donatello's crucible, there is a fourfold smelting of forms, dissolving and reconstituting. First, there is the Master. The second figure is Magdalene, the supreme insider, freed through her kairos story. She finds the right orientation to the primary figure's being—fusing with him, becoming him. Yet, simultaneously, and for the first time, she becomes her own singular self.

The artist is the third figure to enter the crucible of being. Through an immense concentrated feat of inward wrestling, unto death, Donatello turns himself into Magdalene. Becoming her, he is able to retell, from the inside, her unique story. Through her, he subjects himself to the Passion.

Finally, Donatello creates a piece of sculpture which provides viewers with a medium through which they may experience the fourth conflation. The Story comes alive when ordinary individuals are taken out of day-to-day life and its chronos pace, and become suffused with the timeless theme. They themselves are now living instances of the larger truth. Magdalene — when she touches — provides a way to the righting of *being*.

To me, one slight, wooden figure presides over Florence — over all its magnificent works of art and architecture. Magdalene's phantasmal aura is a stillness echoing out from the Cathedral Museum, and through the city.

Pope Gregory the Great, in the sixth century, confirmed a growing tradition of conflating the three women into one — Luke's sinner, Mary of Bethany, and the Mary Magdalene of John's *touch-me-not* scene in the garden. Medieval and Renaissance art followed suit. Magdalene in the garden is typically depicted with a flask or jar of perfume placed nearby.

The link with Mary of Bethany is difficult. Modern attempts to identify the two as the same person have been countered by others, pointing out incompatibilities.[19]

From the *mythos* perspective, there is no problem. This is an archetype with two personae. I have traced the branches which grew from the seed planted by Mark in his sparsely detailed story of the unnamed woman in Bethany. Mark generates the allusion that she is a rich courtesan—by means of sensual imagery, and reference to the expense of the perfume. Luke midrashes her into the wayward woman at Simon's feast. John midrashes her back to Bethany, and precedes the anointing with the Raising of Lazarus. John develops Mark's *insider* theme, making explicit that this is Jesus' central teaching story—focussed on hamartia.

What remains to be explained is why John bifurcates the story between the two Marys. He gives Mary of Bethany attributes from both Mark and Luke: anointing, in Bethany; and the feet, which she wipes with her hair. The precious perfume is worth the identical three hundred denarii. The significant difference is that this Mary is slower to learn than Luke's Magdalene.

John is the only one of the four tellers of the Life to recount a *touch-me-not* episode. His Magdalene is lost, on the Sunday morning in the garden. She behaves like Mary of Bethany before her awakening. There are a range of parallels. As one wept for the loss of her brother, the other weeps for the loss of her teacher. Both cling to the dead. One was keeping oil for the anointing of the dead body; the other seeks that body. Further, the dynamic exchange between attachment and detachment echoes the Bethany transformation in Mary. The Master's abrupt prohibition—*Touch me not!*—repeats the angry snort and the inward shudder.

Little is to be gained from further attempts at linkage. There is merit to Ingrid Rosa Kitzberger's description of the parallels as 'interfigurality'—whereby the reader understands one character in terms of the other.[20]

The texts leave us with a composite story. The motif is firm and clear, while the detail remains blurred and, at times, confused. We may take this as a lesson on how to read stories. It is the shadow form gliding under the surface that matters. Here is a check on the need for clinical consistency. It warns against the anxious craving for pedantic order, which may afflict those lost in the vicinity of some great power of the deep.

Much is to be learned from this story about the process through which a dynamic archetype keeps evolving. Once the basic structure of the building has been given, it keeps getting partially demolished, then restored — walls moved, spaces redefined, furniture and décor replaced. Or, to mix metaphors, what the blueprint form generates is a signature tune.

There is a lesson, too, for the reader. Or for the observer, if the mode of telling is painting, sculpture, theatre, or film. It is to absorb the architecture of the story — by *mythos* osmosis — but then let it find its own spaces and costuming within. Those who witness may find their own lives revealed.

The Magdalene climax is *Touch me not!* The dramatic orchestration of the scene suggests the words are spoken softly, with intimate calm. Within, they harbour a stormy precedent, the shuddering in angry and indignant inner turmoil, which explodes into the bellowed command into the tomb. In turn, the great shout at the dead Lazarus echoes with the last great death cry from the cross.

But the first deliverance here is tragi-comic. There is no more flagrant image of futile being in the culture of the West than the linen-swathed Lazarus hobbling forth from death. It serves as a strategic backdrop to its direct opposite — an empty tomb housing discarded burial wrappings. As the teacher had angrily ordered the stone be removed from Lazarus' tomb, so, with his own tomb, that stone is mysteriously gone.

The twin-personaed Mary moves giddily through the midst of the drama. She answers her brother's mortal stench with costly perfume. She rises from wretched despair at her Master's feet. She is there in the dark before Sunday dawn, not stumbling, and because of the light within. She is welcomed by angels. She meets the gardener. She receives the most intimate words he will ever speak to another human being: *Touch me not!*

CHAPTER NINE

I AM NOT!: JUDAS

What is 'evil'? Herman Melville speculated in his novella *Billy Budd* on whether evil is a natural depravity, inborn in some individuals. A recurring view has been that, from time to time, some malevolent force or energy or spirit—demons, the Devil, Satan—may come from outside and possess people.[1] *Satan* was the Hebrew term for 'the adversary'. As a variant, Dr Jekyll has a dark self—a shadow, other self—that comes out at night, in the form of Mr Hyde.

Or is evil simply an excess of the dark impulses that many humans harbour within—the will to power, the sadistic pleasure in the failure or suffering of others, the exuberant triumph over the defeated or bettered, and a generally aggressive, competitive egomania? The evil person is one in whom there is an uncommonly high ratio of malevolent impulses to benevolent ones. Evil is, then, at one extreme in a continuum of malignity that includes, as the popular sayings recognise, a person being 'a nasty piece of work', and another being 'mean-spirited'. Also, to label a person as evil is graver than to judge an act evil.

'Psychopath' is a modern category for those who, without conscience and remorse, inflict violent and unprovoked harm on others. It delineates some individuals as sub-human. But then, under extreme conditions—of war, scarcity, or tyranny—many seemingly ordinary people carry out unspeakable acts that require a total absence of conscience.

The Jesus story supplies the commanding portrait of evil in the culture of the West. The black stigma of Judas came to mark betrayal, breach of trust, and diabolical malevolence. The Story, moreover, not only supplies a vivid personification of the dark force; it also develops a theory of evil.

We already know Judas. He first appears in Bethany, protesting at the waste of money on very expensive perfume — money that might have been given to the poor. John makes it explicit that his motive is not concern for the poor. By his account, Judas keeps the moneybag for the twelve. John forbiddingly smears his character — as low and mean, and as one who filches money from his companions. Judas is a thief.[2]

Mark had merely alluded to a link between Judas and greed. His emphasis is on the contrast with the woman in Bethany. Judas envies her. He is the only other one at the supper at the house of Simon the Leper who has understood the *I am* teaching. He feels the presence of pneuma. He also knows that he is condemned to fail in these terms. Not having the character, he is what it means to be damned. Furthermore, he sees that this is the moment in which the unnamed woman's life is transformed. Judas understands the beautiful thing she has done, and that she will be remembered. The aroma of precious perfume, as it fills the room, sparks a black fury of rancour in him. There will be no Shining. The abomination of desolation rages to destroy.

Mark's next reference to Judas is during the Last Supper, which he pivots on the warning that one of the twelve will betray the Master. Little more is added. He concludes his account of Judas with the kiss in the garden.

The kiss inflames in the reader the metaphysical shock of evil. Judas could have simply pointed Jesus out to the arresting party. Instead, he chooses to go up to the man who has changed his life, his teacher and master, the man whose extraordinary quality he understands, and to use the most intimate of gestures to single him out. Judas has blown up into something monstrous.

If evil is a state of being all on its own, inherently different from common bad acts and foul doings, however extreme, it is present here in its essential capacity to leave the victim, or the witness, gasping with sickened incomprehension. What motive can possibly explain it? Even to posit a reason is to diminish its magnitude. A type of supernatural blight or awesome contagion has descended over the stage, leaving humans in the vicinity feeling violated, corrupted, wanting to look down and away, to shrink. It is as if their condition has been exposed as irredeemably flawed. The Judas kiss is the paradigm in the West of the act of unspeakable horror—demonic in its aura and voltage.

John expands Mark's short Last Supper episode, making it one of his five vital, impression-point narratives.[3] Judas is central. He is a big man, the virtual equal of Jesus, standing opposite and against him:

> Supper had ended. The devil had already put it into the heart of Judas Iscariot, son of Simon, to betray him.
>
> The Master knew that the father had given everything into his hands, and that he came from God, and was going to God. He rose from supper and disrobed. He took a towel and girded himself. He poured water into a basin and began to wash the feet of his followers, and wipe them with the towel wrapped around him.
>
> He came to Simon Peter, who questioned, 'Master, you are washing my feet?' He replied, 'What I do now you do not know, but you will.'

Peter protested, 'No, you shall never ever wash my feet.' The Master responded, 'If I don't wash you, you have no part with me.'

Simon Peter continued, 'Master, not only my feet, but hands and head.'

'He who is pure needs only his feet washed. You are sound, but not all of you are.'

When he had washed their feet, he put on his robe and sat down again. He said, 'Do you know what I have done to you? You call me Teacher and Master, and it is well you say it, for **I am**. If I—the Master and Teacher—washed your feet, so you ought to wash the feet of one another. I gave the example, and as I did to you, so you should do. Most surely, I say to you, the servant is not greater than the master, nor the messenger than he who sent him. If you know these things, you are fortunate if you do them.'

'I don't speak about all of you. I know whom I have chosen. So that what is written may be fulfilled: "He who munches my bread, lifts his heel against me."⁴ I tell you now, before it happens, so you may trust that **I am**.'

'Most surely, I say to you, he who receives whom I send, receives me. He who receives me, receives the one who sent me.'

When the Master finished speaking he shuddered inwardly, and said, 'Most surely, I say to you that one of you will hand me in.'

The followers looked at one another, at a loss about whom he spoke. Now one of them, the one he loved, was reclining against his chest. Simon Peter nodded to him to inquire who it was. So, leaning closer, he asked, 'Master, who is it?'

'The one to whom I shall give the morsel of bread, after I have dipped it.'

He dipped the bread and gave it to Judas, son of Simon Iscariot. With the bread, the devil entered him. The Master then said to him, 'What you do, do quickly.'

No one reclining there knew why he said this. Some thought that, because Judas kept the moneybag, he had been asked, 'Buy what we need for the feast, or give something to the poor.'

That man, having received the bread, immediately went out. And it was night.

The episode starts with water. The Master strips himself of his worldly clothing, in order to teach Peter and the others about following. He hammers home the point that it is right for them to call him Teacher and Master—for the core is *I am*. If they know this, and serve others from within its legacy, they will do well.

He switches to betrayal. In stripping himself, girding himself in a towel, and taking water, it is as if he has prepared himself for sacrifice. He sets up his own betrayal. There is an early warning, 'You are not all sound.' The teaching about following is not for all of them. He chooses the one who will hand him in. He even chooses to be betrayed. And he provides the reason: the Master and the Teacher may only consummate his leadership and his teaching by delivering himself into the hands of his own scripted doom.

The causes of evil are over-determined. We are told, as a prelude to the Last Supper, that the devil has put betrayal into Judas' heart. So evil is a corruption of the heart. It has entered from outside. In the story proper, the sequence is amended: the devil enters Judas when he eats the bread. The bread itself is poisoned.

But the Master has given the bread. He himself dipped it in wine. Moreover, no one else, during this Last Supper, receives bread. 'I know whom I have chosen.'

Christian churches have generally understood the Last Supper as the building of sacred community—the band of blood brothers. The bread and wine, representing his body and his blood, are offered to the inner circle to bind them in Holy Communion. This understanding is annulled in John's narrative. One piece of bread alone is dipped in wine. It is infused with demonic spirit, and given to Judas. Moreover, only one of the remaining eleven reclining together has the slightest idea about what is going on—the Master makes a point of letting only him know.

The Last Supper is Betrayal. The Master turns this last gathering together with his followers into an unholy lesson on predestination and evil. In effect, he urges ten of them to stick to washing feet, while he proceeds with his destiny. The story mocks the idea of a sacred community.

In the background, like a shadowy curtain hanging behind the reclining diners, are Mark's categories of 'the cup' and 'my hour'.[5] It is the cup of destiny, not mentioned explicitly. In John's opening story, Jesus had turned water into wine. He had, however, been reluctant at Cana—while urged on by his mother—perhaps because he foresaw the second Cana. This time it is another feast, and he does not hesitate. If his mother had to forcefully gesture him over the threshold and into his worldly mission, by now he is in full motion. He uses the wine to charge the bread. Through Judas, it will turn to blood. Water into wine; wine into blood. His kairos hour is at hand.

Unlike Mark's Jesus, he commands. He hands the bread to the one who will hand him in. There is gravity brooding in the darkened upper room. He shudders, and he snaps curtly at Judas,

'What you do, do quickly.' It is so horrible, what is about to happen, that he wants it over with quickly. This twisted, venomous spirit—Judas, son of Simon—is repulsive to watch. Jesus wants his viscerally putrid presence out of the room. Yet Judas is little more than a chosen agent, fulfilling the victim's own script.

The Master has himself been chosen for the cup. The time is fated, and it is now. But within the cup, he initiates his own horror. The hour begins with the handing of the morsel to Judas. To borrow a phrase from Joseph Conrad, this is the nightmare of his choice.

Judas is closest of all to the Master. The intimacy of the kiss is fitting. Judas understands Jesus and his teaching. He is the one who sees the change in Mary of Bethany. *I am* registers on him. He is very near to the Shining himself. But this special affinity establishes an *either-or* condition. He is either an insider or an outsider. Judas cannot bear to be condemned to outsider status. Moreover, he was born who he is, so there is nothing he can do to alter his condition. He knows this, all of it. He knows too much. He knows that 'I am not.'

An entire history of Western optimism has been triggered in reaction to Judas. The terms of his story are just too brutal—that his character is inviolably evil, his fate immovably set. We can hear the mainstream of the culture, crying out for two millennia in protest: *There has to be some freedom!* Led by a vast theology defending free-will, it challenges: *There has to be some individual choice. There has to be some chance of me changing myself. I can improve myself. I can reform being.* But the Master set the terms in the beginning, 'I have chosen whom I have chosen.'

John excludes the kiss from his account of the betrayal in the Garden of Gethsemane. He draws on its implicit power. It is as if, in his version, Jesus kisses Judas, with the wine-soaked bread, which enters the mouth, and with it the devil. Like an automaton, the blackened figure rises on cue from the table and staggers towards the door. His mouth is frozen with what it contains. The breath is sucked out of him. He can hardly move. In the hush that has descended over the room, ten men are fearful that it is they who will betray the Master; and blind to why the speechless twelfth is leaving. This is the night made silent. The Temple veil rustles; the curtain behind the reclining diners trembles. Pneuma is astir.[6]

Not much later that night, in Gethsemane, the actual betrayal serves as postscript to the Last Supper. John's text records Jesus, in the garden, taking the initiative. He approaches Judas, once he sees him and a band of soldiers, and others whom the chief priests have gathered, coming with lanterns and weapons to arrest him. He confronts them, asking whom they seek. They answer, 'Jesus of Nazareth.' He proclaims, '*I am!*' They all reel backwards, and fall down.

The central teaching has accumulated such power that an angry mob frothing for blood is bowled over. One man, speaking two words, now commands the world. In his presence, all those who do not know these things, stumble and crash to the earth.

As the last spoken words to Judas — 'What you do, do quickly' — fused with the choking bread in the mouth, so the Master now saying *I am* rips the feet from under the betrayer, and pitches him down. Here is a two-edged sword of awesome cruelty. Judas, the sinister lethal snake slithering through the night, transmutes at the moment he strikes into Judas the helpless and pathetic victim of his own determined fate. Winded by the potency of the two-word proclamation of *being*, and flattened, all that is left for him is to crawl away.

During the Last Supper, three followers are given significant parts. Judas has primacy. Then there is Peter. He may be about to disown his Master but, compared to Judas, he is sound. Weakness and cowardice do not equate with evil. When Peter, later the same evening, protests to the unnamed girl accusing him — 'I am not!' — it is quite different to the Judas negation.

Then there is the beloved follower, who decades later becomes the John who tells the story.[7] The Master consoles himself with his affectionate affinity to the young man, who is in the place of honour on his right.[8] The intimacy gives him strength. It is compounded by John being chosen, by Peter, as the only one near enough to ask the identity of the betrayer. We are told that John leans even closer to ask the question. It is clear later, from the bewilderment of the other ten about what is given to Judas, and why he departs, that the Master has answered John quietly, so no one else has heard. John is the only one whom he lets know what he is doing.

'What you do, do quickly' means *Get out of my sight!* This ghastly shudder, in recoil at Judas, is softened by the intimate closeness to the beloved follower reclining against his chest. To him, he whispers the truth.

John's Life of Jesus creates a revolutionary metaphysics, the implications of which are still scarcely comprehended. John structures his Story on the pivotal truths he has teased out of Mark. One of these truths is incarnate in Judas, now enlarged into a formidable presence — the polar and dynamic opposite to the Master.

John does not record a Transfiguration — there is no metamorphosis on the high mountain. It is as if he takes the Shining as given, and from the start. He opens the Story with light, writing some of the most hauntingly beautiful words, as translated by William Tyndale, to be found in the English language. The words shine their own light. In the beginning, it was the Master, not God, who created all things:

> In the beginning was the Story, and the Story was with God, and the Story was God.
> He was in the beginning with God. All things came through him, and without him nothing was made, that has come into being. In him was life, and the life was the light of men. And the light shineth in the darkness, but the darkness comprehended it not …
> He was the truth light, which gives light to every man coming into the world. He was in the world, and through him the world came to be, and yet the world knew him not.[9]

John's Jesus, in a teaching episode that precedes the Raising of Lazarus, delivers the cryptic saying, '*Before Abraham was, I am.*' Creation is recast in terms of the eternity of *being*. 'All things came through him, and without him nothing was made, that has come into being.' Jesus is seed and agent. *Mythos* is scripted anew, and history rewritten. *I am forever.*

From this moment, Jewish history is made obsolete. It has lost its primacy. Abraham was merely a chronos figure, with no timelessness of *being*. God created Abraham to initiate the history of the chosen people. That history is superseded, and with it the Law of Moses and the inheritance of King David. There is no redemption in the strong tribal lineage stressed in Jewish culture — one generation begetting the next — nor in the morally upright living stipulated in the Ten Commandments, nor in Temple religion. What is worthy is not redemptive.

The new creative force is *I am*. It needs the Story to come to life. For that, the Master, who is the Story, requires a counterweight. Judas acts as the negative pole, without which the charge will not flow.

John signals his key categories from the beginning. They form a trinity. *I am* is the light. Second, there is pneuma. And there is agapē. They pressure a triple envy in Judas. He encounters the Shining *being* of the Master. He flares up at the agapē shown by Mary of Bethany as she anoints the feet. During the Last Supper, as Judas receives the demonised bread, he finds himself in close proximity to another manifestation of agapē — the beloved follower snuggling up against Jesus.

The Judas story presents a theory of evil. The traditional Christian view, both Catholic and Protestant, has been that evil derives from excessive appetite. The human passions need disciplining or they will break out as deadly sins: vanity, lust, greed, gluttony, jealousy, anger, and indolence.[10] The temptations of the flesh require the counter of suppression and denial of the flesh, whether through religious observance — chastity, fasting, prayer — or hard work in a personal vocation, and selfless communal duties. Virtue follows from curbing desire.

A range of examples of malevolence from today would seem to support this view. There is the jealous wife who schemes to destroy her husband's career. There is the violent drunk who bashes his wife senseless. There is the committee that doesn't appoint the best candidate for a job — out of envy of superior ability. There is the ambitious manager who spreads lies to get a challenger sacked. There is the lazy teacher who inflicts crushing boredom on students. There is the child-molesting priest.

Judas is different. The darkness that takes him over does not stem from an excessive or perverted appetite. The sins of the flesh are not his problem, with the minor exception of John's unnecessary slur on him being a thief. He might alternatively be imagined as a man of great reserve, a model of self-control — of composure. John Claggart, the Judas figure in Melville's *Billy Budd*, is just such a model: also solitary, and rather intellectual. Claggart's evil rises the moment he finds himself in the presence of Billy Budd, a handsome young sailor whom all the other sailors love for his angelic innocence. Billy is totally free from any ill will or ill thought. Claggart has an immediate visceral hatred of a man who walks with grace.

Judas is similar. The fateful misfortune for Judas is to be born into the presence of *I am*. Otherwise he might have led an ordinary and uneventful life. But here is the provocation: he is instantly confronted with what he is not. Just to have entered the magnetic field that is the Teacher exposes his wound—the raw central nerve that defines who he is. What he cannot *be*, he has to destroy. Evil is rooted in *being*, not *doing*. The acts that follow are incidental. It is not envy in the sense of wanting to possess this or that. Judas wants to *be* Jesus. He wants to *be* what he is not. He wants to undo his own creation.

Judas is a man of action. He does not react to his own calamity by sitting around feeling sorry for himself, gloomy with self-pity. He does not complain, blaming circumstances or others, for his anguish. He can still move, but it is entirely in reflex, like a sleepwalking automaton. His *doing* is no more than the howl of wounded *being*.

The primal source of evil is existential lack. It is the hopeless and inescapable inner vacuum of *I am not*. Excessive and illicit appetites only grow if there is chaos at the centre. They are a sort of pandemonium of character.

Judas is different from most of his kind in that he is conscious of his condition. He is not blind. He is not in denial. He is cursed to know, and to know that *I am not*. The light shineth in the darkness, but Judas comprehended it. For this, he is a big man.

We have now reached the inner sanctum of the Master's

radical new conception of the human condition. Everything orbits around living *being*—that of the individual. It is the nucleus that determines all. It is both creator and creation. It is the source and the shaper of the constellation of energies that will drive a life—every human life.

In the beginning was the Master. He sets the form: 'What I do now you do not know, but you will.' Just as Jewish history is made obsolete, so is the external God. Beyond *being*, there is no independent divinity. Beyond being, what exists is the scripted hour, and pneuma. Pneuma 'bloweth where it wills, and thou hearest its sound, but canst not tell whence it cometh, and whither it goeth.'

So the death of God happens at the beginning of the Christian story. In Mark, God appears twice in the first half of the story. Otherwise, he is rarely mentioned, except when linked to Old Testament references.[11] By the last climactic week in Jerusalem, he is gone. John's Life of Jesus is more contradictory. It is as if two texts cohabit side-by-side in John. In one, there is God the father, readily acknowledged by Jesus. In the other, starting with the Prologue, Jesus has replaced the external divinity. This is the Jesus embodying eternal *being* who presides through the impression-point episodes that drive John's story.

Judas has his own cup. It is the same cup held by the Master at the Last Supper. It provides the wine-soaked bread that he takes, hand to hand, like a baton in a relay race. In the darkened room, hushed with the fearful bewilderment of the ten, he places it—the morsel of his destiny—in his mouth. As his teeth munch into bread, Judas' mood darkens. *Who does he think he is, this Galilean charlatan, to humiliate me so! What arrogance! I shall show him that I am no sheepish coward—no Peter. Nor am I some naive, gullible youth—no John.* The hour has tolled.

But Judas chokes. There is a tremor in the room, a draught

whirling around the dim light shining at the centre of the shadowy circle of reclining men, rustling the curtain, now spiralling towards the exiting betrayer. Gasping, he staggers for the door. Behind his broad shoulders he feels the heat of the light flaring with pneuma the god, flaming like a welding torch directed at the back of his neck. He feels the breath being sucked out of him.

The truth light shineth in the darkness. So Peter falls asleep in the unlit garden, drained by failure, and he is condemned to sleep the big sleep. Peter's fate is mild compared with what Judas departs into. It is evoked by the finale to the Last Supper, as the curtain comes down. The climax is what lies through the door. It is described in three of the bleakest words ever written — *ēn de nux*. 'And it was night.'[12]

CHAPTER TEN

HE WHO LEARNS: PILATE

Pontius Pilate is well known in the West. He was the Roman governor who tried Jesus. Caving in to Jewish pressure, he condemned Jesus to death by crucifixion. He then washed his hands before the assembled crowd, proclaiming, 'I am innocent of the blood of this just man.'

Pilate is the popular symbol of weak authority. He is every captain, business executive, president, bishop, senior bureaucrat, work supervisor, committee member, doctor, teacher, and father or mother, who — in the wake of scandal, disaster, or monumental bungle — protests their innocence. *It was not my responsibility ... I didn't know ... It was their fault ... It was an accident ... The circumstances were beyond my control ... I am not to blame ... My hands are clean.*

This is Matthew's Pilate. It is not Mark's Pilate. It is manifestly not John's Pilate.

John orchestrates the two trials of Jesus — before the High Priest, and before Pilate — differently from Mark. He shortens the first trial, held in front of Jewish religious authority, to almost nothing: an incidental pause separating Peter's denial from the Roman trial. John then develops Pilate into a major figure in the drama. Pilate represents the fourth distinct type of follower — after Peter, Magdalene, and Judas:

Then they led the Master from Caiaphas to the Praetorium. It was early morning. They themselves did not enter the Praetorium, lest they be ritually defiled, and so they might eat the Passover meal.

Pilate went out to them, and demanded, 'What accusation do you bring against this man?'

'If this fellow were not an evil-doer,' they answered, 'we would not have handed him over to you.'

Pilate commanded, 'You take him, and judge him according to your law.' The Jews protested, 'We are not permitted to put anyone to death.'

Pilate re-entered the Praetorium. He summoned the Master and questioned, 'Are you the King of the Jews?' He received the reply, 'Are you posing this yourself, or have others told you about me?'

Pilate responded, 'I am not a Jew, am I? Your own people and the chief priests have handed you over to me. What have you done?' The Master said, 'My kingdom is not of this world. If my kingdom was of this world, my subjects would fight to stop me being delivered to the Jews. But now, my kingdom is not from here.'

Pilate questioned further, 'Are you a king, then?' The reply came, 'You say a king, I am. For this, I have been born. For this, I have come into the world, so that I should bear witness to the truth. Every one who is of the truth, hears my voice.'

Pilate said to him, 'What is truth?'

After he had spoken this, he went out again to the Jews and announced, 'I find no fault in him at all. You have a custom that I should free one person for you at Passover. Do you want me to release the King of the Jews?'

They yelled out, 'Not this man, but Barabbas.' (Barabbas was a bandit.)

Pilate took the Master and had him scourged. The soldiers wove a crown of thorns and fixed it upon his head. They threw a purple robe around him and chanted, 'Hail, King of the Jews.' And they repeatedly slapped him over the face.

Pilate went out again to address the crowd, 'Look, I am bringing him out to you, so that you may know that I find no case against him.' The Master followed, wearing the crown of thorns and the purple robe. Pilate said to them, 'Behold the man!'

The chief priests and the temple-police, when they saw him, screamed out, 'Crucify! Crucify him!'

Pilate responded, 'You take him and crucify him, for I find no case against him.' The Jews replied, 'We have a law according to which he ought to die, because he has claimed to be the son of God.'

When Pilate heard this he was more afraid. He returned into the Praetorium and questioned the Master, 'From where are you?'

Receiving no answer, Pilate pressed, 'Are you not speaking to me? Don't you know I have the authority to crucify you, and the authority to release you?' The Master replied, 'You would have no authority over me unless it had been given to you from above. Because of this, the one handing me in does the greater wrong.'

From then on, Pilate sought to release him. But the Jews kept screaming out, 'If you let this fellow go, you are no friend to Caesar. Whoever makes himself a king, speaks against Caesar.'

When Pilate heard this he brought the Master out. He sat down on the judges' bench in a place called the 'Stone Pavement'. It was the preparation day for the Passover, at about the sixth hour — which is noontime. Pilate addressed the Jews, 'Behold your King!'

They screamed, 'Away with him! Away with him! Crucify him!'

Pilate queried, 'Shall I crucify your King?' The chief priests countered, 'We have no king but Caesar.'

So Pilate handed him over to be crucified. They led him away, carrying the cross himself, to Skull Place. There, they crucified him, and with two others, one on either side.

Now Pilate wrote a title, which he put on the cross. It read, 'Jesus of Nazareth, King of the Jews.' Many of the Jews read this inscription, because the place of crucifixion was near the city. It was written in Hebrew, in Greek and in Latin.

Consequently the chief priests of the Jews petitioned Pilate, 'Don't leave written "King of the Jews", but rather "This man claimed to be King of the Jews".'

Pilate answered, 'What I have written, I have written.'[1]

John cuts the main crucifixion story here back to almost nothing. The strong inference is that the reader already knows it from the other three accounts. The references — to mocking, the soldiers, carrying the cross — are minimal. This allows John to bring Pilate forward, and to place him centre-stage.

The narrative is tight. Pilate is the principal figure; Jesus, secondary. This is surprising in that we are at a critical point in the Passion sequence. In fact, John will underplay his final crucifixion scene, injecting far more narrative force into the

Pilate story (which immediately precedes it), and the meeting with Magdalene in the garden (which follows it).

Pilate is pitched into the journey of his life. As Roman governor of the province of Judea, his main residence is in the Mediterranean coastal town of Caesarea. When in Jerusalem, he resides, most likely, in the Royal Palace, built by Herod the Great fifty years earlier. The Praetorium was the garrison headquarters of the provincial governor—and, in this case, part of the palace.[2]

Pilate begins cautiously. He comes out of the Praetorium to meet what seems to be a large crowd of angry Jews, led by their chief priests. He asks for the charge against Jesus. They parry that they would not have brought him if he were not a criminal. For some reason they are evasive, not specifying his crime.

Pilate does not want to get involved. He tells them to use their own legal processes. They remind him that Rome does not allow them to impose capital punishment. Pilate, as governor, does not wish to give away this power. So he goes back into the Praetorium to conduct his own probing of Jesus.

His opening question is blunt: 'Are you the King of the Jews?' Jesus queries whether this is what Pilate wants to ask—or, rather, what he has been told. If he were proclaiming himself as a worldly king, that would indeed threaten Roman authority. As the Jews later insinuate, this is a treasonous claim, one that merits crucifixion.

Pilate's reaction is not to extend his questioning, as might be expected of the province's political head, but to reflect back on himself. 'I am not a Jew, am I?' He has reason to be irritated by a prisoner questioning his motives. His question may be thought of as abruptly and rhetorically dismissive, petulantly stating the obvious. This is unlikely, for his next remark is respectful of Jesus, explaining that his own people have handed him in. Pilate, in effect, excuses himself.

Not being a Jew, Pilate does not know anything about Jesus apart from what he has been told. Pilate further implies that he is detached and objective, and not in alliance with the Jews. He is interested to hear the truth, which he will judge fairly. Perhaps there is even an undertone, in his self-questioning, of complicity with Jesus and some sympathy for him.

Already, the presence of Jesus is afflicting Pilate with the question of *being*—'I am not a Jew, am I?' Pilate's next question, 'What have you done?' is both that of the investigating officer, and personal. By now, the Roman governor seems intrigued.

Pilate is not a Jew, obviously. He may be hinting that he understands Jesus is not the leader of the mob outside, an uncouth oriental rabble with their barbaric dietary superstitions—subjects, John's narrative implies, who are repugnant to this Roman governor. More, if the prisoner is a king (and he has just stated that he has a kingdom) it may be that Pilate himself is one of his subjects.

Pilate probes further on the subject of kingship. By this stage of the dialogue, the questioning sounds naive. It serves to cue the reply that *truth* is the kingdom, and that anyone who belongs to it will hear this man's voice.

'What is truth?' Pilate responds with the first of his five paradigmatic sayings. It comes in the form of a question, suddenly there in the text, standing alone, unexpected, parenthetical. We, the readers, are given no clue as to its intonation—how it was spoken. Is it dismissively rhetorical? Or is it quietly reflective, this Roman posing, for the first time in his life, the question that matters? Or is it simply an exclamation, evoking shock, bursting from Pilate's mouth?

The prisoner has shifted the ground from that of political authority—Pilate's own domain—to that of truth. Jesus, as king of this domain, is leading the governor. Pilate, who understands this, abandons all interest in political charges, and indeed in the trial itself. Instead of probing the facts of the case—the specific truths—as a judge normally would, he switches to the ultimate question. 'What is truth?' will govern the rest of the Pilate story.

Pilate is a man of action. Now galvanised, he returns to address the Jewish mob, delivering his judgment. Roman authority finds Jesus innocent. He then offers the Jews a way out: the Barabbas choice. But the shrewd governor is rebuffed. The cultures clash, the political craft of the Roman countered by the tempestuous fury of the Jews.

The governor changes tactics, taking punishment into his own hands. He has Jesus scourged—a vicious form of whipping, the leather thongs often tipped with metal barbs which ripped out chunks of flesh.[3] He lets his soldiers mock him as a pretend emperor. He then displays the flogged and humiliated Jesus to the crowd, hoping this will slake their thirst for blood. The stratagem fails; instead, it provokes a diabolical frenzy in the mob, screaming for death by crucifixion.

The scene is portentously theatrical. From the Praetorium platform, standing next to the Master—who is crowned in thorns, and robed in purple, his flesh torn, covered in dribbling, congealing blood—Pilate delivers the second of his paradigmatic sayings. **'Behold the man!'**

At this, the crowd beneath, surrounding the platform, explodes in a mass crescendo of chanting, a howling storm of tribal rage. The deafening noise rising up, enveloping and swallowing the two men standing alone, flashes the chorus line, 'Crucify him! Crucify him!' What has provoked them most is the *word*. Pilate signals who Jesus is, if in coded form. He himself is on the threshold of discovery.

Pilate has moved from 'What is truth?' to 'Know the man!' The Greek imperative used here—*Idou*—may be rendered as

'Behold', 'Look', or 'See here'. The renowned Latin translation — *Ecce Homo* — carries a similar range of meanings. The Greek comes from the verb, *eidō*, meaning 'I see'. But the Greek equally means, in the derivative form of *oida*, 'I know'. In fact, the very name of Oedipus — spelt *Oidipous* in Greek — has coded in its first syllable the double meaning of swollen and knowing. Oedipus is, by name, literally both 'swollen-foot' and 'knowing-foot'. He takes, on foot, the journey of knowledge.

Pilate has built into his proclamation before the Jewish people the imperative 'Know!' With this word, he acknowledges Jesus.

'The man' is what Pilate presents to the world, in public on the Praetorium stage. Here stands the human ideal, the Platonic form of being human. *Here before you, observe quintessential humanity. Know what it is. Know who you are.*[4] But it is not clear how much, or precisely what, Pilate understands. Early in the trial, he himself had asked, 'Who am I?' In response, Jesus played with his own double identity of king, and *I am*.

There is also a subtle play on the words spoken to King David in the Hebrew Bible, which mark the turning point in his story — the point at which fortune swings against the greatest of Jewish political leaders. Nathan the prophet signals to David that he has lost favour with God by stating, 'You are the man!'[5] A divine curse will follow. Pilate's, 'Behold the man!' supersedes the curse. Both scenes take place in Jerusalem.[6]

Mark's Life of Jesus recorded the centurion at the crucifixion exclaiming, 'Truly, this man was the son of God!' Mark went on to blur the identities of the centurion and Pilate. John goes further, midrashing the centurion into Pilate.

In response to further howls of 'Crucify him!' Pilate becomes exasperated. He tells the crowd that it should crucify him, proclaiming for the third time that he finds no case against Jesus. This forces the Jews to switch the political charge to a religious one. Jesus has claimed to be the son of God. This is blasphemy, and Jewish law — in the Book of Leviticus — decrees the death sentence for blasphemy.[7]

At this, we are told that Pilate is suddenly more afraid. Why? The only objective threat to him is political: that Jesus might be a rebel against Roman authority. But the Jews have switched their charge away from treason. This seems to trigger further *truth* agitation in Pilate. Suddenly, he needs to know more.

So he takes Jesus back inside the Praetorium, and puts to him the third of his paradigmatic sayings. **'From where are you?'**

He receives no reply. He tries ineffectually to threaten Jesus, by warning him that he, Pilate, has the power to crucify him. He is told that if he has authority over Jesus, that comes from above. Here is the oblique answer to his worried, 'From where are you?'

Indeed, from where does the Master come? We recall that in the next major episode — two days later — he will reappear early on the Sunday morning, in the garden outside the empty tomb. Magdalene will mistake him for the gardener. His identity is growing more obscure. Further, Pilate may be playing with the present tense of the verb 'to be'. 'You are' cues its grammatical predecessor, 'I am'. His question has buried within, 'From whence *I am?'* Pilate asks into the origins of *being*.

Jesus had, in his earlier teaching, provided part of an answer. 'Before Abraham was, *I am.'* In the beginning there was primal being. *Being* is forever.

The Jews then intensify their threat by telling Pilate that he risks angering Caesar if he lets Jesus go. Pilate dare not risk riots in Jerusalem, nor risk word getting back to Rome that he has been lax in punishing those who question Caesar's authority.

He leaves the Praetorium and proceeds to a place called the Stone Pavement, and takes his seat on the Judge's Bench. The judgment he then delivers is not what either the reader of the story or the Jews expect. It takes the form of a three-word imperative, and targets the Jews, not Jesus: **'Behold your King!'**

The sheer brilliance of Pilate—both insightful and sharply clever—has never been recognised. It is on full display in these three words. At first reading, he taunts the Jews. According to the Hebrew holy texts, God is their king.[8] By their law, a man claiming to be king of the sacred realm commits the ultimate blasphemy. Such a man transgresses the First Commandment, delivered by God to Moses on Mt Sinai.

'Behold your King!' has sometimes been interpreted as ironical, as mocking Jesus.[9] But if it were, the Jewish mob would not have responded in outrage, screaming, 'Away with him! Away with him! Crucify him!' If anything, Pilate has touched the *messiah* nerve, arousing the fear in the Jews that this may be the 'anointed one', sent by their God to save them—and they are about to kill him. Pilate's immediate follow-up query, 'Shall I crucify your King?' suggests that he is, quite deliberately, needling that nerve.

Pilate also makes explicit to the Jews that they are asking a Roman to put one of their own to death—indeed, their king.[10] Here, perhaps, is John's radical midrash of Pilate washing his hands of the blood of an innocent man. This narrative portrays Pilate as decisive, taking the initiative, rather than weak, as in Matthew's hand-washing scene.

The words may also be read as 'Know your King!' The deeply serious and troubled Pilate attempts to tell the Jews what they least want to know. Again, their screams drown him out—screams that block their own ears. Truth is lethal, so it must be crucified. The howling crowd in Jerusalem, led by the chief priests, seeks to restore the standard human condition—oblivion. *Truth is not-oblivion.*

Pilate, in his new role as teacher, has proclaimed to the Jewish people that there is one of them—one of their own, and a man—who is a king. The chief priests lamely and deceitfully parry that Caesar is their only king.

Pilate also voices what will become the judgment of history. The next two thousand years will demonstrate that the Jews did, in fact, produce one man of towering, world-historical significance. This is him—the man they are in a fury to kill. That is the secular historical judgment. In the West, the sacred historical judgment is just as unequivocal. The ultimate kingdom is that of Truth, the kingdom over which this man reigns.

Pilate places the final, fifth seal on his sequence of revelations. From 'What is truth?' he progressed to 'Know the man!' Then, 'From where are you?' he moved finally to 'Behold your King!' Now he speaks his last words to the leaders of the Jewish crowd, abruptly and categorically: **'What I have written, I have written.'**

Pilate will no longer be swayed. The words are gnomic, brooking no retort, yet charging that there is a deeper truth coded in his words—one that the crowd probably does not understand. *Whether you do, or you don't, does not concern me. I am not about to explain myself.* In any case, these words are untranslatable.

Pilate closes his own story by taking on the mantle of prophetic authority. Of course, the surface reference is to the words that the governor has had inscribed on the cross. If, however, they were the true subject-matter of his retort, he would have spoken more plainly. He might have said something like, 'The inscription stands', or 'I have no reason to change the wording.'

Why does he choose to inscribe the words, 'King of the Jews'? Formally, Pilate is the governor who has judged this man guilty. The charge is treason—Jesus is a rebel against Roman authority.

The crime is written above the convicted man's head, in order to inform the public of the offence. But John's story makes it clear that Pilate's intention is not to mock Jesus, whom he holds in ultimate respect.

Pilate's real text lies behind the literal words. Scripted in Hebrew, in Greek, and in Latin, it is universal, thereby superseding all languages. It may only be deciphered by retracing the story. Pilate has unwittingly laid out his Ariadne thread to lead the reader along his own journey by means of paradigmatic sayings. What opened with 'What is truth?' climaxes in 'What I have written, I have written.'

This is the indelible script of Truth. Yet it remains obscure. What has Pilate really written? He has, in effect, replaced the crown of thorns with a new crown, in the form of an inscription written on a board nailed to the cross above Jesus' head. This is his new title, in three languages. It proclaims him King. Pilate has used his authority to crown the Master as *King of Truth*. He provides the answer to his own defining question.

Pilate is everyman, and more. This story has not been about Jesus' guilt, or Jewish rancour. Its substance is Pilate's trust. Those interpreters who have placed Pilate in some spiritual no-man's-land between denial and belief underestimate him — for he does not reject or deny.[11] Pilate is not Peter. He takes the same journey as Oedipus, that of self-knowledge. And he learns — to know the man. By the end, he is very close.

Pilate represents borderline *I am*.

He has enough inner strength to plot his own course through a political challenge that threatens his career, even his life — emperors had a habit of executing disgraced officials. Like Magdalene, he switches his life-direction, and in a single brief moment. He bows down before the *truth* question, and before the man who lives it. It is Pilate who will always be remembered as the one who stood alongside the Master, high on the Praetorium platform, above a mob screaming, 'Crucify, Crucify him!' He answered, 'Know the man!'

Pilate is in the vicinity of what matters, and he knows it. His fate is to have been cast into this place and time, to move side by side, in dialogue and action, with the Master. In this, he is like no one else. Pilate's self-possession means that *being here* counts—reflected in the fact that it is he who stakes out the metaphysical terrain with his five sayings. He is no passive, weak bystander. *Being* is presence.

Little detail of what Pilate learns is shared with the reader. This is odd, for we all walk most of the time, through this narrative, in the shoes of the Roman governor. Perhaps that is the point: not to provide us with specific knowledge. We are left, rather, with a sense of the man—a shimmering, silhouetted emanation of his large and almost commanding presence, probing *truth*, probing *being*.

The Pilate sequence begins in the early morning. Daybreak indicates rising light. It comes through he who learns. Pilate delivers his sentence at noon—in the full glare of high noon. The trial has taken six hours or so, enough time for the Roman governor's slow awakening.

The Pilate story provides its own light for penetrating the obscurity that surrounds it. In this, it is archetypal. As with all big *mythos* stories, progress depends on finding the Shining midrash. Another eighteen hundred years would pass before the story seeded.

Herman Melville completed *Billy Budd–Sailor* in 1891, a few months before his death. A novella (a long short story), it was not published until 1924.

Pilate is a political man. Politics is his vocation; which means that, in effect, he has taken an oath to a higher calling. His principal duty is to the political office that he holds — his oath to Caesar. In practice, this means serving the interests of Rome in Judea by keeping order. Grappling with what makes a good political leader becomes, through the narrative, a vehicle for the *being* question.

In Melville's story, Pilate is recast as a naval captain — Captain Vere, whose name means *truth*. Pilate's self-identifying question, 'What is truth?', is scripted into the captain's nature. Melville, further, draws on the merging of the personas of Pilate and the centurion. A centurion was a Roman captain, if military rather than naval. Captain Vere commands the British warship *Bellipotent* in the year 1797, during the Napoleonic Wars.

Billy Budd joins the ship. He is twenty-one, of great physical beauty, also immensely strong. But he is most striking for his virtue and un-selfconscious honesty. He has no awareness of evil. Likened to an angel, he is nicknamed 'Baby Budd'. The crew of hard-bitten sailors come to love him — doing his washing, making him things.

John Claggart, the 35-year-old master-at-arms — the policeman on board — hates Billy. Claggart is tall, spare, austere, and distinguished-looking: pale, with silky black curls, and an intellectual cast. He trumps up a charge of mutiny against Billy, which he reports to the captain.

Captain Vere finds Claggart vaguely repellent. He calls for Billy and asks the master-at-arms to repeat the charge to the young sailor's face. Billy turns pale at the lie, responding with 'a strange dumb gesturing and gurgling' — he has a speech impediment, a stutter, but he sings beautifully. Vere tells him in a tender, fatherly tone to take his time in giving his reply. The paralysis brought on by inner torture breaks. Billy's right arm shoots forward, his fist striking Claggart in the middle of the forehead. The master-at-arms drops to the deck—dead.

Captain Vere utters, in a whisper, 'Fated boy.' He soon follows, as he looks down at the corpse, 'Struck dead by an angel of God! Yet the angel must hang!'

The captain sets up a drumhead court. Billy protests that he is not a mutineer, but true to the king. Vere replies with suppressed emotion, 'I believe you, my man.' To which Billy responds gratefully, and without a stutter, 'God will bless you for that, your honour!' He adds, 'Could I have used my tongue I would not have struck him. But he lied foully to my face and in presence of my captain.'

Captain Vere then instructs the court that, as sailors in the British navy, their allegiance is to the king. They are governed by the king's law, which in this case means the Mutiny Act. According to the Articles of War, if a man strikes a superior, and the blow kills, the act is a capital crime. Irrespective of intention, it must receive the death penalty. Duty to the king overrides private conscience.

He adds a practical argument. There has been a mutiny recently on a British warship—known as the Great Mutiny of 1797—and all naval hands are still on edge. Sailors are simple men who know the law. If the captain shows clemency, it will be taken as weakness—that he is fearful of his crew. It will compromise discipline on board the *Bellipotent*, making it more vulnerable to mutiny. These are times of national danger, under threat from Napoleon and the French.

Billy Budd is condemned to death, and hanged from the mainsail yardarm early the next morning. At the last moment, he utters in a clear melody, like a singing bird, 'God bless Captain Vere!'

Soon after, the *Bellipotent* falls into an engagement with a

French warship—the *Atheist*. Captain Vere is wounded. A few days later he dies, murmuring the words, 'Billy Budd, Billy Budd.'

Captain Vere is Pilate revisited. Circumstances, in combination with his office, require that he hang an innocent man; worse, an angel of God. That angel loves his captain. Indeed, it is more important to Baby Budd that his captain believes him—that he is not a mutineer, and true to the king—than that he is about to die. Billy shows no fear of death, sleeping soundly during the night.

Captain Truth knows. Indeed, he knows everything, apart from the most important thing of all: whether he himself can be redeemed from doing what he now does.

Until this moment, he had been able to answer the *being* question—who am I? He is a captain. He has taken an oath to something fixed and timeless, bigger than himself, something with its own incontrovertible laws—his vocation. He is honour-bound to obey it. He is *being*-bound to obey it. Were he to decide that this was all too difficult, and switch roles from captain to man of compassionate conscience, he would be nobody—perhaps even lesser than a Claggart, who at least has a Judas identity. Other officers on board, in fact, urge him to postpone his decision, leaving judgment to the admiral. But Vere is not one to shift responsibility; and, in any case, his job is to maintain the *Bellipotent* as an effective fighting warship, ready for action.

Captain Vere is summed up in the name of his ship: 'beautiful power'. He is the quintessential man of politics, at its best. Politics, as a necessary fact of human life, is, of its nature, about the use of power—even violence—to achieve given ends. Good politics is the putting of power to benevolent use, in the service of the people and their well-being.

Captain Vere embodies the four classical character virtues. He is a *just* man. He has *practical wisdom*—he draws on his sharp insight into the nature of men, his knowledge of his position, and his common sense, in order to manage the crisis on board the *Bellipotent*. His temperament is *balanced*—moderate, not given to excessive emotion, nor the exercise of judgment coloured by passion. He is, fourthly, *courageous*—having the moral fortitude to act knowing the dreadful personal consequences of what he decides to do.

This is the difficult decision of his life. Vere is no harsh disciplinarian, not given to rigidly implementing the law according to its strictest letter. If he were narrow-minded—lacking in imagination—the decision would be easier. He dislikes Claggart. The captain inclines to the view that malicious envy of such proportions receives its just punishment in the form of a fatal blow to the forehead. He admires Billy with a paternal affection. He knows that his crew loves Billy, and that he risks arousing their hatred by punishing him.

Captain Vere has reflected deeply on his calling. He was known to have said, 'With mankind, forms, measured forms, are everything.' This could be Plato—the principal philosopher of the West—speaking. All humans are responsible for maintaining forms. A captain is merely representative. If the forms weaken, there will be mutiny, the community of sailors will disintegrate, and the ship will be rendered useless. The angel of God is a necessary martyr to the king's forms—the angel himself knows this. So it is in all walks of life, where there are many and diverse ships that need steering. Such is the human order.

Vere is also aware that he cannot condemn an innocent man to death and escape bloodguilt. He cannot wash his hands of this tragic affair. He is about to oversee a violation of sacred order. In the scale of things, this is of far greater moment than maintaining discipline on the *Bellipotent*. The captain may be about to damn himself eternally. When he whispered 'Fated boy', he should rather have mouthed, 'Fated man.'

It is Captain Vere whom fate has struck. And he is everyone who walks this pathway to *being*—that of vocation, or a chosen life-activity. On the vocation path, the kairos hour now sounds.

The questions surge and pound like stormy waves. Does the captain become the one who learns—to *Watch*? There he is at early light, the restive, haunted sailors crowding the deck, Billy up above, strung to the yardarm, the first rays of dawn striking him, and the voice singing forth melodiously over the decks of the *Bellipotent*, 'God bless Captain Vere!' Is the captain awake to this, the Mary-of-Bethany moment? He surely, now, echoing Pilate, asks himself, 'What is truth?' His *being*—scripted in his name—is in doubt. Through acting truthfully to his calling, he has pitched himself into the nether gloom of unbelief.

Captain Truth is in the process of withering to a black stump. By being the best that a captain can be, he destroys captaincy. His vocation is annihilated. How can he continue in charge of his ship, of any ship, after he has killed the angel of God? How can he continue *being* anything? Indeed, in the next kairos moment, the captain will die at the hands of atheism. Likely, death comes as relief. Which poses the ultimate question for the Pilate story: does vocation only reach its full consummation—its maturity—when it turns into tragic vocation?

There are a handful of familiar justifications for any person's chosen central life-activity—whether it be holding office (like that of captain), being a mother, or father, a sportsman or woman, or taking any job seriously, throwing one's heart and soul into it. A vocation is useful to others; it serves the common good. It earns an income, providing for self and dependents. It is a vehicle for demonstrating character, and for employing inherited qualities and talents to good ends. It provides the backbone for a balanced and fulfilling life. It is a secular form of worship, a means for developing a sort of concentrated inwardness through which mind, body, and the external world may achieve a harmonious oneness — giving some sense of higher belonging.

But Captain Vere's story implies that these reasons are superficial. They engage merely with the preliminaries — set in the antechamber of vocation. Vere comes to understand that until his sense of himself as a captain is charred to a black stump, he is nowhere.[12]

The captain is taught that there are different orders of *being*. Billy belongs to a higher one. That Billy is perfectly happy to accept an unjust punishment, as long as he has his captain's trust, signals the inferiority of the middle, ethical human order. Its realm is that of the moral law, of just men acting well, of the punishment of evil, of the king's forms, and of common vocation. Billy Budd puts Captain Vere in his lower place. He teaches him that unless he can rise to where he himself belongs, he will remain a dead man walking, if an admirable and a good one. This is the same lesson that Pilate learns from Jesus. And Jesus and Billy are both judged according to the same false charge — of rebellion, or mutiny.

Billy knows his captain, and how close to damnation he has pitched himself. He knows that only the angel of God can save Captain Vere. His dying words are uttered in devotion — perhaps even the reason for this angel's existence. Sung as if they were choired from the heavens, the aim of 'God bless Captain Vere' is not, as it might seem, to forgive. It is to signal that the fated man may be fine. Like the final words spoken by the Master, to the fallen woman at the house of Simon the Pharisee, they intimate a righting of being. From within the charged air, as the first rays of sunlight strike the hanged angel, at this point of near-unbearable, climactic intensity in the story — and in the life of Vere — there is hope of a sacred encounter.

Vere reborn — how might he be? In what form might he appear? That he is killed by the French *Atheist* becomes a metaphor for his truth. Soon after the burial at sea of Billy Budd, his captain-self is mortally wounded whilst carrying out his duty in the cauldron of battle. He is a captain no more. Atheism — no belief — is now what threatens him mortally. If Vere does not trust, he is finished.

Several days later, lying prostrate, he is able to break free from his dumb-struck state. He looks upwards in the moment of death. His condition is that of the mad boy, writhing on the ground, frothing at the mouth, picturing the Transfigured Jesus. The story leaves open the question of whether, or not, Captain Vere sees the Shining. He can focus, and murmur, 'Billy Budd, Billy Budd. From where are you?'

Vere's story is about himself — the one named *truth* — and it is driven by the Pilate question. 'What is truth?' Vere learns that there are two quite distinct and incompatible orders. There is the truth of captaincy, which he has mastered. And there is Billy.

Vere and Pilate are one and the same, but with stories that reveal different facets of the borderline condition. The Vere story pays more attention to what happens before the kairos moment — filling out the form of the good political leader. With Pilate, this is merely sketched, in passing. His story concentrates on what happens afterwards, in the pursuit of truth.

Pilate remains in office, and his final words are captain-like: 'What I have written, I have written.' Were we to know his private thoughts, a few days later, they might well echo Vere's dying words, 'Billy Budd. Billy Budd.'

Such private reflections midrash, in John's Life of Jesus, as it continues on after Pilate's exit. They appear in the next big episode, at dawn in the garden. Magdalene speaks a single word, in recognition and acknowledgement, reverently, lovingly: 'Teacher.' Captains Pilate and Vere, as one, aspire to be her.

We, the readers, are on the threshold of being able to say of Pilate, as of Captain Vere, 'Know the man!' With Magdalene, he is the most interesting of the five followers of Jesus.

Such is borderline *I am*.

CHAPTER ELEVEN

LET HIM BE!

In him was life, and the life was the light of men. And the light shineth in the darkness, but the darkness comprehended it not ...

He was the truth light, which gives light to every man coming into the world. He was in the world, and through him the world came to be, and yet the world knew him not.

Why does John open the Story with the Shining? For every person, he seems to be saying, the struggle to *be* takes place in the darkness. *I am* is buried deep within, down in the dark of the housing character. It is shrouded in oblivion.

Yet it is given. It was there in the beginning—in the form of eternal *being*. Every man coming into the world has his share of the all-creative presence. However, without the truth light, it will remain sunk in the darkness. There is Dark *being*; there is Shining *being*.

This is abstract. What might it actually mean, brought down to earth, in the thick of real life lived in the human world? The challenge to make *being* legible is crucial for Mark and John. They take different paths. Mark chooses to look principally at Jesus himself, and his life; secondarily, at his followers. He records the existential tragedy of the Master, told from the inside. John reverses focus. His Jesus is not a figure with whom the reader identifies—he is too super-human, too magisterial for that. John approaches the enigma of *being* through the followers.

There are five different modes of following. Mark mapped out the blueprint for all five, some with no more than a canny outline trace. John filled out these archetypal modes. So far, we have considered four: Peter, Magdalene, Judas, and Pilate.

The fifth is the storyteller.

What do we know about John? The author of the fourth Life of Jesus identifies himself, at the end, as the follower loved by Jesus. He has generally been known as the 'beloved disciple'—notably, the one who, during the Last Supper, reclines against Jesus' chest and is told the identity of the betrayer.

Around 180AD Irenaeus identified the author as John, one of the twelve, who lived at Ephesus until the end of the first century; as a boy, Irenaeus had known the Bishop of Smyrna, who claimed to have known John.[1] Circumstantial evidence from within the text supports this identification of the author as John, a Galilee fisherman, the brother of James, and the son of Zebedee.

In Mark—as later in Matthew and Luke—James and John are the sons of Zebedee. Mark's Jesus even gives them a nickname: 'sons of thunder'. With Peter, they make up the favoured three followers. However, the fourth Life drops all of this. There are no favoured three. In fact, the three are replaced by one, who is *beloved*—the word is *agapē*. Even more intriguingly, John is never mentioned by name. The Baptist is the sole 'John' who is acknowledged.

Only six of the twelve followers are named, and even then only intermittently through the text — Andrew, Simon Peter, Philip, Nathanial, Judas, and Thomas. There is, in addition, a mention, in the final chapter, of the sons of Zebedee, but they are not explicitly named. The author seems quite deliberately reluctant to do so, for some reason.

There are five separate episodes in John's Story in which the unnamed *beloved follower* appears. The first is the Last Supper. 'One of the followers, whom the Master loved', is snuggling against his chest. It is the night before the crucifixion, on the threshold of the end, and this is the first reference to the beloved follower. He only appears on stage in the last act. Neither John nor the sons of Zebedee have been mentioned previously — not even at the outset, when Jesus calls the twelve to follow him.

Renaissance and neo-classical painting will take up the implication that the beloved follower is youthful. Raphael and Poussin, notably, conjure a young man, fresh-faced and open to life, with a self-sufficiency and poise beyond his years, intensely engaged by the events into which he is cast. He looks on with a mixture of dread and curiosity. For them, he is the principal one who learns by observing — in contrast with Magdalene, whose awakening requires doing.[2]

The fourth Life casts the beloved follower as the third watcher — he has been preceded by a blind man and by Mary of Bethany. Pilate, the fourth, is still to come. At the height of the Last Supper drama, he is chosen by the Master as his intimate.

A second possible appearance of the beloved follower occurs after Gethsemane. Peter shadows the arresting party, accompanied by another one of the twelve. The other was known to the High Priest and let into the courtyard with Jesus. Peter is left standing outside, so the other speaks to the young woman keeping the door and gets him admitted. It is at this point that the girl recognises Peter as a follower of Jesus. He responds with his first denial — 'I am not.'

The third episode has the beloved follower identified explicitly. It is the scene of crucifixion. Jesus is on the cross:

> Standing by the cross were his mother, his mother's sister, Mary the wife of Clopas, and Mary Magdalene. When the Master saw his mother and the follower whom he loved standing by, he addressed his mother, 'Woman, behold your son!' He then told the follower, 'Behold your mother!' From that hour, the follower made her his own.

The fourth Life of Jesus had as its opening event the marriage at Cana — and it was disturbingly incomplete. At Cana, the Master had dismissively addressed his mother, 'Woman, what have I to do with you? My hour has not yet come.' Now his hour has come. He addresses her again, 'Woman'. This is her first reappearance in the story since Cana. From the cross, her son commands, rather than dismisses.

The Cana episode is finally completed. He places her — not as *his* mother. The implication seems to be, and this is harsh, that his opening rebuff, 'What have I to do with you?' should be read as *I am not your son! I have no mother. This, my beloved follower, is your son. As I love him, so you should love him.*

John's story has no birth narrative. The only reference in the entire text to a human father is by the Jews, soon after the walking-on-water scene, when questioning his claim to divine origins: 'Is not this Jesus, the son of Joseph, whose father and mother we know?' The Jews do not understand that *genesis* is not normal biological birth. *In the beginning was the Story.* The text reinforces the point by opening its first piece of narrative action at Cana. Jesus is there with his mother, telling her he has no mother.

Let us go back to the very beginning. The Master enters fully mature, in the form of the Shining. He is the light and the life through whom the world came to be. 'Before Abraham was, *I am.*' *Being* is not born of woman. He makes this explicit in his first encounter after Cana and the cleansing of the Temple—with Nicodemus. Nicodemus is told that unless he is born again he will not enter the sacred realm. He questions how a man can enter his mother's womb a second time. The Master replies that a man must be born from water and pneuma.

He shows a fatherly affection towards the beloved follower. As there was intimacy at the Last Supper, there is intimacy from the cross. Although, in terms of primal being, the Master has no human family, he creates a surrogate one. 'You, know your son!' 'You, know your mother!' It is an inversion of what, centuries later in the Middle Ages, will become the *Pietà* archetype—the mother cradling her dead son's body. His command from the cross places the mother in the beloved follower's caring arms. The follower makes her his own.[3] He has been given a family—which makes sense of the fact that in John's text, up until this point, against all three Synoptic versions, the beloved follower has neither brother nor father. This text, like Mark's, is worked with intricate care.

In addition, 'Woman, behold your son!' may be read from a different angle.[4] There is a shadowing echo in the words. The Master is also referring to himself—as her son. If we retranslate his address as 'Woman, know your son' this scene joins the sequence of recognition episodes. What starts with the angry snort to awaken Mary of Bethany, and then continues with Pilate's revelation 'Know the man', ends with his mother. As he spoke knowingly at the Last Supper to the beloved follower, so he now addresses his mother. That the son she finally knows is about to breathe his last overcasts the crucifixion in tragic poignancy.

The fourth episode in which the beloved follower appears is that of 'touch me not' at Sunday dawn. Magdalene, on finding the tomb empty, runs to fetch Peter and the follower. On the return, he outruns Peter—another possible indication of his youth. He stoops, looks inside, sees the linen cloths, but does not enter. He waits—perhaps out of deference to Peter, perhaps out of modesty. Or is it sacred fear?

Time is compressed at the climax of the Passion. The Last Supper took place a little more than forty-eight hours earlier, and it was there that he had leaned close against the Master, heard of the betrayer, then watched on with dread as Judas exited into night. The long darkness since that moment was punctured by the words from the cross, intimate, spoken to him, making him the bequest of a new family—the whole scene bleak with horror, yet underwritten by trust in him.

This Sunday, the first rays of the new dawn lighten the gloom, but not inside—for the tomb is empty, apart from folded white burial cloths. Would not John, indeed anyone, be stricken? *What is in there? Is it a holy of holies, or an abomination of desolation? Surely I am looking into the mystery site of a happening beyond normal human comprehension, charged with forces of demonic metamorphosis. Is it, perhaps, the site of some Shining god who might incinerate the first mortal intruder to glimpse his face?* The new son, like the weeping Magdalene, might wail, *Where is my beloved Master?*

Peter arrives and enters the tomb. He shows no sign of reticence—another cue to his brute insensitivity. *I am not* continues his perpetual stumble. Now, the beloved follower also enters. The story registers sparely, 'he saw, and he trusted'. The two men then return home.

The fifth and final episode takes place some time later, on the Sea of Galilee. It is the fishing scene in which the Master reappears and questions Peter three times as to whether he loves him. Apart from Peter, six followers are present: Thomas, Nathanial, the sons of Zebedee, and two others.

The beloved follower is also named, later on, as one of the seven gathered there. He plays one of three major parts in this scene — with the Master and Peter. So, his identity becomes clearer. He must be either a son of Zebedee or one of the two other unnamed followers. Let us assume, for the moment, that he is John, son of Zebedee.

Peter and John are paired in all of these five episodes. The exception is the scene at the foot of the cross; but, even there, Peter's absence is loaded, as a kind of anti-presence, given that the darkness of his denial still shadows the others. In each of the pairings, Peter is shown up badly as the one who gets things wrong.

At the Last Supper, John is chosen as the single insider — to be quietly told the truth of what is happening. Peter is left outside, confused and agitated. At the cross, John is trusted with the care of the mother. At the empty tomb, John shows true sacred fear, and *trusts*, whereas Peter rushes up, charges inside, stumbles around, sees nothing, then goes home. The final encounter, by the Sea of Galilee, focuses on the contrast between philia and agapē. The triple questioning of Peter represents a type of last judgment — that the only love of which he is capable is philia. John, like Magdalene, is already identified with agapē: it is the nature of the Master's own feeling towards him.

These pairings are carefully orchestrated by the narrator. They leave a richly toned picture of two contrasting modes of relationship between master and follower. Further, it is in tune with the composition as a whole that John is the 'other follower' in the second episode — the one who accompanies Peter after Gethsemane, and who knows the High Priest. In effect, he delivers Peter into the arms of his fate by introducing him to the servant girl keeping the door. John has her trust, as he does the trust of her master, the High Priest. If she recognises Peter as a follower, surely she recognises John, too. But John has no need to deny anything—he accompanies Jesus into the courtyard, so it is plain he is a follower.

The ease with which John passes from one enemy group to the other suggests that his presence is unthreatening. There is perhaps a youthful innocence to him, a lack of guile—perhaps a type of charisma that makes it difficult for others to think ill of him.

This midrash of Peter's denial has drawn out the inference in Mark that the servant girl confronts Peter, not because of the surface fact that he is a follower, but because she reads his character as deceitful and cowardly. She is alerted by his shiftiness, evoked in the story by his skulking along behind, and hanging round outside the door. Outraged at his denial—*I am not!*—she serves as an anonymous agent of the Master's truth. She instinctively understands hamartia, the unredeemable warp of this flawed being.

In other words, John has unwittingly led Peter to his doom. His role in this scene is more than it appears. He shares an affinity with the servant girl. Together they extend the exclusion of Peter that started, in John's text, at the Last Supper.

It is understandable that Peter should turn against John. The sequence of events in which they participate together provides fertile soil for envy. While Peter is bewilderingly obtuse, he does finally react. It comes at the very end, by the Sea of Galilee, after the triple grilling about philia, after he has been instructed to 'Follow!' His exit scene takes the form of an angry spasm. Peter turns around and sees the beloved follower. He snaps, 'But Master, this one, what about him?' He receives the petulant reply, 'If I want him to abide until I come, what is that to you? You, follow me.'

That the Master is irritated by Peter's question may suggest that he has picked up some hostility of intent. It is none of Peter's business what is required of John. The two of them belong to different orders of being.

These are the last words the Master speaks. The narrative ends with a two-headed reference. Peter is instructed, 'You, follow me.' John is addressed obliquely, 'If I want him to abide until I come.' The Greek verb for 'abide' — *menō* — can also mean 'stay', 'tarry', 'wait', or 'stand fast'.

In John's Story, the Last Supper is followed by four chapters of Jesus' teachings.[5] They open:

> In my father's house are many mansions ... And if I go and prepare a place for you, I will come again and receive you to myself. So that where **I am**, there you may also be ... **I am** the way, and the truth, and the life.

As *being* came into the world not born of woman, it departs not extinguished by death. It will return. Although absent, it will prepare the way. In the meantime, the indirect advice to John is simple. *There is nothing particularly you have to do. There is nowhere in particular you have to go. You do not need to change — to become something that you are not. There is no need, in your case, to reform being.* The strong inference is that John is fine as he is.

'Abide' is the climax to the five beloved-follower episodes. It suggests that John is at home in the world, at home in himself. In his opening scene, the casual ease with which he snuggled against the Master's chest implied a harmony in relation to *I am*. He moves smoothly into the domain of the High Priest. He is the only one of the twelve at the crucifixion. While fishing on the Sea of Galilee, he is the first of the seven to recognise the Master. This follows on directly, in his biography, or autobiography, from the conclusion to the empty-tomb scene. There, he was the one who finally saw, and trusted. Here, he is the one who sees clearly, like Magdalene.

If poise of *being* is what characterises John, there is little for the Master to say. In effect, his final words, triggered by Peter, are, 'Let him *be!*' In fact, these are exactly the last words he speaks about Mary of Bethany, in response to Judas — 'Let her be!'

Peter is told to follow and to serve: to build churches. This is not John's way. The one who abides in the mansion of *being* — who just *is* — becomes the storyteller. To do that, he must wait many years, even decades, perhaps till very late in a long life.[6] And the mansion of being is sited within, not at any human place of worship — whether up some holy mountain or in Jerusalem. This is precisely what the Master tells the Samaritan woman at the well: the only worship that counts is worship of 'pneuma the god'.[7]

D id John write the fourth Life of Jesus? Today, most scholars assume not.[8] They read the last chapter, recording the encounter with the seven followers by the Sea of Galilee, as an epilogue, appended to the narrative proper. Yet there is no textual evidence for this — the 'epilogue' is included in all early manuscripts. Raymond E. Brown speculates, with others, that the fourth Gospel is the outcome of one among a number of traditions of Jesus stories, and that the 'beloved disciple' was the source of this tradition. He was a minor follower, not one of the twelve. One of the beloved disciple's own followers then wrote it, later on.[9] This is sheer guesswork.

The final chapter adds substantive content to the story. The happenings beside the Sea of Galilee are essential completions to the portraits of both Peter and John. This is not an epilogue. It is not some tacked-on afterthought. It is a finale.

The Master's final words were, 'If I want him to abide until I come, what is that to you. You, follow me.' Immediately after them, the narrator adds, referring to 'him':

> This is the follower who testifies to these things, and wrote
> them, and we know that his testimony is true.

The beloved follower says he wrote the fourth Life. He does so in a carefully scripted ending, which is a necessary and well-integrated part of the whole. There is an authorial virtuosity here beyond the talent of a hack editor. Why should he be doubted?

The case for John's authenticity is strengthened by comparison with Mark. The writer has wrestled from the beginning with the first Life, seeking to digest the cryptic signs that show the way so as to provide his own version of the *truth light*. And, like Mark, he signals his own identity indirectly. Neither storyteller names himself.

Mark's narrator leaves a series of obscure clues to his identity through the text. John's midrash of this is not to include the sons of Zebedee among the twelve until his last chapter. This omission is striking, given the prominence of the favoured three in all Synoptic accounts. It plants a seed of suspicion.

Both narrators are young men, with the implication of innocence, or purity of character. In the one case, there is the composite portrait of Legion, a fleeing young man stripped bare of concealing clothing, and one dressed in white linen. In the other, there is the trusted follower who comes to trust—enshrined in agapē.

There are parallels with the differing representations of Jesus. Just as Mark's Jesus is unsure of his way and emotionally volatile, his narrator incorporates within himself the wildness of Legion, the panicky flight of the naked young man, and the achieved calm inside the empty tomb. In contrast, John's Jesus is composed and magisterial, and his narrator is steady and resolute. And just as there is an explosive existential drama binding master and writer in Mark, so there is the constancy of the shared bond of agapē in John. The beloved follower is the human counterpart to Jesus—becoming his mother's son.

As the beloved follower has the key vantage-point at the Last Supper, in order to tell the story from the inside, he is present at the crucifixion. This is John's most radical departure from the Synoptic accounts. Mark's Jesus dies alone. There is no one to whom he has been close—followers or family—in the vicinity of the Cross. In John's version the intimates are all present: Magdalene, the beloved follower, as well as his mother. Jesus calmly organises his surrogate family.

The alternative crucifixion stories fit the contrasting portraits of the Master. They also fit the differing portraits of the special follower as storyteller. Mark flits around in the outer shadows of the action, only finding his bearings at the very end when he takes centre-stage inside the empty tomb. He addresses the reader, person to person.

John leaves himself out of the story until the Last Supper—where he becomes a major figure. He is suddenly and dramatically present, thereafter cumulatively increasing his authority to tell the story. *One* replaces the Synoptic *three*. He being the one, and only one, loved by the Master, spotlights his unique status. Not naming himself serves as a method to create mystery-loaded legitimacy. It is tactful. As Nietzsche put it, 'Whatever is profound loves masks.'

The chosen follower as insider then closes the narrative by switching the focus to himself. He is the new embodiment of *being.* One commentator has called him 'the most profound theological personality of the New Testament'.[10]

Let him *be!* The beloved follower is companion to Magdalene. The fruit of his experience will be to tell the story; her gift was *touch.* His lesson seems to hinge on learning to know *being,* so as to tell its story. It follows that there are two sacred gifts: the power of touch and the power of storytelling. They symbolise everything that matters. Agapē is common to both.

The John example speaks to every individual at the time of metaphysical judgment, on those days spent in reflection about oneself and one's life. The common pathway in search of bearings, some dignity, and a vindication is off the mark. Forget all such life-questions as: *What have I achieved? What have I learnt? Who have I become? What do I believe?* Answers to such questions are without significance. There is only one existential testimony that matters: *I know that I am!* Anyone who can truthfully speak their own ease of *being,* with surety, as the single and essential knowing, says enough. They verify an island of calm within the ocean of eternity.

The beloved follower is the one who abides. He dwells in the mansion of being. Invisible until needed at the Last Supper, his role there was simply to recline close by, listen, and watch. After Gethsemane he does no more than accompany the Master and get Peter admitted to the High Priest's house. At the crucifixion he is the intimate bystander. On the Sunday morning his role is again one of witness. And on the Galilee beach all he does is recognise the Master and overhear the reprimand to Peter, 'Let him *be!*' He needs no instruction. He is a lesson in simply being there, open and alert.

The story signals this leading motif in its opening chapter (verse 38). The first two followers mentioned are Andrew and an unnamed one—likely John himself. Jesus asks, as they tag along behind him, 'What are you seeking?' They respond, 'Master, where do you dwell?' They use the same Greek verb *menō*, which equally means 'abide'. So the key question is established at the outset.

John is the insider who does not need a traumatic initiation. He is the prototypal human — as truth-light *being*. As such, there is no need for metamorphosis — he is not a Magdalene. Nor is he borderline *I am* — not a Pilate. His story is one of emerging slowly as he learns. There is an ease to his being in the world, although he looks on, from intimate proximity, at the events that determine his life with a mixture of searching and dread. What he sees drives him to retell the story.

What does it mean to tell the story? How can John's particular achievement be generalised to other humans living their very different lives? Make sure you are there, his example proclaims, in intimate proximity. His instruction is to abide, to dwell, to wait — and to watch! Your psychic orientation is also given — that of agapē, questioning with reverence and dread. Then retell the story, just as I — John — retell Mark's story. Retell the story from within yourself, from within your own particular *being* emerging from the shadows, at your own Last Supper. Abide in the darkness until you start to see. Then, when the time comes, transcribe what has been given, what it is that oscillates around your kairos hour.

What I have written, I have written.

THE TWO DEATHS

Humans die two deaths. They live two lives. Two dwell in one. I don't mean here that they die twice, although they may. Augustine held that to be possible, with the soul sometimes dying before the body. Likewise, a kairos death may happen long before the chronos end. The Story has rather left the imprint of two distinct types of human death.

Jesus is twofold. There are two crucifixions. There are two Passions—that is, two modes of experience and suffering. The end of the metaphysical road that governs every life diverges, as if one way plunges into a dark tunnel and the other rises, magisterially, up onto an overpass.

Mark's Jesus comes first. His life reaches its consummation in tragedy—a godless and profane one—and a great death scream from the cross, questioning the sense of it all. Everything he has tried and everything he has suffered has been for … what? In rising anger at the rapidly approaching kairos hour, he had withered the healthy fig down to a black stump. *Over there, by this road winding from Bethany up to Jerusalem, that is me and my fate*, he seemed to proclaim. Then, collapsing to the ground in the pitch-black olive grove, in the misery and woe of forsakenness, he cursed his leading followers to sleep the big sleep. His exit from life drove him through pressing crowds who were out of their exploding minds with hatred, chanting, 'Crucify him! Crucify him!' Up on the cross, his only companion was the darkness that came over the land at noon, three hours in. Nature's order showed sympathy, its eerie black silence portending the gale of avenging pneuma that would rise over the Jerusalem hills with the last echo of his death bellow.

This is the first, and tragic, death. It projects its own logic backwards across the life that precedes it. The life will only make sense if the death does. As in the Story, what comes before it is a prelude — the way into the death Passion.

In life as lived, it may not seem like this. Peter stepped out of ordinary life as a husband and fisherman to follow the Master. But once he gained a sighting of the new way, he stumbled in fear. He then attempted to return to his old life, catching fish by the Sea of Galilee.

The second death, as the second life, is John's Jesus. It develops out of the first. The Master enters, shining. He begins his mission by reluctantly turning wedding water into wine, then evicts the unholy humans and their profane goods from the Jerusalem Temple. Through all of the pivotal, impression-point scenes, he directs events with deliberate precision. This holds for his teaching of Mary by bringing Lazarus back to life; using the Last Supper to choose Judas; turning the encounter with Pilate into a truth trial of the Roman governor; completing Magdalene's initiation in the garden with the touch-me-not transmission of being; and the final directions given to Peter and John by the Sea of Galilee.

There are occasional tremors of emotion, as with the angry snort at Mary of Bethany, or the request that Judas do what he has to do quickly. But they do not disrupt the abiding sense of a man in command of his destiny.

This Story is not tragic. Death is incidental. From the Cross he ties up loose surrogate-family ends. There is no suggestion of

Mark's *forsakenness*. In this version, there has been no agony in the garden; there is no death scream. The crucifixion itself is of minor impact in the narrative; apart from his brief exchange with his mother, it is little more than a punctuation mark separating the Pilate episode from the meeting with Magdalene afterwards.

When the Master asserts, '*I am*. Don't fear', the words come with a calming authority. They do not induce the big fear over stormy water. While his teaching centres on himself, he stands apart from it. And his presence is strangely uninterrupted by death. It comes with little surprise to the reader when he appears at Sunday dawn in the Garden, or later by the Sea of Galilee. *I am* carries the poise of eternity.

Pneuma the god has been his companion, providing a cocoon of inspired being, both in this life and beyond. For those he walks among on earth, his presence is formidable, stopping them in their normal tracks, overawing their minds. Yet the nucleus of his being seems to hover outside the human plane. So he is not beset by normal fears of the *hour*, or of approaching *not-being*. Mortality is unproblematic for John's Jesus.

He leaves three parting gifts. Pilate is given a glimpse of Truth — and he begins to write with authority. Magdalene is given the 'touch me not' interdiction, forbidding attachment, so that she, from out of the love which is her element, may, in the end, turn into him. She is an angel of agapē — and *daimōn*. John is told simply to be who he is. In time, the beloved follower will tell the story.

Humans lead two parallel lives: one tragic, one eternal. Balance is everything. Here is the deepest of metaphysical truths. For many, the first, tragic death seems to be overwhelming, if only unconsciously, terrorising everyday life with its vagrant anxieties.

Magdalene experiences tragic death herself, then finds the

threshold of the higher death: she is there at first light, then swings backwards and forwards between weeping/clinging and touching/glorying. What happens in her mundane after-life is left open. Some have imagined her gaining the power, like Legion, and going out into the world as emissary, as servant — the saint of touch. Others, notably Donatello, have meditated on her later being, and found it an agony of self-negation, straining to become the one she has lost.

There are other paths, ones that lose their way before reaching the clearing in which the two deaths await. Death is not at issue for Judas, for he is so consumed by his lack in life. Hamlet, a Judas minus Jesus, has no one to guide him, therefore no one to envy, and is just depressed by his *I am not* — or, as he puts it, 'not to be'. Although he talks a lot about death, what he longs for is a final oblivion to anaesthetise the pain of living. Both Judas and Hamlet exit into night. Death, in neither of the Big Story senses, is for them.

Pilate comes close to achieving the second, higher death. With his dying breath — murmuring 'Billy Budd! Billy Budd!' — he reaches up for the truth-light.

John is born in tune with the higher death. There is a dimension of other-worldly innocence to him — in contrast with the earthiness that predominates in the young Magdalene. We meet him — the beloved one — snuggling up against the Master at the Last Supper. He witnesses, from close by, the dread of the Judas betrayal, Peter's denial, and the crucifixion of his teacher. He needed this education into what humans do — how vile and weak they can be. Otherwise he would not comprehend Mark, digest what he had written, and be able to elaborate it later, in his own way.

The Story is the seed. And what a seed! Out of the dark, over two millennia, it has generated vast kingdoms of enchantment.

For instance, today, in a largely dechurched West, Christmas for children remains beautiful and inspired—with re-enactments of the birth in the Bethlehem manger, three wise men from the east, and shepherds guided by a star, all accompanied by joyfully reverent carols.

> Silent night, holy night;
> All is calm, all is bright
> Round yon virgin mother and child.
> Holy infant so tender and mild,
> Sleep in heavenly peace.
> Sleep in heavenly peace.

The magical fantasy of the birth is a corrective to the harrowing story of the existential Jesus. Children attempt the Homeric, *Odyssey* approach to life—as fun and adventure, ending in a death that comes, hopefully, 'as mild as air'.

But, in the West, such lightness of *being* depends on the vitality source. It was Mark who found and tapped that source. He gave shape to the *mystery*. The Story, in the beginning, is the fathomless reservoir of energy—surging, irrepressible—out of which the culture and its civilisation was made. What empires of stone and mind have been built in prolific midrashes of the Jesus essence!

One of the lessons has been that the story will only work for the person who manages to retell it from within, making it their own. I am a witness to this process, and to the effect that retelling the story may have. Once the idea came to me to write this book, the texts—Mark and, subordinately, John—took over. They drove me. My working method was simply to put my head down, fashioning the detail, trying to get the form right. The journey was comparatively smooth. By the end, the one conspicuous surprise for me is that I have gained little detachment—indeed, as much as one can be sure about these obscure things, none at all. Once having entered the task, and become immersed in it, I don't seem able to climb back outside. I have little idea of what I have done as the author—whether it has worked, or even what that might mean. I am in there, down inside, with only the dim sense that I have been captured by a long and complete dark saying.

The two deaths fuse in John's Last Supper. They become one. Let us imagine what it was like in that Jerusalem upper room on the Thursday night. Nicholas Poussin, the painter, helps us to picture the scene in his *Last Supper*, which now hangs in Edinburgh.

In the darkened room, the backdrop stirs—the curtain closing off the rear. Lamp-light flickers dimly over the gathering. Twelve men are reclining, Roman-style, around a low table set with bread and wine. No one eats or drinks. The Master, at the centre, holds the poisoned cup up, cushioning it in his left, upturned palm—its crucible form forward, as if floating in the midst of the scene, attracting the cone of light, its bounded circles signalling the closure of the script. In the thickening, brooding hush, all is set, determined, trapped inside time, like this closed upper room.

He points with his right index finger back, at himself. No longer is there any beyond. The after-tremor will come soon, later this night in Gethsemane, when he affirms, '*I am!*' and everyone falls down.

At the table, Peter reels backwards, away from the Master, afraid that he is the betrayer. 'Not I?' he stammers. Judas has already risen and left the circle. He heads for the door, his back to the others, choking on the wine-soaked morsel. He is about to plunge into night.

Pneuma the god works its elusive spell. It eddies around the room, ebbing and flowing, brushing the curtain, threatening to snuff out the light, then flaring it up — flaming. One moment it concentrates near the door, a wind vortex sucking the life out of Judas, suffocating him. The next it sits still, compressed, over the cup, bathing the Master in its eerie serenity. The others are left gasping for breath.

John, the beloved follower, knows. He lurches upright, his body rigid, mouth dropping open, freezing with the horror — at Judas leaving, at his ten fellows agog with uncomprehending fear, and at his own rush of imaginings of what is about to happen. Dread of the kairos hour is reflected in his witnessing face.

He sees, in a blur, his Master close by, the man, the hovering cup, the pointing hand. Yet something is different about him — something is wrong. His eyes have retracted into a distant unknown, deep within himself, yet out and away. He is no longer here. A phantasm presides at the table. Solitary unto itself, it has withdrawn its attention completely from anyone else in the room, from everything else. Yet somehow it remains, a concentrated presence, an eternal luminous thereness, as John fathoms it in the gloom.

In the shadows, looking on and serving, is the youthful Mark, robed in white linen, the storyteller to be — the first of four to come.

When Mark came to write the story, he adapted this scene and projected it into the empty tomb. There, inside the dark, it was the same Last Supper enigma of presence and absence. The young narrator, like a spectre clothed in supernatural white, appearing from nowhere, welcomed the reader. And he calmly urged that there was no cause for alarm.

ACKNOWLEDGMENTS

Many have assisted me with this book, directly and indirectly.

The La Trobe Reading Group has made a singular contribution, in its collective reading, chapter by chapter, of books from the Bible. I am especially indebted to the members of the 1998 and 2003 groups who read Mark; and those of the 2001 and 2006 groups who read John.

The following read the manuscript at different stages of its development and made helpful comments: Wendy Bowler, Anna Branford, Chris Cheah, Nigel Cooper, Stephen Crittenden, Mary Cunnane, Richard Gill, Peter Murphy, Mike Richards, Ian Roberts, and Sally Warhaft.

My daughter, Khadija, made several strategic interventions. My partner, Eva, has been a constant and discerning companion throughout the course of writing.

The staff at Scribe has contributed its distinctive cheerfulness and high competence. Henry Rosenbloom, the publisher, has combined vision and enthusiasm for the book with scrupulous editing of the text. As always, it has been a pleasure to work with him. And a special thanks to Sandy Cull, the cover designer.

NOTES

The Enigma of Being

1 J. D. Denniston and D. L. Page, *Aeschylus Agamemnon*, Oxford University Press, Oxford, 1957, pp. 169–70. Paul uses *ainigma* in his famous phrase translated in the King James Bible as 'through a glass darkly' (I Corinthians 13: 12). Tyndale had rendered it 'in a glass even in dark speaking'. 'Dark saying' has the advantage over 'dark speaking' of incorporating the suggestion of riddle or aphorism.

2 This is Nietzsche's formulation, in the theory of culture developed in his *The Birth of Tragedy*.

3 The turn of philosophy back to *being* was led by Martin Heidegger.

4 Gallup polled regular American church attendance at 35 per cent in December 2004. However, this was a poll-based survey — asking people themselves about their behaviour — rather than a count-based one registering numbers entering the church doors. Sociologists have calculated that poll figures for church attendance should be discounted by as much as a half, to take account of the degree to which people exaggerate or lie on this subject — whether out of guilt, self-deception, or in the belief they will help the local church by claiming they attend regularly when they don't.

For instance, C. Kirk Hadaway and P. L. Morler studied Protestant and Catholic attendance counts and found the rate at about half the poll figure ('Did You Really Go to Church This Week? Behind the Poll Data', *The Christian Century*, 6 May 1998). Hadaway's 2005 figure is 21 per cent regular attendance (private communication).

What we may conclude is that between 17 per cent and 25 per cent of Americans regularly attend church in the early years of the twenty-first century.

5 In Australia, the 2001 National Church Life Survey put the weekly attendance at Christian churches as 8.8 per cent of the total population

(*2001 Church Attendance Estimates*, Occasional Paper No. 3, J. Bellamy and K. Castle, February 2004). The Catholic component was 15 per cent of Catholics attending weekly, which equates to 4 per cent of the total population. This figure seems pretty reliable, as it was based on comprehensive surveying of parishes across the country over four weeks (information from Bob Dixon, director of Pastoral Projects Office of the Australian Catholic Bishops Conference). The Protestant figures appear more vulnerable, and need discounting. We may conclude that between 6 per cent and 8 per cent of the Australian population attended a Christian church weekly in 2001. The figure is declining.

The British figure looks like roughly 5 per cent, with France and Germany lower again.

6 Bloom, *Jesus and Yahweh*, p. 64.

7 I have explored this search for secular altars in the everyday world in an earlier book, *Ego and Soul: the Modern West in Search of Meaning*.

8 I shall be using the Fourth Revised Edition, from 1994. This is the United Bible Societies Greek New Testament edition, derived from the famous Nestle–Aland edition, first printed in 1898.

9 The two significant changes since the time of the King James translation are the excision of John's story of the woman taken in adultery, and of the second half of Mark's final chapter (16: 9–20). Neither appears in the earliest manuscripts.

10 R. E. Brown assumes some time in the 60s or just after 70AD. He assumes that Matthew and Luke wrote ten to 20 years after Mark, and John between 90 and 100 (*An Introduction to the New Testament*, p. 7).

11 Moloney, *Mark*, pp. 7 and 9.

12 Aristotle uses *mythos* in a narrower sense in his theory of tragedy (*Poetics*, s. 1450). *Muthos* means the narrative plot — the synthesis of doings, or, differently put, the combination of actions (*sunthesin tōn pragmatōn*). Aristotle holds *muthos* to be the foundation (*archē*) and soul (*psuchē*) of tragedy — in contrast with the other elements of individual character (*ēthos*) and thinking (*dianoia*).

Aristotle held Homer to be the master of tragedy.

13 L. T. Johnson, 'The Quest for the Historical Jesus', in Crossan, J. D., Johnson, L. T. & Kelber, W. H., *The Jesus Controversy*, p. 89.

14 Wilde, p. 929.

15 R. E. Brown, *An Introduction to the New Testament*, pp. 153–4.

16 Bultmann, *Theology of the New Testament*, vol. 1, p. 4.

17 Harold Bloom, *Shakespeare*, Riverhead, New York, 1998, pp. xviii–xix.

18 Bloom, *Jesus and Yahweh*, p. 65.

19 To provide just one indicator, Stephen Prothero records that in 2003 the American Library of Congress held 17,000 or so books about Jesus, the figure mounting rapidly. It was twice as many as on the runner-up, Shakespeare (p. 11).

1. The Sower

1 Transliteration from the Greek script will follow the convention used in *The New Shorter Oxford English Dictionary*, 1993.

2 In fact, in the early manuscripts all words are written wholly in uppercase, with the first letter undistinguished.

3 The Greek original for 'unsound pneuma' is *pneuma akatharton*, with 'uncatharted' usually translated as 'unclean'. It may equally imply 'impure', 'unfree', or 'unsound'. Aristotle uses catharsis in his theory of tragedy in the sense, close to that in modern English, of a purging of emotions — especially fear.

4 John 3:8 and 4: 24.

5 Bultmann stresses that the Jesus of the Gospels lived as a Jewish rabbi, or teacher: 'He was called, so to speak, "Professor", "learned Doctor".' The implication is that he had been formally schooled as a teacher. His disciples are more accurately described as pupils, with whom he disputed questions of the Law (*Jesus and the Word*, pp. 57–61).

J. R. Donahue observes that Mark's Gospel makes far more reference than the other two synoptics to Jesus as a teacher. Yet it contains far less actual teaching of Jesus ('Jesus as the Parable of God in the Gospel of Mark', *Interpretation*, 32 (1978), p. 373).

6 Crossan, *Jesus*, p. 26.

7 Isaiah's meaning was straightforward: under God's instruction to make 'not understanding' and 'not perceiving' a punishment on the evil people (Isaiah 6: 9–12). Matthew laboriously rationalises Mark back to Isaiah, then for double measure he contrasts the disciples with the outsiders — 'blessed are your eyes for they see, and your ears for they hear' (13: 13–17). Thus he erases Mark's enigma and inverts his meaning.

8 Kermode makes this point (pp. 29–30).

9 Mary Ann Tolbert picks up the link of Peter with stony ground (pp. 145–6, 154–6).

10 Matthew, ever seeking to normalise Mark, excising enigma and fear, downplays the significance of the sower parable by placing it much later in his narrative — in the thirteenth of twenty-eight chapters. He makes *Petros* the rock on which the church will be built (16:18).

11 Mark 1: 29–31.

12 The Greek noun, *pistis,* rendered here as 'trust', is almost always translated in the New Testament as 'faith' or 'belief'. 'Trust' is equally legitimate. It more faithfully reflects the tenor of the teaching of Mark's existential Jesus. And it avoids the deadening effect that church doctrine has had on both words, 'faith' and 'belief'.

13 Throughout, *grammateis* will be translated as 'intellectuals'. The orthodox translation is 'scribes'. The Greek means clerks, secretaries, or those who write, but with the possible inflection of letters and learning. The Jewish 'scribe' was an interpreter and teacher of the religious texts, a scholar.

   The French, *clerc,* carries with it the parallel range of associations from clerk to cleric to intellectual. Julien Benda's 1929 polemic, *La Trahison des clercs,* was translated into English as *The Treason of the Intellectuals.* 'Scribe' is archaic, apart from its obscure Biblical resonance.

14 Michael Murphy uses it in this sense — off the target — in relation to golf and to life in a chapter titled 'The Hamartiology of Golf' (*Golf in the Kingdom*, Penguin, New York, 1997).

15 This image of the tree is from Simone Weil ('Human Personality', included in *The Simone Weil Reader*, ed. George A. Panichas, David McKay, New York, 1977, p. 328).

16 Mark's sequence has been reordered in this passage. The teaching about profaning pneuma comes after the healings, just before the parable of the sower.

17 Matthew will repicture Jesus as a moral teacher — principally through the inclusion of the lengthy Sermon on the Mount. Matthew thereby normalises Jesus as a more conventional religious leader.

18 The linking of fear and pneuma is, at this point in the story, an extrapolation. It will be filled out when Jesus crosses the sea for the second time with the twelve.

19 There are two other early healings, of a man with unsound pneuma and a leper; they have only a minor dramatic impact within the narrative.

20 Frank Kermode interprets Mark's text as structured on 'impression points' (p. 16). The term comes originally from Wilhelm Dilthey, the German being *Eindruckspunkt,* a biographical point or feature from which the whole form, or *gestalt,* of a person's life may be derived.

21 In this he is like Hamlet. Indeed, Hamlet, best known by his inward and gloomy monologues, may be taken as one of the greatest midrashes of Mark's Jesus.

22 J. D. Crossan notes another possible mustard tree association. In the Mediterranean region the wild mustard propagates vigorously and is hard to contain (*Jesus*, p. 65).

2. Fearing the Great Fear

1 The Greek *kurios* has traditionally been translated as 'Lord'. Wherever in the text the term relates to Jesus I render it by the equally legitimate translation, 'Master'. 'Chief' or 'principal' might also be used. 'Master' carries an allied resonance to the main term of reference Mark uses for Jesus — 'teacher'.

2 I have chosen to translate the Greek noun *eleos* as 'empathy'. It also carries a range of associations to 'compassion', 'pity', and 'mercy'.

3 It is the 'power' (*dunamis*) that goes out of him — the strength, might, or force. Towards the end of the story he will refer to himself, sitting near the 'power' — not near God.

4 Plato introduced the category of 'right fear' — a person should be taught what to fear, that there are transgressions of laws that are shameful and unforgivable (*The Laws*, book I, 647a–d).

5 A prototypical example of 'initiation' in the anthropological literature is that of the Australian Aborigines — see, for instance, Robert Tonkinson (ch. 4).

6 This will develop into the folklore of Salomé and the dance of seven veils. Ernest Renan, in his *Life of Jesus*, assumed Salomé was naked, and argues that a dance like this was accepted in nearby Syria as appropriate when performed for a distinguished person (p. 208). It is a common scholarly reading that the dance was sexually provocative. Joel Marcus assumes that Salomé was, at the time, an unmarried teenager (pp. 394–401).

   A number of scholars have noted that, on the one hand, it is not plausible that a Herodian princess would have been allowed to demean herself by dancing at court; on the other, that the court was secular and notoriously decadent, and so anything was possible.

7 Herodias was a granddaughter of Herod the Great and, consequently, her marriage to Herod Antipas — one of Herod's sons — bordered on incest. John the Baptist was thus echoing a popular view. It was common in the irreligious family of the Herods to intermarry. There is further suggestion that the historical Herodias was violent and ambitious, despising Judaism and its laws, while her second husband was weak.

8 Euripides explores this in his final play, *The Bacchae*.

9 For example, Titian: *Salomé with the Head of John the Baptist, and Herodias*, c.1560–70. The complex of castration and male masochism, sometimes combined with homosexual motifs, is also illustrated in the two other beheading stories commonly depicted in painting and sculpture: Judith and Holofernes (examples by Donatello, Veronese, and Caravaggio)

and David and Goliath (examples by Donatello, Verrocchio, and Caravaggio). The theory linking beheading with castration, and castration anxiety, was developed by Freud.

10 Crossan's view is that John the Baptist was an 'apocalyptic prophet' in the classical Jewish mode, announcing 'the imminent advent of an avenging God' (*Jesus*, p. 38). As such, he was not at all a precursor of Jesus. Herod Antipas acted against him because of the apocalyptic hopes he was stimulating in the people.

11 Kierkegaard, in his theory of the three stages — the aesthetic, the ethical, and the religious — argues that passion is only found in the third stage (*Fear and Trembling*, p. 130). For an outline of the theory of the three stages, see my *The Wreck of Western Culture* (ch. 10).

12 Luke will midrash the walking-on-water scene into his powerful post-Resurrection story of the encounter between an unrecognised Jesus and two men on the Road to Emmaus.

13 Kierkegaard, *Fear and Trembling*, p. 76.

14 Kelber makes this point (p. 37).

15 This is Kermode's conclusion in relation to a later numerological puzzle in Mark (p. 46). Kermode uses the analogy of the riddle of how to fit five elephants into a Volkswagen, noting that it is only when you stop thinking about the obvious thing — size — that the answer becomes clear: two in the front and three in the back. Legions of other scholars have fallen for the trap of trying to make sense of the numbers in this feeding parable, and in a sequel in which Jesus feeds four thousand. For example, Kelber (ch. 2) identifies the five thousand as Jews and the four thousand as Gentiles.

16 Legion's address to the Master, 'son of the highest god', is Hellenistic not Jewish terminology, as if his link is to the Greek divinities. The Gerasene region south-east of the Sea of Galilee that Legion came from was largely non-Jewish. Hence the herd of pigs.

17 Henry James introduces the category of 'sacred rage' in his novel *The Ambassadors* — see my *The Wreck of Western Culture* (ch. 12).

3. Fire on the Mountain

1 A film of 1995, titled *Dead Man Walking*, drew on the same lineage.

2 John's midrash of the healing of the blind man continues this doubling-up of identity. The man who was born blind is the prototype for humans at their best. He has spent his life sitting and begging — a metaphor for ordinary, profane *being*. Once he receives sight he knows, and proclaims in response to queries about his identity, '*I am!*' He is the

only one in either of Mark's or John's Life, apart from Jesus, who says this of himself. He goes on to teach with confidence and authority.

3 I Corinthians 13:12. Paul's words are themselves a variant of Mark 8:24 on seeing men like trees walking.

4 Many scholars have accepted that Mark's Jesus does not call himself the *messiah*. This recognition has generated an interpretation of Mark's strategy that came to be known as the 'Messianic secret', initiated by Wilhelm Wrede in 1901. Wrede makes the distinction between the belief of later followers that Jesus was the messiah and the non-messianic earthly Jesus. The messianic understanding of Jesus comes as a result of the Resurrection (Wrede, pp. 229–36). Bultmann concludes, 'The synoptic tradition leaves no doubt about it that *Jesus' life and work* measured by traditional messianic ideas *was not messianic.*' (*Theology of the New Testament*, vol. 1, p. 27)

Kelber notes that while it is initially unclear to the reader whether Peter's, 'You are the Christ.' is an accurate identification, by the end of the episode Mark has made it clear that it is not (ch.3).

5 The modern scholarly consensus is that (1) 'son of man' is a genuine Jesus usage; (2) it is not derived from Old Testament sources although there is a hint of precedent in Daniel; (3) it is awkward in Greek and does not draw on Hellenistic sources. By contrast, there is much scholarly doubt about the authenticity of the terms 'messiah' and 'Son of God', reading them as later additions to the texts rather than terms used by Jesus himself. For an overview of the 'son of man' literature see R. E. Brown, *The Death of the Messiah*, pp. 506–15. Brown is puzzled as to what the term might mean.

By the way, the conclusion that 'son of man' is unGreek is questionable, given that the common way of naming heroes in Homer's *Iliad* is 'son of x' — a means for respecting the father's glory.

Crossan interprets 'son of man' as a low-key expression meaning little more than 'mortal' (*Jesus*, pp. 49–53). Miles makes the same point, arguing that both classical Hebrew and Aramaic are weak in adjectives, so 'son of man' is simply a way of saying 'human being' (p. 35).

6 Mark 3: 28.

7 In English this episode is known as The Transfiguration. The Greek verb is *metamorphoō* — to change, transform, or transfigure.

8 There are exceptions among the Christian churches, notably in the Pentecostalist tradition.

9 Exodus 14:19–26. Poussin, in his painting of the *Crossing of the Red Sea* (c.1635) in Melbourne, reverses the links, using the surface story of Moses saving his people from Egyptian captivity as the turning point

for the birth of Christian Shining. His black cloud both curses Moses and prepares the way for the new order, led by a Mary figure and a baby redeemer.

10 Matthew will spend a lot of effort countering Mark's non-Jewish Jesus, restoring links with the Hebrew heritage. Crossan reads Matthew and Luke as the 'messiah' gospels (*Jesus*, p. 19).

11 There is Old Testament precedent in that the skin of Moses' face shines when he comes down the mountain after receiving the tablets of the Ten Commandments (Exodus 34: 29, 35). There are Greek precedents, too, starting with Homer, who frequently has gods or goddesses bathing their favourite heroes in golden light, making them seem more than human.

12 Bloom, *Jesus and Yahweh*, p. 60.

13 In *The Transfiguration*, Raphael includes Peter twice. While he appears with James and John up the mountain, his major role is in the lower left foreground, where he sits in a precariously unstable position (that is, stumbles) straddling water — his medium. He is counterpoised to the mad boy, whom he is failing to cure. And he is visually paired, in identification, with Moses and his law — they also look alike, and Peter holds open a large book.

Here is yet another signal of the sheer metaphysical brilliance of Raphael, arguably the first person after Mark and John with deep insight into the story they tell.

4. The Black Stump

1 Kelber, p. 58. My interpretation of the entry into Jerusalem episode has affinities with that of Kelber.

2 Zechariah 9:9.

3 A reading supported by the midrash into Sancho Panza and his donkey, starring in arguably the most brilliant comic-serious creation in Western literature, *Don Quixote* (1604;1614). John Ford will also use the comic-serious play of the man riding on the donkey in his film tribute to the American Abraham, *Young Mr Lincoln* (1939).

4 Depicted, for instance, in Titian's painting of *Bacchus and Ariadne* (1522).

5 Kelber, p. 62 .

6 Crossan notes precedents for the Mount of Olives being used as a base for an invading army from which to attack Jerusalem (*Jesus*, p. 42).

7 Deuteronomy 6: 4–5 and Leviticus 19: 18.

8 Daniel 7: 13–14.

9 The woman in Bethany and the preceding 'watch' incantation combine to generate a sequence of great Renaissance midrashes in the theme of the *Annunciation* — with the young virgin Mary the one who understands how to bide her time while she watches. For example, Poussin's 1657 *Annunciation* in the National Gallery in London.

10 Michael D. Gouldner, *Luke — a New Paradigm*, Sheffield Academic Press, Sheffield, 1989, p. 399.

11 Matthew too picks up the association, in his account having Judas paid thirty pieces of silver — exactly a tenth of the value of the perfume.

5. And It Was Night

1 The words with which John ends his account of the Last Supper, as Judas exits into endless night — *ēn de nux*.

2 Zechariah 13: 7.

3 On whether to translate the Greek verb *aparnesthai* as 'deny' or 'disown', see R. E. Brown, *The Death of the Messiah*, p. 137.

4 'Enough' in this speech translates the Greek word *apechei*. This word has troubled scholars. On some of the range of possible translations, see R. E. Brown, *The Death of the Messiah*, pp. 1379–83.

5 Raymond Chandler will use the phrase, in his novella titled *The Big Sleep*. The title is a midrash of Mark, as is the construction, adapting 'fear the great fear'.

6 Mark does not have her explicitly kissing him. Luke takes what is implicit in the anointing of the head with precious oil to cast Mary Magdalene as prostrate at his feet, wiping them with her hair and kissing them.

7 A Caravaggio-style painting of *Peter's Denial*, attributed to Pensionante del Saraceni, held in the Vatican Museum, underscores the age difference, and brilliantly projects the girl's outrage.

8 Erich Auerbach, in his book *Mimesis*, suggests that there are a number of aspects of Mark's story of Peter's Denial that are quite new in literature — including the focus on common people rather than the upper classes (pp. 40–9).

9 The Biblical scholars range in their opinion of the disciples. Many seek to save them by one means or another. Kelber does not. The most influential recognition of the disciples' unredeemable state is that of Weeden, who sums up:

'I conclude that Mark is assiduously involved in a vendetta against the disciples. He is intent on totally discrediting them. He paints them as obtuse, obdurate, recalcitrant men who at first are unperceptive of Jesus' messiahship, then oppose its style and character, and finally totally reject it. As the *coup de grace*, Mark closes his Gospel without rehabilitating the disciples.' (pp. 50–1)

10 Joseph Conrad will midrash some secular aspects of the young man, in his novella *Heart of Darkness* (1899), into the harlequin, an enigmatic young Russian dressed in a coat of many colours—the only character in the story who can move at will, freely, through the African jungle.

11 Kermode devotes a chapter to 'the boy in the shirt' (ch. 3).

12 The English word composed from the Greek, *melas*—black and *cholē*—anger or bile.

13 Mark does not specify that it is a garden. He refers to a 'place' called Gethsemane, which by implication is on or near the Mount of Olives. Of the four canonical storytellers, it is only John who will refer to a garden, where Jesus often went, and where he goes after the Last Supper, and in which he is betrayed and arrested. John does not name it.

   R. E. Brown concludes, 'One may assume that on the Mount of Olives there was a plot of land or garden with olive trees and an oil press, bearing the name Gethsemane.' (*The Death of the Messiah*, p. 149.)

14 *Paschō* projects a range of meanings: to happen to a person; to experience, whether good or bad; to suffer. Thus it contains within itself the equation of living (which depends on experiencing) with suffering. If you want to live, rather than vegetate in oblivion, suffering is at the core of experience.

15 Holbein uses the image of the skull in his huge painting *The Ambassadors* (1533) to put the challenge of death to humanist culture—see my *The Wreck of Western Culture* (ch. 3). Carpaccio, in a painting of the *Christ Entombment*, shows the corpse laid out on a marble slab on ground littered with skulls and skeletons. In this case, the Christ is serene, triumphant over the nihilism of death.

16 So Hamlet meditates on the meaning of death—and life—with the skull of the court jester, Yorick, in his hands.

17 Bach will evoke the dark, melancholic tones of precisely this moment in his cantata, *Ich Habe Genug*, the title translating literally from the German as 'I have enough.'

6. The Empty Tomb

1 One of many Greek parallels, or influences, is that *The Iliad* ends with three grieving women at a burial, that of Hektor—Crossan, 'Historical

Jesus as Risen Lord', in Crossan, Johnson & Kelber, *The Jesus Controversy*, p. 27.

This story, like *The Iliad*, ends with a funeral. Here, it is a strange obituary delivered from an empty tomb—symbol of non-lethal death. Also, the cry from the cross echoes Achilles bellowing out three times from the ditch protecting the Greek ships from the Trojans, a cry of both grief and war, of both unbearable suffering and a challenge to live (*The Iliad*, book 18, lines 215–29).

Mark's story, written in Greek, does not read like any of its Old Testament predecessors—in narrative type, in method, or in tone. Its form most resembles that of classical Greek tragedy. (Gilbert G. Bilezikian notes that Greek tragedies were commonly performed and studied in Mark's day—p. 28.) It involves the annihilation of the self—the *alētheia* (truth) that frees the self. It climaxes in the death of death, which means a-lethal annihilation. As with Oedipus, the narrative is one of mounting suffering while all normal human hopes for a happy life—the pleasures of family, friendship, of power and its benevolent use, of worldly success, status, and wealth—are obliterated.

As with the Greek precedent, fate broods over the action, its binding thread controlling the way, inexorably working its pitiless fill, determining the *hour*. And there are Greek *daimones*, demi-gods or spirits which possess the humans from time to time, or permanently, swaying their moods, driving their moves.

There is some accord here with the general statement of Dennis R. MacDonald that Mark's genre is that of the Homeric prose epic (p. 3). However, MacDonald makes an implausible case linking Mark's Jesus with Odysseus, based on far-fetched parallel passage comparisons. As much as there is an antecedent to Mark, it is Greek tragedy. To the degree that there is a character predecessor to Mark's Jesus, and this is severely circumscribed, it is Homer's tragic hero, Achilles.

Bilezikian reads Jesus in the tradition of the Greek tragic hero (especially pp. 109–12). He uses Aristotle to provide his model of tragedy, which works only in a very loose sense, and has a critical problem—Aristotle's hero falls because of a flaw in his own character.

2 Joan L. Mitchell wants to redeem the three women by arguing that their fear is numinous (ch. 6). Others also try to explain away the fear; for example, David Catchpole reads it as 'awe-inspired reaction to a heavenly epiphany' ('The Fearful Silence of the Women at the Tomb', *Journal of Theology for Southern Africa*, 18 (1977), pp. 3–10). The

argument is hard to credit, given the prominence of 'fear' in Mark as unambiguously negative.

In general, feminist scholarship has been keen to find a prominent role for women in Mark as true disciples — not difficult to do — yet has tended to avoid the most significant of them all, the woman in Bethany. For instance, see E. S. Malbon, 'Fallible Followers: Women and Men in the Gospel of Mark', *Semeia*, 28 (1983), pp. 29–48. Malbon does later distinguish between 'fallible followers' and 'exemplars', and shifts the anointing woman into the latter category ('The Major Importance of Minor Characters in Mark', in E. S. Malbon & E. V. McKnight (eds.), *The New Literary Criticism and the New Testament*, p. 69).

3 A number of scholars link the young man in the empty tomb with the unknown follower who flees naked — e.g. Allan K. Jenkins, 'Young man or Angel?', *Expository Times*, no. 94, 1983, p. 239; and James G. Williams, p. 85. H. Waetjen identifies the two as one, and gives them Joseph attributes ('The Ending of Mark and the Gospel's Shift in Eschatology', *Annual of the Swedish Theological Institute*, 4 (1965)). R. Scroggs and K. Groff identify the doubled-up figure with the Christian initiate in baptism ('Baptism in Mark: Dying and Rising with Christ', *Journal of Biblical Literature*, 92 (1973), pp. 536–40).

Albert Vanhoye links the young man who flees with Jesus himself, using different associations — Resurrection ones — than those developed here. He puts it that, 'Jesus finds himself in the same predicament as the young man; he has nothing but a cloth to cover him … But, like the young man, he leaves the cloth and escapes.' (*'La fuite du jeune homme nu'*, *Biblica*, 52 (1971), pp. 402–406.)

Michael Patella links the two young men, and both with baptism (p. 112). He starts the series of shared identities with Bartimaeus, a second blind man whom Jesus healed — whose story I have not included. The tie for Patella is that Bartimaeus throws off his cloak before being healed. Perhaps this is right; perhaps not. Starting the sequence with Legion, as I have in my reading, makes Bartimaeus superfluous. Patella finds in Bartimaeus' name, meaning 'son of Timaeus', a reference to Plato's cosmological Dialogue *Timaeus* — he notes some obscure astrological links between Plato and Mark.

4 Kelber's conclusion is that the mystery in the first Gospel does not reside with the twelve, as the apostolic tradition would have it, but with the death, which is accessible to all who read about it ('Apostolic Tradition and the Form of the Gospel', in Fernando F. Segovia (ed.), p. 42). Kelber endorses Moltmann's view that Mark redirects Christology away from the risen Lord toward the earthly Jesus.

In the same essay, Kelber counters the range of scholars who have attempted to save the twelve from Mark's systematic denigration. Above all, he questions whether the three references to a meeting with the disciples after his death in Galilee—the post-Resurrection meeting—are meant to redeem them. He notes that the references are timid in the narrative as a whole; and, in the final case, in Chapter 16, the women do not pass on the young man's instruction to the twelve. Indeed, the women, like the twelve, are distanced as outsiders (p. 36).

5 Nietzsche, *Beyond Good and Evil*, section 40.

6 James G. Williams refers to it as the 'master parable' (p. 116).

7 Crossan is open to the possibility of 'Mark himself obliquely and indirectly signing his narrative', while he himself speculates the author might have been the woman in Bethany (*Jesus*, p. 192).

Some scholars have identified Mark as the John Mark mentioned in Acts—for example, Theodor Zahn, sections 51–3; and Josef Schmid, p. 8.

J. H. McIndoe gives added weight to this link by assuming that the Last Supper took place in the home of Mary, the mother of John Mark, where the young son might have heard the words spoken, especially to Peter, thus making sense of the phrase 'and to Peter' added inside the tomb (The Young Man at the Tomb', *Expository Times*, no. 80, 1969, pp. 125–8).

The doyen of modern Biblical scholars, R. E. Brown, dismisses these links as 'imaginative flights of fancy' (*The Death of the Messiah*, p. 299). Brown elsewhere shows his unmusicality in relation to the way narrative works in a doctrine-bound disparaging of Kermode's *The Genesis of Secrecy*: 'Leaving aside the critiques of Kermode's book as to whether he has understood exegesis and has not substituted art for science, one may object that he has isolated Mark's writing from its ultimate Christian theology.' (*An Introduction to the New Testament*, pp. 153–4).

Francis J. Moloney provides a lucid and cautious overview of who Mark may have been, and where he may have written (*Mark*, ch. 1).

8 A large majority of Biblical scholars assume that Mark's Gospel was written around 70AD, or a few years earlier or later. If they are right—and there is no historical evidence pointing in any direction here—it is plausible that an author who was twenty at the time of the crucifixion should be writing the story down for posterity in his fifties.

Kelber assumes a date for Mark after the Roman–Jewish war of 66–74AD, speculating that Chapter 13 contains references to the destruction of the Temple in 70AD—for instance, that the 'abomination of desolation' is a reference to the conquering Roman general, Titus (p. 13). Moloney agrees with Kelber (*Mark*, p. 11). R. E. Brown inclines to an earlier date (*An Introduction to the New Testament,* p. 164).

9 This is a technique used frequently by Shakespeare, in epilogues. In his final play, *The Tempest,* it is the principal character, Prospero, alone on stage, who addresses the audience. *Midsummer Night's Dream* is closer to Mark in that it has Puck, a principal character who has flitted around on the margins of the action, deliver the epilogue.

10 Tolbert observes that Mark's perfect disciple is the audience itself (p. 297).

11 I have elsewhere called this a Dreaming theory of culture, drawing on the terminology of the Australian Aborigines, and argued that every culture is, at its core, a body of timeless archetypal or Dreaming stories (*The Western Dreaming*). This is close to the classical Greek understanding of *mythos*.

7. Peter the Outsider and the Churches

1 Most Biblical scholars are, understandably, uncomfortable with a text that has Peter, the leading disciple and founder of the church, cursing Jesus. Helmut Merkel accepts the obvious, while surveying different interpretations of the 'curse' ('Peter's Curse', in Ernest Bammel, (ed.), ch. 5)

2 A summary of Peter in the Gospel of Mark, and a sketch of varying scholarly interpretation, is provided in Chapter 5 of *Peter in the New Testament,* edited by Raymond E. Brown, Karl P. Donfried, and John Reumann.

3 John 12: 26.

4 John 13: 8.

5 John 21: 22. In this last exchange, the Master separates off the role of Peter from that of John. I take up this distinction later, in Chapter 11.

    T. L. Brodie suggests that John represents the contemplative face of the church; Peter, the official one (pp. 563–4).

6 The Old Masters will typically picture Peter as a simple-minded, grey-bearded rustic, sometimes with the comic edge of the fogey or dotard.

8. Magdalene the Insider

1 Magdalene is explicit as the lead theme in *The Da Vinci Code*. This novel's worldwide sales have been in the order of 50 million since it

was first published in 2003.

2 Kermode makes this point, in relation to the Judas story (pp. 81–96).

3 Matthew does no more than clumsily retell Mark's version (Matthew 26: 6–13).

4 Luke 7: 36–50.

5 Oscar Wilde has an edifying reading of this — a midrash in itself. Mary Magdalene had seven lovers, one of whom gave her the alabaster flask (*De Profundis*, p. 932). There is support for this, whether Wilde had picked it up or not, in John's early story of the Samaritan woman at the well. This woman has Magdalene attributes: she is a woman meeting Jesus alone in a remote place; he knows she is living with a man out of wedlock; and she has had five husbands. The episode at the well insinuates the loaded subtext that Jesus himself is her current 'man' (the Greek word — *andros* — means both man and husband).

6 Raphael, in his *Transfiguration*, positions a powerful young woman, with Magdalene attributes, in the centre-foreground. She points to the mad boy as if she has just realised that he is the one. It seems the 'divine Raphael' has also merged the episode of the mad boy with the Magdalene story.

7 Titian paints Magdalene as a fleshy, earthy young woman who has indulged heedlessly in the pleasures of life.

8 Poussin paints the scene of Magdalene at the house of Simon the Pharisee in these terms — in his 1647 *Sacrament of Penance*.

9 Both Mark and Luke use the Greek — *to alabastron* — for the alabaster flask. An alabastron was a term in itself for a container for perfume, often ceramic — sometimes alabaster.

10 John 12: 1–8.

11 Luke provides a parallel scene to contrast the sisters — in a story of Jesus visiting their village. Mary sits at his feet listening to his teaching, while Martha busies herself with the profane business of serving food (Luke 11: 38–42).

John has likely merged the moral of this Martha–Mary story into his account of the Raising of Lazarus. The probability of this is strengthened by the fact that John also describes Martha as serving food, in his second Bethany episode.

12 R. E. Brown, *The Gospel According to John*, vol. 1, pp. 425–6.

13 R. E. Brown translates it as 'shuddered' (*The Gospel According to John*, vol. 1, p. 426).

14 F. J. Moloney is one Biblical scholar who accepts that Jesus is angry with Mary. He interprets the cause as her weeping with 'the Jews' — she has joined their world. Jesus is 'severely disappointed' with her, given

that she had shown signs of belief. Moloney translates Jesus' reaction to Mary's tears as 'frustrated and angry disappointment, and deep, shuddering internal emotion' (*Signs and Shadows*, pp. 166–7).

15 Poussin picks up this link, placing Judas beside Simon in his painting of *The Sacrament of Penance*. In fact, Poussin splits Judas into two figures, themselves reclining side by side, on the right hand of Simon. Both Simon and Judas wear headscarves with inscriptions on them, written in Hebrew, proclaiming that they believe in the letter of the law.

16 Barocci's *Noli Me Tangere* is a striking example.

17 *Haptō* was also used to mean 'bind' by Homer.

18 Pope Benedict XVI's first encyclical, released in 2006 — *Deus Caritas Est* — attempts a partly similar dialectic between eros and agapē.

19 For example, J. H. Bernard, vol. 2, p. 657. Alban Goodier imagines that Mary of Bethany spent her youth in the town of Magdala, renowned for its lax morals and common prostitution (*The Public Life of Our Lord Jesus Christ*, vol. 2, pp. 266–8, 357–65). R. E. Brown puts a case for separating the stories (*The Gospel According to John*, vol. 1, pp. 450–1).

20 Kitzberger plausibly argues that John makes many references back to the Synoptics. This means that John and his readers knew the three earlier Lives of Jesus. Kitzberger interprets, for instance, Mary of Bethany wiping away the precious oil with her hair as an explicit reference to Luke's story of the sinner, drawing on its narrative flavouring (p. 579).

9. I Am Not!: Judas

1 J. M. Coetzee ruminates that evil may stimulate a satanic energy, as for instance when a hangman exceeds his commission and obscenely mocks the man who is about to die at his hands ('The Problem of Evil', included in his novel, *Elizabeth Costello*, Vintage, London, 2003, p. 177). This sounds like a type of sadism. Sadism is elemental and universal, noted as early as *The Iliad*, notably in the blood-lust aroused in the gentlest warrior of all, Patroklus, when he gets carried away in the heat of battle. Patroklus, too, mocks one of the doomed enemy as he is dying (*The Iliad*, Book 16).

2 The association with filthy lucre, in combination with John's collective denigration of 'the Jews', will feed the anti-Semitic caricature that would be used by Christians to justify a long history of Jewish persecution in Europe. George Steiner reflects on the power of John's telling of the Last Supper, and in particular its setting up of Judas as the caricature 'Jew', in 'Two Suppers', *No Passion Spent*, pp. 409–19.

3   The others are the Raising of Lazarus, Mary Magdalene in the garden, the trial before Pilate, and the Peter–John ending. The meeting with the Samaritan woman at the well (4: 4–43) and the healing of the blind man (9: 1–41) almost qualify as two more.

4   The quotation is from Psalms 41: 9, but with John replacing the verb 'eat' with the earthier 'munch'.

5   Poussin paints such a curtain in his second version of *The Sacrament of Eucharist*, better titled *The Last Supper*. This is his meditation on the Last Supper, based on John's account. The curtain doubles up as the veil in the Jerusalem Temple.

6   This is how Poussin depicts Judas exiting the Last Supper.

7   There is a large volume of scholarship on the identity of the 'beloved disciple', on that of John, and on the authorship of John's Gospel. It is addressed in Chapter 11.

8   Henry van den Bussche argues that the text makes this clear. Given that John is resting against Jesus' chest, eastern eating customs place him on the right (p. 383).

9   This rendition is largely Tyndale. The significant differences are that 'Story' has replaced 'word'; and 'he' has replaced the 'it' that was in the beginning with God — as oddly translated by Tyndale. Above all, the rhythms of word and sequence created by Tyndale are preserved.

10 This list endures in the 1994 *Catechism of the Catholic Church* (section 1866), where the seven are called 'capital sins'.

11 The dozen references in Mark to what is usually translated as 'the kingdom of God' could just as plausibly be rendered as 'the divine realm' or even 'the sacred order'.

12 Bussche points to this as the moment of supreme combat between light and darkness (p. 384).

10. He Who Learns: Pilate

1   In this translation, I have taken account of R. E. Brown's rendering of John's version of the Roman Trial, and his notes on the Greek text (*The Gospel According to John*, vol. 2, pp. 843–920).

2   On the likely historical site of the Praetorium, see R. E. Brown, *The Gospel According to John*, vol. 2, p. 845.

3   Mel Gibson's 2004 film *The Passion* dramatised the gruesome cruelty of scourging.

4   C. K. Barrett draws links with Jewish and Hellenistic myths of the primal man (*The New Testament Background: Selected Documents*, SPCK, London, 1956, p. 450).

5   II Samuel 12: 7.

6   R. E. Brown reads Pilate's words differently, as signalling to the Jewish crowd that Jesus is a pathetic figure — 'Look at this poor fellow here!' (*The Death of the Messiah*, vol. 1, p. 828). Bultmann held the same view (*The Gospel of John*, p. 659). So did Rudolf Schnackenburg, who saw Pilate himself as scornful of Jesus (pp. 256–7).

7   Leviticus 24: 16.

8   For example, I Samuel 8: 4–10.

9   For example, Bultmann (*The Gospel of John*, p. 665).

10 This is R. E. Brown's reading (*The Death of the Messiah*, vol. 1, p. 848).

11 This is R.E. Brown's position (*The Gospel According to John*, vol. 2, p. 864).

12 In the formative Hindu story cycle, the *Mahabharata*, there is an episode with some similarity. Eklavya becomes higher than his vocation as the greatest archer, by willingly cutting off his right thumb.

11. Let Him Be!

1   R. E. Brown, *An Introduction to the New Testament*, p. 368.

2   Raphael notably in his *Deposition* and *Transfiguration*; Poussin in his second *Sacrament of Penance* and *Last Supper*.

3   This may be taken further. Matthew and Luke's birth stories link the families of Jesus and John the Baptist — leading to the convention, much later, in paintings of the Holy Family of including the two mothers and the two infants. Toddler Jesus and toddler John the Baptist often play together. In John's reworking, it is Jesus and the *beloved follower* — the other John — who are intimate.

4   I am indebted to Anna Branford for this reading.

5   These four chapters — 14 to 17 — interrupt the narrative, disrupt it. They are preceded by the intense drama of the Martha, Mary, and Lazarus story, closely followed by the Last Supper. Chapter 18 takes up where the Last Supper left off, moving directly to Gethsemane.

Scholars have provided a range of explanations for this awkward and lengthy insertion in the narrative. Rudolf Bultmann is intriguing. He argues that the four chapters belong with the Last Supper that immediately precedes them, and serve as Christ's farewell to his own — what he said at the Last Supper (*The Gospel of John — a Commentary*, pp. 458–61). The Fourth Gospel provides a 'tremendous concentration on the last night'. Bultmann further contends that the chapters are in the wrong order. They should start with 17: 1–26, which serves as a farewell prayer. The rest of the text should then follow, acting as a series of farewell discourses.

The *mythos* reading of the texts, which predicates this book, points to an alternative interpretation. With these chapters bracketed out, the seven consecutive chapters — 11 to 13 followed by 18 to 21 — achieve a continuous narrative with a cumulative dramatic intensity equal to Mark. These seven chapters, with the Prologue, make John's Life of Jesus the *tour de force* that it is.

Further, the content of Chapters 14 to 17 is esoteric teaching, employing abstract categories — in this, it is like the Prologue. However, the Prologue is stylistically tight, spare, and beautifully worked, whereas these four chapters are rambling, jumbled, and often contradictory. Why so sloppy and out of character for John? It may be that the writer does not care much. He has inserted them unwillingly, against his own narrative purpose.

One possible explanation is provided by the content. Much of it is doctrine — doctrine suitable for church building. We recall that John has changed direction from Mark, on the need for churches. He may have decided that his Jesus was duty-bound to provide some guidance — for human communities that bind and secure, that follow and serve.

6 One reason for the delay may be that John, who presumably started adult life as an illiterate Galilee fisherman, will need time to educate himself as a writer.

7 John 4: 21–24.

8 There are a dozen-or-so scholars since the Second World War who identify John the son of Zebedee as the author (Charlesworth, pp. 205–13). James H. Charlesworth provides a clear and thorough overview of the issues at stake in identifying the 'beloved disciple', and the range of scholarly opinion and argument — his book was published in 1995. He mars his work with the far-fetched hypothesis that doubting Thomas was the beloved follower.

9 R. E. Brown, *An Introduction to the New Testament*, pp. 368–71.

10 Colson, p. 25.

BIBLIOGRAPHY

The Bible, translations into English: King James Authorized Version, New Revised Standard Version, and William Tyndale's New Testament.

The Greek New Testament, fourth revised edition, eds. Barbara Aland, Kurt Aland, Johannes Karavidopoulos, Carlo M. Martini, and Bruce M. Metzger, Deutsche Bibelgesellschaft, Stuttgart, 1994

A Greek-English Lexicon, with a revised supplement, 1996, compiled by Henry George Liddell and Robert Scott, Oxford University Press, Oxford, 1996

Aeschylus, *Agamemnon,* trans. Richmond Lattimore, University of Chicago Press, Chicago, 1953

Alter, Robert & Kermode, Frank, *The Literary Guide to the Bible,* Harvard, Cambridge, Mass., 1987

Armstrong, Karen, *A History of God,* Knopf, New York, 1994

Aristotle, *Poetics,* with trans. by S. H. Butcher, Dover, New York, 1951

Auerbach, Erich, *Mimesis,* trans. Willard R. Trask, Princeton University Press, Princeton, 1953

Bammel, Ernst, *The Trial of Jesus,* SCM, London, 1970

Bernard, J. H., *A Critical and Exegetical Commentary on the Gospel According to John,* 2 vols., T. & T. Clark, Edinburgh, 1928

Best, Ernest (ed.), *Mark: The Gospel as Story,* T. & T. Clark, Edinburgh, 1983

Bilezekian, Gilbert G., *The Liberated Gospel: A Comparison of the Gospel of Mark and Greek Tragedy,* Baker, Grand Rapids, 1977

Bloom, Harold, *Jesus and Yahweh: the Names Divine,* Riverhead Books, New York, 2005

Bowersock, Glen W., *Fiction as History: Nero to Julian,* University of California Press, Berkeley, 1994

Brodie, Thomas L., *The Gospel According to John*, Oxford University Press, New York, 1993

Brown, Peter, *The Rise of Western Christendom*, 2nd edn, Blackwell, Oxford, 2003

Brown, Raymond E., *The Death of the Messiah*, 2 vols., Doubleday, New York, 1994

Brown, Raymond E., *The Gospel According to John*, 2 vols., Doubleday, New York, 1966

Brown, Raymond E., *An Introduction to the New Testament*, Doubleday, New York, 1996

Brown, Raymond E., *A Risen Christ in Eastertime*, Liturgical Press, Collegeville, Minn., 1991

Brown, Raymond E., Donfried, Karl P. & Reumann, John (eds.), *Peter in the New Testament*, Chapman, London, 1974

Bultmann, Rudolf, *The Gospel of John: A Commentary*, trans. G. R. Beasley-Murray, Blackwell, Oxford, 1971

Bultmann, Rudolf, *Jesus and the Word*, trans. Louise Pettibone Smith & Ermine Huntress Lantero, Scribner, New York, 1958

Bultmann, Rudolf, *Theology of the New Testament*, 2 vols., trans. Kendrick Grobel, SCM, 1952, 1955

Bussche, Henry van den, *Jean*, Desclée De Brouwer, Bruges, 1967

Calasso, Roberto, *The Marriage of Cadmus and Harmony*, trans. T. Parks, Knopf, New York, 1993

Carroll, John, *Ego and Soul: The Modern West in Search of Meaning*, HarperCollins, Sydney, 1998

Carroll, John, *The Western Dreaming*, HarperCollins, Sydney, 2001

Carroll, John, *The Wreck of Western Culture: Humanism Revisited*, Scribe, Melbourne, 2004

Charlesworth, James H., *The Beloved Disciple*, Trinity Press International, Valley Forge, Penn., 1995

Colson, Jean, *L'Énigme de disciple que Jésus aimait*, Théologie historique 10, Beauchesne et ses fils, Paris, 1968

Crossan, John Dominic, *Jesus: A Revolutionary Biography*, HarperCollins, New York, 1994.

Crossan, J. D., Johnson, L. T. & Kelber, W. H., *The Jesus Controversy*, Trinity Press International, Harrisburg, PA, 1999

Donahue, John R. & Harrington, Daniel J., *The Gospel of Mark*, Liturgical Press, Collegeville Minn., 2002

Fiorenza, Elisabeth Schüssler, *In Memory of Her*, SCM, London, 1983

Frye, Northrop, *Anatomy of Criticism*, Princeton University Press, Princeton, 1957

Goodier, Alban, *The Public Life of our Lord Jesus Christ*, 4 vols., Burns, Oates & Washbourne, London, 1930

Goulder, Michael D., *Midrash and Lection in Matthew*, SPCK, London, 1974

Grant, Michael, *Jesus*, Weidenfeld & Nicolson, London, 1977

Hock, Ronald F.; Chance, J. Bradley; & Perkins, Judith (eds.), *Ancient Fiction and Early Christian Narrative*, Scholars Press, Atlanta, 1998

Homer, *The Iliad*, trans. Richmond Lattimore, University of Chicago Press, Chicago, 1951

Homer, *The Odyssey*, trans. Robert Fitzgerald, Heinemann, London, 1962

Kelber, Werner H., *Mark's Story of Jesus*, Fortress Press, Philadelphia, 1978

Kermode, Frank, *The Genesis of Secrecy*, Harvard University Press, Cambridge, Mass., 1979

Kierkegaard, Soren, *Concluding Unscientific Postscript*, trans. D. F. Swenson, Princeton University Press, Princeton, 1968

Kierkegaard, Soren, *Fear and Trembling*, trans. Walter Lowrie, Princeton University Press, Princeton, 1954

Kitzberger, Ingrid R., 'Mary of Bethany and Mary of Magdala: Two Female Characters in the Johannine Passion Narrative: A Feminist Narrative-Critical Reader-Response', *New Testament Studies*, no. 41, 1995

Kragerud, Alv, *Der Lieblingsjünger im Johannesevangelium*, Osloer Universitätsverlag, Oslo, 1959

Macdonald, Dennis R., *The Homeric Epics and the Gospel of Mark*, Yale University Press, New Haven, 2000

Magness, J. Lee, *Sense and Absence*, Scholars Press, Atlanta, 1986

Maisch, Ingrid, *Mary Magdalene*, trans. Linda M. Maloney, Liturgical Press, Collegeville, Minn., 1996

Malbon, Elizabeth Struthers, *Narrative Space and Mythic Meaning in Mark*, Sheffield Academic Press, Sheffield, 1991

Malbon, Elizabeth Struthers & McKnight, Edgar V. (eds.), *The New Literary Criticism and the New Testament*, Sheffield Academic Press, Sheffield, 1994

Marcus, Joel, *Mark 1–8*, Doubleday, New York, 2000

Miles, Jack, *Christ: A Crisis in the Life of God*, Arrow, London, 2001

Mitchell, Joan L., *Beyond Fear and Silence: A Feminist-Literary Reading of Mark*, Continuum, New York, 2001

Moloney, Francis J., *Glory not Dishonor, Reading John 13-21*, Fortress, Minneapolis, 1998

Moloney, Francis J., *The Gospel of Mark*, Hendrickson, Peabody Mass., 2002

Moloney, Francis J., *Mark: Storyteller, Interpreter, Evangelist*, Hendrickson,

Peabody Mass., 2004

Moloney, Francis J., *Signs and Shadows, Reading John 5-12*, Fortress, Minneapolis, 1996

Nietzsche, Friedrich, *Die Geburt der Tragödie (The Birth of Tragedy)*, Goldmann, Munich, 1969

Nietzsche, Friedrich, *Jenseits von Gut und Böse (Beyond Good and Evil)*, Goldmann, Munich, 1969

Patella, Michael, *Lord of the Cosmos: Mithras, Paul and the Gospel of Mark*, T. & T. Clark, New York, 2006

Petersen, Norman R., *Literary Criticism for New Testament Critics*, Fortress Press, Philadelphia, 1978

Prothero, Stephen, *American Jesus*, Farrar, Strauss & Giroux, New York, 2003

Qualls, Barry V., 'Saint Mark Says They Mustn't', *Raritan* VIII: 4 (Spring 1989)

Renan, Ernest, *Life of Jesus*, Modern Library, New York, 1927

Rhoads, David & Michie, Donald, *Mark as Story*, Fortress Press, Philadelphia, 1982

Rieff, Philip, *My Life among the Deathworks*, University of Virginia Press, Charlottesville, 2006

Robbins, Vernon K., *Jesus the Teacher, a Socio-Rhetorical Interpretation of Mark*, Fortress Press, Philadelphia, 1984

Segovia, Fernando F. (ed.), *Discipleship in the New Testament*, Fortress Press, Philadelphia, 1985

Schmid, Josef, *The Regensburg New Testament: The Gospel according to Mark*, trans. Kevin Condon, Mercier, New York, 1968

Schnackenburg, Rudolf, *The Gospel According to St John*, vol. 3, trans. David Smith & G. A. Kon, Crossroad, New York, 1982

Sophocles, *Oedipus the King*, trans. Richard Grene, University of Chicago Press, Chicago, 1942

Steiner, George, *No Passion Spent*, Faber and Faber, London, 1996

Swete, Henry Barclay, *The Gospel According to St Mark*, Macmillan, London, 1913

Taylor, Vincent, *The Gospel According to St Mark*, Macmillan, London, 1952

Telford, William R. (ed.), *The Interpretation of Mark*, T&T Clark, Edinburgh, 1985

Thompson, Mary R., *Mary of Magdala*, Paulist Press, Mahwah, New Jersey, 1995

Tolbert, Mary Ann, *Sowing the Gospel: Mark's World in Literary-Historical Perspective*, Fortress Press, Minneapolis, 1989

Tonkinson, Robert, *The Mardudjara Aborigines*, Holt, Rinehart and Winston, New York, 1978

Tuckett, Christopher (ed.), *The Messianic Secret*, SPCK, London, 1983

Weeden, Theodore J., *Mark: Traditions in Conflict*, Fortress Press, Philadelphia, 1971

Wilde, Oscar, *Complete Works*, Collins, London, 1966

Williams, Bernard, *Shame and Necessity*, University of California Press, Berkeley, 1993

Williams, James G., *Gospel Against Parable*, Almond, Sheffield, 1985

Wrede, William, *The Messianic Secret*, Clarke, London, 1971

Zahn, Theodor, *Einleitung in das Neue Testament*, 3rd ed., Deichert, Leipzig, 1907

INDEX

John Carroll is professor of sociology at La Trobe University in Melbourne. His recent books include *Ego and Soul: The Modern West in Search of Meaning, Terror: A Meditation on the Meaning of September 11,* and *The Wreck of Western Culture: Humanism Revisited.*